Guide to
Working
Abroad

The Daily Telegraph

Guide to
Working
Abroad

**Twenty-First
EDITION**

Godfrey Golzen

PERSONAL
BANKING
International

**KOGAN
PAGE**

First published in 1977

Twenty-first edition 1999

Apart from any fair dealing for the purposes of research or private study, or criticism or review, as permitted under the Copyright, Designs and Patents Act, 1988, this publication may only be reproduced, stored or transmitted, in any form or by any means, with the prior permission in writing of the publishers, or in the case of reprographic reproduction in accordance with the terms of licences issued by the Copyright Licensing Agency. Enquiries concerning reproduction outside those terms should be sent to the publishers at the undermentioned address:

Kogan Page Limited
120 Pentonville Road
London N1 9JN

' Godfrey Golzen and contributors 1977, 1979, 1980, 1981, 1982, 1983, 1984, 1985, 1986, 1987, 1988, 1989, 1990, 1991
' Kogan Page Ltd and contributors 1992, 1993, 1994, 1995, 1996, 1997, 1999

Every effort has been made to ensure information in this book is up to date at the time of printing. Where no revisions to country profiles were received from individual embassies the text from the twentieth edition has been used.

British Library Cataloguing in Publication Data

A CIP record for this book is available from the British Library.

ISBN 0 7494 2881 3

Typeset by Saxon Graphics Ltd, Derby
Printed in Great Britain by Bell and Bain Ltd., Glasgow

Contents

Contents

Acknowledgements

Many individuals and organisations have helped us with information and advice on various aspects of working and living abroad, and in updating information for this edition. We wish to extend our thanks to Margaret Stewart for her contributions to several previous editions; Tony Smith of the International Safety Council, Chicago, for writing the Introduction in Part 1; Susan Jackson for writing the chapter on the education of expatriates children; the Centre for International Briefing, Farnham Castle, Surrey; the Department for International Development for information on the situation in developing countries; the European Council of International Schools; Innes Anderson of Anderson Sinclair & Co for detailed advice on the financial planning chapter; Colin Bexon of Hay Management Consultants for information on job opportunities; R J B Anderton of Anderton & Son for his help on the chapter on letting your home; Niki Chesworth for updating the chapter on taxation; Louis Conrad of the Conrad School of Languages for help on the section on learning a language; the members of foreign embassies and high commissions in London and the press offices of various government departments (particularly DSS, DfEE, HM Customs) who have helped in the revision of the text; and readers who have written in with criticisms, information and suggestions.

Preface

With the economic groupings that are beginning to replace national boundaries, in the business world at any rate, the word abroad is becoming less meaningful, except when long-haul journeys and major cultural differences are involved.

Rewards are also converging among countries. There are however still differences in gross managerial salaries between various European countries, though in the case of net figures, these are less marked when you take into account the effect of taxes and social security contributions. For instance, the Union Bank of Switzerland s latest survey (Prices and Earnings Around the Globe) shows that the gross salary of a departmental manager in Frankfurt is over a third higher than his or her counterpart in London, but the gap between their take-home pay is much less. But the tendency towards convergence, particularly at more senior levels in the same business sectors in European countries is bound to be accentuated as we move towards European Monetary Union. Indeed it is becoming clear at conferences on global remuneration policies that even in countries like China and the republics of the former Soviet Union where in the past managers have been very poorly paid in comparison with the West the move is quite sharply upwards. In the emerging economies the dearth of talent combining local know-how with the ability to apply western business methods means that locals who possess this combination can get even more than western expats.

However, the picture is confused by currency instability. Even within Europe, the pound has moved sharply upwards against other currencies over the last year, a situation which may not last if an overvalued pound leads to a UK recession. Elsewhere, economic crises such as in many parts of Asia, and speculative moves such as are occurring against the South African rand at the time of writing, can seriously erode the value of a reward package. In some cases employers have used Harold Wilson s notorious the pound in your pocket argument (ie that devaluation did not affect purchasing power within the country which was devaluing its currency) as a reason for not increasing salaries that have been affected by currency swings. That, for instance, was how one US company justified its decision not to adjust the salary of an expatriate in Malyasia to take into account a 25 per cent fall in the value of the ringgit. But it is not an argument that should be accepted by an expatriate in a similar position. Apart from the fact that devaluations do affect the prices of goods and services sooner rather than later, increasingly expatriate salaries are benchmarked against global standards in relation to the industry and job level concerned. So if the package you are being offered falls below that, it is a signal to either negotiate, look for another job or not to accept the offer if it is being made in connection with a new appointment. Nor do you need to resort to buying expensive salary surveys these are made for client companies and priced accordingly to find out what the going rates are. It s simply a question of keeping an eye on job advertisements at the appropriate level in the media or, as people are increasingly doing, looking up Internet job sites, such as The Monsterboard.

Expatriate Pay and Prices

Jobs abroad tend to be better paid than their equivalent in the home country, irrespective of what that home country is. The structure which is most widely used consists of a base salary, equivalent to home base pay, plus a highly variable uplift factor to compensate for higher taxes and social security charges (the UK percentage of 26.4 on an average departmental manager s salary is fairly low, by global standards), accommodation (you may have to maintain a house or flat in your home country as well as in the one to which you are moving), school fees, medical costs, travel home, lifestyle costs (if you need to entertain or belong to a club and general inconvenience and disturbance).

However, it s the money you take home that counts, not the actual amount. The much quoted Big Mac index periodically published in *The Economist*, presents a rough and ready but telling picture in this regard. It takes the price of a MacDonald Hamburger in 35 countries as an index of purchasing power and hence of the real value of their currency. Most recently this shows that a Big Mac, priced at $2.56 in the USA, costs appreciably more in Switzerland, France, Germany, the UK and Scandinavia and appreciably less in many parts of Asia, Southern and East Africa and Eastern Europe. Thus a salary which sounds impressive in Switzerland where the Big Mac costs 50 per cent more than in the USA may not buy as much as you might think, whereas the reverse might be true in Australia, where it cost over 30 per cent less. That is also a fair reflection of relative living costs. The latest survey of Worldwide Living Costs, produced by *Employment Conditions Abroad*, shows that the 15 most expensive cities to live in are:

Tokyo
Osaka
Hong Kong
Oslo
Zurich
Libreville
London
Paris
Geneva
Moscow
Vienna
Copenhagen
Stockholm
Tel Aviv
Beijing

At the other end of the scale, Bombay, Tehran, Harare and Jakarta are right at the bottom of the ladder.

Surprisingly, Rome is well down at 57th place out of 119, which does not correspond to the experience of people who have lived there. However, it is sometimes not entirely clear on what basis these and other surveys are compiled. Do they all compare like with like criteria for example how living costs are viewed by people, with and without families, and with similar spending habits? The best plan if you are faced with the prospect of an appointment abroad is to make an exploratory visit and this is what most companies are now offering. Equally, if you are going under your own steam as you can do within the countries of the European Community make very sure that you are aware of what it s really like to live there. A memorable holiday in the Costa Packet is not necessarily a guarantee that life from November to March will be of the same standard. Consider:

- the price of the typical items in your weekly shopping trolley
- rental in the kind of area you would like to live, if the employer is not paying for that
- transport costs
- utilities gas, phone, electricity
- journey time to work
- local schooling, if available, and the effects of that on your children s education when you return to base
- work opportunities for your spouse if he or she has a career
- the climate throughout the year

Expatriate Pay Trends

The growth in cross-border transfers that all employers are reporting not just within Western Europe but between all OECD countries and many emerging economies (16,000 foreign companies are reported to be active in China) means a boom in expatriate employment. At the same time companies are trying very hard to contain costs. That means that many of the perks associated with expat status are being eroded; in fact, in the case of transfers to countries that are regarded as being pleasant to live in Europe, the USA, Canada, Australia and New Zealand they are disappearing altogether, with the exception of cost of living allowances. A survey conducted last year by the accountants, Price Waterhouse, showed that a third of companies pay no incentive for people to work abroad at all and that 25 per cent do not even pay a relocation allowance, though most do pay for temporary accommodation for some weeks after arrival. There is some indication that this hard line is having to be softened in the light of the skills shortage, so another trend is to control costs by moving towards so-called cafeteria benefits: expats are simply given a lump sum on top of the weighted basic (home base pay plus local adjustment) and left to their own discretion about how to spend it.

On the whole, the laws of supply and demand dictate the following: the less desirable the location, the scarcer your skill or the more urgently the employer needs to fill a particular position, the greater your bargaining power and the more the employer will be prepared to stretch a few points on salary and benefits. Again one has to repeat the message that outside Europe it is well worth finding out what the hazards are in accepting a post. Crime rates in a number of emerging economies, notably Africa, Latin America and the former Soviet Union are high enough to be a real deterrent, except possibly, for young single men.

Shark nets

Some expatriate assignments, notably those in Middle Eastern countries and those in highly difficult locations, do offer the chance to accumulate considerable capital sums. That brings the risk of unwise investments and of hard sales pitches from unscrupulous financial advisers, many of whom travel abroad to drum up business as do some perfectly respectable ones, of course. Regulatory bodies, such as the Personal Investment Authority (PIA) and LAUTRO, exercise some control in the UK, but their writ does not run abroad. However, one precaution that is worth taking is to ask financial advisers who may approach you while you are working abroad whether they are approved by the relevant UK regulatory bodies. If they say they are they should provide documentary proof before you make any commitment to them.

As far as making your own judgements on investment is concerned, the dreadful story of the Lloyd s names carries its own lessons. Beware of any schemes to invest in property, objects or special situations, unless you really know what you are doing. As a piece of general advice, Richard Stevenson of Innes Anderson, a firm of financial consultants specialising in the expatriate market, believes that managed currency funds are currently the best buy for those who want to combine safety with some degree of capital appreciation. But for those who go abroad on one-year assignments long enough to escape UK income tax for the period in question Louise Botting, formerly of BBC *Moneybox* fame, believes that a straightforward offshore high interest bank account may well be the best bet.

The spouse problem

The big problems that remain unsolved are the loss of income from a spouse salary and the disruption of a spouse career. By that term we generally mean a wife, since the number of married women employed as expatriate managers remains negligible. But the Price Waterhouse survey indicated that employers persist in the rather old-fashioned view that where the husband goes, the wife will follow. This is no longer automatically the case. Many married women now have careers of their own which they may not be able to pursue in the host country. The survey showed that this was the main reason why managers, when offered an expatriate posting, turned it down.

A few companies do make an effort to find a job for the spouse, but they admit it is very difficult. Some are even prepared to allow for a loss of spouse income in computing the salary package. Others are apparently considering the possibility, at least within Europe, of commuting expatriates. Paying for a weekly airline ticket could well work out cheaper than meeting all the costs of an expatriate assignment. Clearly, this is a matter that will have to be sorted out with employers, if and when it arises. The role of non-married partners is, of course, even more problematic.

Expatriate assignments and careers

If the financial incentive is less compelling than it used to be, what are the career effects? The trend in expatriate employment is heading towards a pattern of two tiers and so two, different, kinds of career. The upper tier is an aspect of management development part of the process of moving managers around to expose them to various management scenarios and experiences. In this case, the period spent abroad may be comparatively short two or three years is the usual spell. The other one more closely resembles expatriate employment in the way it appeared in earlier editions of this book: a more opportunistic, adventure and lifestyle-driven approach to an individually determined career.

Except in the Third World and in developing countries, the role of the expat in its previous sense may be coming to an end; that is, the highly paid business or technical mercenary, moving from one overseas posting to another, cocooned from the local community by skilfully designed tax-avoidance devices and a range of fringe benefits which back at base could only be matched, perhaps, by the most senior board members. For that reason, expats seldom returned home to an ordinary line management career. In fact, they often retired abroad after spending their working lives there.

As far as the developed economies of Europe, the USA and Australasia are concerned, the picture has been changing rapidly. In these countries today s expatriate manager will often belong to the upper tier; typically he will be a high-flyer, in his mid-30s, being groomed for greater things in his home company by being given a taste as well as a test of general management, often as chief executive officer of an overseas subsidiary.*

Recent studies of the careers of top managers in large companies have shown that a high proportion have worked abroad in a senior position at some point. The advantages of this are seen to be, exposure to responsibility across a wide range of management functions, usually at an early age, the development of overseas experience and contacts, and the chance to learn another language.

However, those who are thinking of going abroad as part of a career development plan within the organisation to which they wish to return should make sure that such experience will be val-

---

* We use the personal pronoun in its unisex sense throughout the book, though it must be said that female expatriate managers are still a rarity.

ued. There are firms where jobs abroad, intentionally or otherwise, are a kind of corporate Siberia. The Price Waterhouse survey to which we have previously referred confirms that this remains a fear, particularly in the light of the fact that the duration of the average expatriate assignment is between three and five years. Bearing in mind that such assignments often occur during the crucial career years between 30 and 35, it is vital that the good corporate intentions, that will no doubt be expressed at the outset of the assignment, will actually be maintained. Positive signs of this are the following:

- Proper briefing procedures on working and living aspects of the assignment before departure. Also, advice on personal finance and taxation aspects and what to do about UK property, dependants, school-age children, etc while working abroad.
- A salary policy that fits coherently into the home salary and benefit structure, so that when you return it will be at the level you would have reached had you been progressing successfully within the home company.
- The existence of channels of communication for keeping in regular touch, not just on business matters, but on corporate affairs generally.
- Full exchange of views, up to contact at the most senior levels appropriate, while on home leave.
- A coherent policy for bringing returnees into functions, posts and areas of responsibility where their experience is used properly.
- The presence within the company of managers in senior positions who have themselves worked abroad.

In fact, opportunities are increasing for students to work abroad, either before graduation or as an aspect of postgraduate fulfilment. The University of London Careers Service, 50 Gordon Square, London WC1H 0PQ (tel: 0171 554 4500; fax: 0171 383 5876), provides a wide range of careers guidance and resources services to students and graduates, including interviews and advice. Their library holds most of the current directories and information on 38 countries.

HOW TO ORGANISE YOUR INTERNATIONAL REMOVAL

The first steps you should take are to determine which of your household furniture and personal possessions you wish to take with you to your new home, and which you are going to leave behind, perhaps in storage until you return.

It is often useful to find out something about the kind of property available at your destination. Is it likely to have fitted wardrobes? Do UK electrical appliances work in the country you are moving to? If not can they be adapted and if so how much will this cost? The answers to these kind of questions can help you reach a decision. What is the value of items of furniture at your destination? If the item is expensive to buy new at your destination and the secondhand value in the UK is not good then it makes sense to take it with you. As a general rule furniture that has been purchased within the last five years, and all types of antique furniture are well worth taking with you as their value overseas is often greater than it is here.

When you have decided which items are going with you then it's time to phone your removal company and arrange for their representative to come to your home to survey your household effects. During the survey the representative will compile an inventory of the items that you wish to take with you, assess the packing requirement and estimate the weight and volume of your possessions. The weight and volume will be crucial to the overall price paid and is usually expressed in Cubic Feet/Lbs or Cubic Metres/Kilos.

Once the remover has completed the survey a cost estimate for the removal of your possessions can be prepared.

An international removal is comprised of three important steps. Firstly there is the packing of your possessions (the origin service) which involves carefully ensuring that all items are wrapped in protective materials and all small articles eg glassware, are boxed in sturdy export cartons and cases. For delicate items of furniture, eg a grandfather clock, a special custom built crate may also have to be made. Once the packing has been completed your possessions can then be loaded and for surface transportation this will be either into a removal van or a 20ft or 40ft steel container. For air transportation, and for some surface destinations the loading will be into a wooden case, often referred to as a lift van. A lift van gives additional protection to high value possessions and is constructed so that it can fit neatly inside either a removal van or a steel container.

The second step to be carried out is the transportation which will either be by road, sea or air. The remover will select the most appropriate vehicle, ship or aeroplane according to the route and your final destination.

Once the transportation has been completed and your possessions have arrived at their destination the third step (the destination service) can begin. The remover will, through his colleague at your destination, arrange customs clearance, delivery and unpacking of your effects into your new home.

In other words the reverse of the packing services at origin will take place during the destination service.

Many of the leading international removers are shareholders in OMNI, Overseas Moving Network Incorporated, which is a consortium of the leading removers of the World welded together into a tight knit organisation designed to give high quality service at many worldwide locations. If you choose to move with an OMNI remover then smoothness and quality should be the passowrds of your relocation. John Mason International, with offices in London, Liverpool and Manchester, are one of the leading OMNI members in the United Kingdom.

Several advisers specialise in certain areas of the world. To those outside the University of London, there are small charges for these services.

Cultural adaptation

Beginning early in this way provides a good background for upper tier and, indeed, second tier expatriates because what employers are increasingly looking for is that elusive creature, the international manager.

Whereas the idea of going native used to be anathema, absorbing and being absorbed by the culture of the host country is now encouraged. The international manager is someone who feels almost as at home in Munich, Milan or Melbourne as he does in Manchester, who at least in developed countries sends his children to a host nation school, who becomes involved in the social life of the local community and who, together with his wife and family, is ready to become, if he is not already, fluent in the local language. The idea is that when he returns home, he will have developed a range of networks which will stand him and his company in good stead in the new world of global trading. In later stages of the guide, we stress again and again the importance of adapting to what the local culture has to offer. The expatriate who must have cornflakes for breakfast will find life abroad psychologically tough, as well as more expensive, than it need be.

Cultural adaptation is perhaps less important for the second tier, but even there expatriates need to be sensitive to the local scene, local customs and etiquette. The colonial era, in which expatriates simply told the locals what to do, has been overtaken by a new demand for skills transfer. This is shown by the increasing number of local companies who are recruiting expatriates in areas where there is still a local skills shortage. Principally, these companies are found in developing and newly industrialised countries but, where they are to be found, British and European technicians are having to compete for jobs with applicants from Asia who, as well as being highly qualified, are also prepared to work for less money and with poorer amenities.

Local employers in developing and newly industrialised countries

There has been a slow but perceptible shift towards local companies as well as governments becoming expatriate employers. This can present certain hazards in countries where the role of the employee is a lowly one by definition, irrespective of the seniority of the job, and where British expatriates are now quite often competing with qualified people from developing countries such as Pakistan, Egypt and Korea. It is important in those cases that acceptable contracts of employment are negotiated beforehand and that nothing vital should be left to verbal understandings .

A cautionary tale, which many expatriates recognised as typical in at least some of its elements, was a story published in *The Daily Telegraph* under the title Top Pay Doesn t Come Cheap . Its author came to a verbal agreement with a Saudi employer in London. A few days after arriving in the country, he was handed a contract of employment at a substantially lower salary than the one that had been agreed. He was then told that he would be working in Bahrain, not Saudi Arabia. Bahrain is actually a more pleasant location, but the arbitrary change of plan was a symptom of the fact that there was a difference between his job title and his status, which was that of a servant a highly placed servant whose professional standing and career credentials are now being recognised by the award of a senior job title. But he was treated as a servant, subject to a good deal of verbal bullying and a limited amount of trust, until he was fired on a pretext after 11 months.

The moral of the story is not that foreign employers are a bad lot, but that when working for locally owned companies in developing and newly industrialised countries you should have a contract, binding in the law of the country to which you are going, before you depart. The fact that your employer wore a good suit and interviewed you in a swish European office means very little when you get out there to work for him.

The growth of local employment has also had another effect of which readers should be aware. People going out to work for British or multinational firms could rely on them to come to their aid if they ran into personal difficulties with local laws (even if their case was not a particularly deserving one!) or to get them out of the country if political conditions made this necessary. Working for a foreign employer may make it necessary to rely for protection on British diplomatic channels. Their role has been much criticised according to the Foreign Office this is because the limits of what British embassy and consular people can and cannot do has not been understood. Readers are advised to look at the guidance given on this in Chapter 8, as well as to take to heart the information that is provided on local business and social etiquette in the Middle and Far East. The instability of the international job market, on account of both economic and political factors, has had the effect of making overseas contract periods much shorter sometimes by accident, sometimes by design. One does not have to look very far around the world of 1998 to spot a number of places where expatriates must bear in mind at least the possibility of an unexpected return home.

The pattern of the book

In what is now its twenty-first edition, the general pattern of the book follows the formula which readers have in the past found helpful. Thus, while talking about salary benefits and tax levels in a way which will assist the reader to evaluate and compare jobs which he is applying for or has been offered, the book is equally concerned with giving brief descriptions of living and working conditions, compiled as far as possible from first-hand sources, in the countries that we have identified as being the principal areas of opportunity or interest (the two are unfortunately not necessarily the same thing) for expatriates.

Obviously, in a book of this nature the scope for going into detail is limited; so what we have done is, first, to answer what we believe are the main questions people raise about the general implications of going to work abroad: how it affects their status as UK taxpayers; what happens to their entitlement to UK welfare benefits; what to do about letting their home; what action to take about children s education, and so forth. Then, in the second part of the book, we have given surveys of various countries, which will enable readers to get some idea of what life there might be like. The information, gathered largely from 1997-8 sources, is as up to date and accurate as we have been able to make it. At the same time we must issue the usual disclaimers about not being held responsible for errors, first, because even the reporting of facts can sometimes be a subjective business and, second, because inflation a world-wide phenomenon tends to date figures quickly. However, the slow-down in inflation to single figures in most countries, other than those with obvious political or economic problems, has meant that cost of living figures have not had to be drastically altered. Exchange rate fluctuations are a bigger problem. Because of these, any sterling figures given should be treated as being indicative rather than precise. You will obviously check with your bank what your pound is worth. (In countries with a dollar currency, the figures quoted are understood to be in local, not US, dollars.)

We should like to hear from anybody who has more current information or who has suggestions for including additional material or more country surveys, which may be incorporated in future editions.

We have made some obvious but intentional omissions. One of these is the question of health. We cannot over-emphasise the need for you to seek expert advice well in advance of your proposed trip abroad. Several organisations specialising in travel medicine are listed below. One important piece of additional advice do not take any drugs to a Third World or developing country unless they are prescribed and labelled.

The Malaria Reference Laboratory at the London School of Hygiene and Tropical Medicine (Keppel Street, London WC1E 7HT; tel: 0171 636 8636, fax: 0171 436 5389) runs a helpline on 0891 600350 (49p per minute or 39p per minute cheap rate).

MASTA (Medical Advisory Service for Travellers Abroad) offers health briefs on 230 countries. Information can also be obtained direct from MASTA on 0171 631 4408, and from their Traveller s Health Line on 0891 224100 (49p per minute, 39p cheap rate).

Preventative advice, an extensive range of health products and immunisation can be obtained from the Travel Clinic, Hospital for Tropical Diseases, 4 St Pancras Way, London NW1 0PE. For information, call their Healthline on 0839 337733 (49p per minute or 39p per minute cheap rate); to make an appointment, telephone 0171 388 9600.

There is a nationwide network of British Airways Travel Clinics. Call 01276 685040 for details of your nearest clinic. Details are also available on the British Airways website, www.british-airways.com. There are currently 37 clinics nationwide, plus one in Johannesburg and one in Cape Town.

The clinics offer a one-stop service with immunisation, health protection items such as mosquito nets and water purification tablets, and anti-malarial tablets. A particular feature is a personalised health brief, combining a personal medical check-up with very up-to-date information on the countries (or combination of countries) to be visited from the MASTA database which covers more than 250 countries and includes the latest data from the Foreign Office. Central billing for companies can be arranged to cover all their employees who travel abroad.

One service geared particularly to the intending expatriate is a detailed health brief, an extensive individual health report on the country concerned. This costs £29.50.

There is, however, one major, international health hazard that has come to the fore since earlier editions of this book: the problem of AIDS. It has reached epidemic proportions in some parts of Africa and other developing countries. It is no longer sufficient to warn expatriates against the dangers of promiscuity. People can become infected through transfusions of infected blood or treatment with instruments that have not been properly sterilised. Expatriates are now advised to contact British embassies or high commissions, who keep registers of reliable blood donors among the expatriate community. The British Airways Travel Clinics are affiliated to the Geneva-based international charity, the Bloodcare Foundation, which can send screened and tested blood worldwide. Cover is available for individuals or families, or for a company, on a monthly or yearly basis.

It is also inadvisable in many countries to attend local doctors or dentists clinics unless they are known to enforce the highest standards of hygiene.

Those working in Saudi Arabia should note that they will have to produce a doctor s certificate to show that they are HIV negative. It has been pointed out that this can raise problems when applying for medical insurance. Even the answer yes to the question Have you ever been HIV tested? can raise the suspicion that your lifestyle exposes you to the risk of AIDS. Thus, if you have been HIV tested in connection with an assignment to Saudi Arabia, you should point this out if the question arises on medical insurance forms.

An extremely useful leaflet *Travellers Guide to Health* covering prevention and planning, emergency care, international health care agreements and a copy of form E111, can be obtained from your GP, or through the Health Literature Line on 0800 555 777. A comprehensive guide is available in the form of *Health Information for Overseas Travel* (The Stationery Office, £7.95). This detailed work is primarily intended for reference by GPs, but for *serious* travellers, it will be found most useful, providing a thorough guide to disease risk, immunisation, other hazards and child-specific information.

Social security is dealt with in a general chapter but the systems in individual countries are not covered in any detail. Benefits and contributions are constantly fluctuating and up-to-date information can be obtained from the appropriate embassies or high commissions, or from the Department of Social Security (see page 365).

We have kept lists of addresses to the minimum. The location of embassies and consulates can best be established from the *London Diplomatic List*, an invaluable list of all the representatives of foreign states and Commonwealth countries based in London, together with a directory of international organisations. Published by The Stationery Office and available through their regional bookshops, agents, other booksellers, or direct to the The Stationery Office Publications Centre, PO Box 276, London SW8 5DT, tel: 0171 873 9090; fax: 0171 873 8200; price £4.95. Prospective workers overseas should contact the legation s legal or labour counsellor or the embassy s information department.

Godfrey Golzen

Part 1
General Aspects

Introduction

Tony Smith

Job prospects for UK expatriates

The reputation of British expatriates is still highly regarded abroad and their salary rates are very competitive against labour recruited from the USA and the other Western European states. In reality, US and European contractors frequently turn to the United Kingdom to recruit workers for their overseas projects at salary rates below those demanded by their own nationals. This type of contract is normally lucrative in salary terms for the UK national and has the added advantage that the contractor frequently provides good living and contract conditions.

The ability to earn significant salaries overseas, together with the chance to avoid UK taxes, sounds like Utopia. However, in fact, the expatriate worker is faced with a new set of problems. Many of these will be outside work and will involve his family and social life. Working abroad requires a substantial adjustment in attitudes towards work and life in general. The ability to adapt to the new environment is absolutely essential, together with a willingness to make the best of things as they are in the new surroundings. Attempting to change the new surroundings to a British way of life is bound to be frustrated and to result in the resentment of the host country.

Lucrative overseas employment can solve many problems and may seem like the answer to a prayer. But it also creates problems, which may result in broken marriages, ruined careers and disturbed children. In accepting a job overseas you are taking a substantial risk and you should calculate how big the risk is in your particular case. Very often you will find that there is a direct correlation between risk and salary. For example, working for a major company such as British Aerospace in Saudi Arabia carries much less risk than working for a Saudi company. The rate of pay offered will probably be very different, with the Saudi company offering much higher pay, but the security and facilities which British Aerospace provide would not be available. However, even working for British Aerospace will not stop or cure all the problems caused by working overseas. It will also not give workers immunity if they break the laws of the host country.

People work overseas for many different reasons and are motivated to do so by many different things. It is difficult to believe anyone who says that money is not one of the major incentives. The duration of overseas employment is also varied. Some people just work a one- or two-year contract to help pay off the mortgage, or to produce the capital to start a business. However, such short-term contracts attract many applications and usually tend to be taken up by permanent expatriates   those people who have spent much of their working lives abroad.

Career development is another common reason for working abroad and is particularly important and frequent for those working in multinational and international companies, government bodies, banks and organisations with large export markets.

An expatriate returning to the UK faces as many adjustments to life and work as he does in going out to an overseas job. Picking up the threads of a career in the UK can be extremely difficult and overseas experience is not always regarded favourably. Employers with no previous experience in overseas work themselves may think that you are returning from a very alien and low technology environment, and doubt your ability to cope with new technology and life in the UK.

Recruiting organisations need to find workers who can perform a specified job in an overseas environment. It is easy to find candidates who can do the job in a British environment but only a small proportion can survive and succeed overseas. Their second task is to ensure that any applicant they select is aware of all the problems and difficulties he is likely to encounter in the country he is going to work in. They do not want the candidate to be surprised by conditions when he arrives, resulting in a premature termination of contract. This is bad for the individual and may affect his future employment prospects. It is bad for the company since it is very disruptive and involves them in substantial replacement costs. It is bad for the agent since it undermines the confidence of the client and can also turn him totally against the idea of using British workers.

Given that you have decided, after careful consideration of your family and your career, to find work overseas, you will need to identify the best way of achieving this, and to decide in which overseas countries you wish to work. Working in the Middle East is very different from working in Africa, which is also poles apart from working in the USA, Europe or the Far East.

The overall number of jobs for UK expatriates has declined quite markedly in recent years and the jobs most affected are for unskilled, semi-skilled, skilled, clerical and administrative workers. Many of these types of job are now filled by workers from the Far East and the Indian sub-continent where wage rates are much lower. The same market forces have resulted in some of the more senior jobs which have traditionally been filled by Americans being switched to less costly British labour.

The world-wide recession of recent years has resulted in reduced opportunities for expatriates. Companies have been forced to reduce expatriate salaries and benefits.

Frequently, salaries are only 10 20 per cent above current UK rates, but of course the ability to avoid tax and deductions from salary and the receipt of free accommodation and other benefits still make contracts financially attractive.

How to find work overseas

Having decided that you wish to work overseas you should:

1. Look at whether there are any opportunities for overseas employment within your own company. This has the advantage that a period of work overseas could be fitted into your overall career plan, which would alleviate any problems you would face in re-establishing yourself in the UK after your period of overseas work.

2. Look at British (and multinational) companies which can offer the chance to work overseas as part of your overall career development.
3. Look at foreign companies which are recruiting from the UK labour market. These fall into two categories: (a) foreign companies recruiting UK nationals to work in their own country; (b) foreign companies recruiting employees to work in other countries.
4. Assess the opportunities that exist with overseas government bodies, voluntary work overseas, overseas development aid programmes, United Nations and World Bank projects. These jobs are virtually always in the poorer and developing countries.
5. Since some jobs are never advertised and are filled by some agencies from their candidate registers, it is important to have your details on file with the major international recruitment agencies. Some welcome the receipt of rØsumØs and application forms, but others are not interested and rely entirely on advertising to fill their jobs. There are a number of highly reputable and professional agencies specialising in overseas jobs and you can be sure that if they hold an employment agencies licence they are bound by rules which ensure proper service to clients and job-seekers.

Family considerations

Perhaps the most fundamental question an expatriate must resolve is whether he is going to take up a post on bachelor/unaccompanied status or whether he is looking for married/accompanied postings. Many people who apply for overseas jobs have not thought out the problems and have not reached a family agreement on the type of posting required. One of the major irritations affecting international recruiters is that some candidates apply for single-status jobs and then at the final interview state they are only prepared to accept a married status situation. This results in a complete waste of time and money for both parties and is guaranteed to reduce your chances of getting employment through that agent.

Before you even decide to apply for an overseas job you must discuss and agree with your family the status of posting that you are prepared to take, the countries you would want to work in, and the minimum remuneration and benefits package you will accept. Only when you have decided these points are you in a position to start making job applications.

The following sections offer a brief outline of life and work in particular localities and may help you to identify which geographical area will suit you best.

North America

United States of America

The USA is a particularly popular location for expatriates, but very few applicants can hope to achieve their ambition to work there. The recession badly affected job opportunities in the USA and competition is very strong. It is only possible to recruit in job categories which cannot be filled indigenously. The most likely categories to succeed are highly qualified engineers and managers in high-technology fields, physiotherapists, occupational therapists and scientists. Even the offer of a job does not guarantee early entry into the USA. Permanent relocation can take 12 months to clear the US authorities. For those looking for short-duration employment there is a temporary visa programme which allows short-duration hire in areas of extreme demand such as electronic engineering and computing. Employment is for one year only although it is sometimes possible to get extensions up to a maximum period of three years.

In weighing up whether the USA suits your requirements you will find that it is not an area which allows you to make substantial savings, and that the increased salaries offered are easily disposed of through the many social and recreational facilities available. The USA is in many ways an easy place to settle in, since we speak the same language and our ways of life are also somewhat similar. If you decide that the USA is for you then you will need to be very patient and be prepared to wait up to one year to get there. Housing is not normally provided by employers and you will have to meet all living and housing costs out of your salary. Remember too that you may become eligible for the military draft and US tax, and it has been quite a shock to some expatriates to find Uncle Sam and the IRS interested in them.

Canada

Canada s way of life and standard of living are in many ways very similar to the USAs. However, there are quite significant differences, the most obvious being the dual language system of French and English. Expatriates relocating to Quebec province will find that knowledge of French is essential from a business point of view. Entry into Canada is a much easier and quicker process than into the USA with Canada accepting more than 10,000 UK nationals each year. There are two basic routes of entry. The first is employment authorisation, which is the entry of foreign workers into Canada who have first negotiated a job with a Canadian employer. The employer in turn obtains permission from his employment centre in Canada to offer the post to a foreign national. This permission is now given reluctantly and only if your employment would not adversely affect the job opportunities of Canadian residents. The second route is permanent residence, and this involves applying for an immigrant visa and meeting the requirements of the Canadian Immigration Act. Selection for this scheme works on a points system and it is very helpful to have a job offer before applying.

There is a demand for engineers, accountants, computing staff, skilled tradesmen, industrial chemists, medical and nursing staff. Canada appears to be an easy country to settle in and well over a million UK nationals have emigrated there since 1945. But some people have found it hard there because of the harsh winter climate and the difficulty of finding new friends. A short holiday in Canada is probably a good way of deciding if Canada is for you and will give an opportunity to assess employment prospects.

Europe

The completion of the single market heralded much wider job mobility within the European Union and major companies are travelling across national frontiers to fill key positions. Britons are attracted to mainland Europe since salaries in many EU countries are currently higher than in the UK.

The changes within Eastern European countries, allowing free travel and the right to work abroad, are having a significant impact. This could put pressure on some expatriate opportunities since the salary expectations of Eastern Europeans are substantially below those of workers in the UK and its EU partners.

Outside the Union the picture is very different. Nearly all the non-EU European countries exercise very strong control over work permits and immigration, and often the only way around these barriers is marriage to a national of the country concerned. This may seem rather a high price to pay for finding a job. Language may also be a problem throughout most European countries and in nearly all cases a knowledge of the language of the country is essential. An exception to this is the case of short duration contracts for skilled tradespeople, particularly in Germany and the Netherlands. However, work in this area has seen many abuses by potential employers and agents, and anyone accepting these contracts would be well advised to check out the potential employer. This will avoid travelling across Europe only to find that no job exists or that it is a very different proposition from that which had been promised. Germany s attempt to put the brake on immigration indicates that the domestic scene there has its problems.

Middle East

There are still opportunities for British expatriates to work in the Middle East and over half of these vacancies are in Saudi Arabia. The demand comes from both the commercial and public sector, with contract conditions which range from the superb to the absolute rock bottom. In the past few years there have been delays and cancellations of many major projects in the Middle East, with a substantial reduction in expatriate opportunities although the demand for UK workers was less affected than for other nationals. Recruitment for the region has shown significant recovery following the Gulf War, although the situation still remains volatile.

Saudi Arabia

There are jobs in British, US, German, French, Dutch and multinational and Saudi companies. Many expatriates live in self-contained compounds, some of which contain swimming pools, shops, squash courts, video, TV and other excellent facilities, including restaurants. Some of these compounds provide a very high standard of living and are suitable for families. But many compounds are bachelor only, and the conditions are very basic and much like an army camp. Most Saudi companies and other companies with small-scale businesses and projects will provide accommodation in villas or apartments which are located in the community. Much of this accommodation is adequate and British expatriates can expect to get at least their own bedroom and shared commonroom facilities.

There is a strictly limited number of visas for wives and children, and these are normally available to staff who are qualified to at least HNC standard or where the employer can make out a special case. Whether you live in a compound, villa or apartment you will be bound by the following strict rules:

1. Women are generally not allowed to work.
2. Women are not allowed to drive.
3. Women cannot leave the house unless accompanied, even for simple things like shopping.
4. No alcohol is allowed.
5. No pork or pork products are allowed.
6. Social contact between men and women is extremely limited.
7. The normal working week is five and a half or six ten-hour days.

The effect of these rules may mean that a wife is a prisoner in the home for long periods and her life can be more difficult than her husband s. It demands a ready ability to amuse oneself for long periods. Rules in Saudi Arabia are rigidly enforced and it is foolish to break them, since penalties are very harsh by Western standards.

Other countries in the Middle East

Other Middle Eastern countries also provide jobs for British workers, albeit a smaller volume. The most significant markets are

Bahrain, Dubai, Abu Dhabi, Qatar, Oman and Sharjah. Lebanon is also now slowly emerging from the years of civil war. Conditions vary considerably in the region and are generally more liberal than in Saudi Arabia. Bahrain and Dubai are the most popular locations in the Gulf with British expatriates because life is easier and there are fewer restrictions. Rates of pay tend to reflect conditions, with Saudi Arabia paying highest and Bahrain at the lower end of the scale. All salaries in the Gulf States are free of local tax and there is free movement of currency to the United Kingdom or elsewhere. Opportunities throughout the Middle East generally provide the chance to make significant savings.

North Africa

The countries in the area which offer the greatest number of opportunities are Libya, Egypt and Tunisia.

Libya provides the greatest number of jobs and these are mainly concerned with various facets of the Libyan oil industry.

Expatriates are generally well treated and are welcomed by the local population. The oil companies take very good care of their workers and there is no harassment of workers by the authorities. Work for oil companies is either head office based, and in this case is generally in a major city and offers married status contracts, or is desert based. Desert based posts are always bachelor status and all-found in terms of accommodation, food and recreational facilities, and involve rotational work cycles. Rotations range from 35 days on, 21 days off, to 90 days on with 21 days off. On each rotation round-trip air tickets are provided. Salaries are paid offshore in US dollars or pounds sterling without deduction. Workers are normally safeguarded against any UK tax liability. These positions offer high levels of savings.

Libya is a Moslem country, but it is much less strict than Saudi Arabia. Women can go out unaccompanied, work and drive, and enjoy a reasonable social life.

Currently Britain does not enjoy diplomatic relations with Libya and UK interests are taken care of by the British Interests Section of the Italian Embassy. One should realise that government help might be difficult to obtain in times of emergency and UN sanctions are in force at the time of writing.

Consumer goods are scarce and are very highly priced in Libya and are better bought outside the country. Fresh foods are freely available including meat (except pork), vegetables, fruit, bread, rice, sugar etc. Processed foods are more expensive than in the UK. The importation of liquor is prohibited.

The number of openings in Egypt has increased, particularly since the country started to receive greater US and foreign aid, but there are threats to foreigners from Islamic fundamentalists. There are also a small number of jobs available in Tunisia where it is useful to be able to speak French. The present political turmoil in Algeria rules it out of the picture for all but the foolhardy.

West Africa

The main country for expatriate recruitment in this area is Nigeria which recruits substantially from the UK. The main requirements are in engineering and management. Work permits are difficult to obtain and applications have to be fully documented to prove the expertise of the individual. People taking up employment in Nigeria need to take care of both their property and themselves since there is a significant incidence of theft and aggravated robbery. Many companies provide employees with assistance to ensure their safety and security. Local taxation tends to be punitive throughout the region.

East Africa

The opportunities in this area have greatly diminished and Kenya is the only country offering significant prospects. It can provide a high standard of living and an attractive way of life, but taxes are high and remittances outside the country are restricted.

Central Africa

The prime opportunities in this area are to be found in Zambia, which recruits substantial numbers of UK expatriates for work in the copper belt. Zambia offers a pleasant way of life although certain commodities become scarce from time to time. At times personal security has been a problem. Salaries are only moderate, and annual remittances are not likely to exceed £6000 per annum. Zimbabwe is offering new opportunities for British expatriates, mostly on short-term contracts, although some longer-term (four- to five-year) contracts are available.

South Africa

There has always been a large number of opportunities in South Africa for British workers. The country enjoys a superb climate and offers good living conditions for expatriates and it would be seen as an ideal place to work were it not for the volatile political and racial situation and the need for a high level of personal security.

The Far East

The Far East is now often referred to as the Asia Pacific Rim , a loose term which includes south-east Asia, Japan, Korea, and in view of the economic structure of the region, often embraces Australia as well.

The troubles of these tiger economies have, of course, been well charted over the last year, though reports from the region suggest that their impact on the job market for expatriates may have been overstated. There have certainly been major cutbacks in capital projects   hotels, prestige offices, major engineering projects and the like   but businesses in the region have continued to trade vigorously and indeed some commentators have seen signs of an economic upturn, driven by what are now sharply devalued currencies in most of the region. There is also a continuing and growing demand for people with IT skills.

The two major economies that have not devalued are China and Taiwan. There is an enormous amount of economic activity going on in China in which foreign firms are heavily involved. According to a report in the Economist (24.10.98) currently some 120,000 foreign enterprises or joint ventures employ about 17m people, though it is always difficult to get reliable figures about China, where the comparison of apples with pears is endemic   the pace of change and development varies widely in different parts of that huge country, though statistics tend to be presented in the aggregate. Thus other estimates put significant foreign participation much lower. A recent conference at IMD suggested that 16,000 western firms are currently active in China, predominantly in Hong Kong and the coastal cities.

Job opportunities for westerners with Chinese enterprises are virtually non-existent, though there is considerable scope for racial Chinese who have been educated in Europe or America. Primarily, though, jobs on offer in the Pacific rim countries are with western firms, not with local companies. Indeed the cultural differences between Asia and the West could make it difficult for a western manager to work in any but the most sophisticated Asian business environments a point neatly illustrated in a novel by Paul Theroux, *Saint Jack*. Though written more than a decade ago, cultural factors do not change much within that kind of time span.

Australia

There are very few opportunities outside the formal emigration process and in-company relocation. If you are interested in individual relocation it is best to contact Australia House to find out which jobs are likely to get acceptance for immigration. Immigration policy encourages the entrepreneur willing to invest and set up a business which might provide more jobs.

South America and the West Indies

There are very limited opportunities for British expatriates in South America. Invariably a fluent knowledge of Spanish or Portuguese (depending on precise location) is essential. Economically, South America falls mainly under US influence and turns more readily to the North American market for recruitment. However, the conflicts in Central America and the security problems of some South American countries have reduced the number of Americans willing to consider posts in the area. Living standards are high but so is inflation. In many locations theft is rife and precautions need to be taken to protect yourself and your property. The West Indies now offers few expatriate opportunities and these are keenly contested because of the good climate and living conditions.

Conclusion

You may think that the facts portrayed paint a rather gloomy picture of the opportunities available. However, the rewards can be high and work abroad usually offers the chance to make significant savings. The amount of your savings depends largely on the location chosen and your attitude to life abroad.

Perhaps the expatriate who finds life the most difficult is the married man with teenage children since in many countries secondary education is either unavailable or extremely expensive. The alternative of a UK boarding school is also expensive, and tends to break up the family unit.

We strongly recommend that if you are seriously contemplating a job overseas you should research the job market very carefully. You should try to decide whether you have the ability to survive and succeed overseas and whether, where appropriate, your family can also adapt to the new life style. Once you have made this decision honestly you must identify the countries which offer the rewards and the conditions you require.

1

The Overseas Job Market

It is difficult, if not impossible, to form any precise idea of the number of UK citizens currently working overseas. Despite the flood of human resource statistics which flows from Whitehall, there is no central register of expatriates. The broad trend can, however, be adduced by examining people s intentions, looking at the range of jobs on offer, and the numbers of applications for particular posts. The peak was probably reached in 1976. Thereafter, rising unemployment in many countries, political uncertainties in the Middle East and parts of Africa and perhaps more optimism about prospects at home combined to make people more cautious. Moreover, reductions in UK tax rates tended to reduce financial incentives to work and live overseas.

Expatriate employment, though continuing to be an attractive prospect to UK job seekers, is no longer the Klondike it used to be. At present only the most intrepid and seasoned expatriates are prepared to take up Middle East postings, although rebuilding in the Lebanon could offer some interesting opportunities if the situation there returns to stability, following the latest setback. Balance of trade and political problems have affected the expatriate job market in Africa and Latin America, though the Far East and Pacific have continued relatively stable. Compensating factors are a continuing demand in specific areas of employment, notably in the financial and retail service sectors and the growth in short-term contracts.

This shading off has been accompanied by a trend towards greater stability in salaries, as well as some degree of uniformity in the remuneration packages being offered by different employers for comparable jobs, as competition for expatriate labour diminishes. In many parts of the world remuneration in sterling terms has only risen by the level of UK inflation.

Opportunities have diminished more markedly at technician and supervisory levels, because of competition from qualified personnel in developing countries who are prepared to accept much lower salaries, and also because of the gradual emergence of skilled workers among local nationals as the fruits of training schemes come on-stream. On the other hand, at more senior grades the relatively low level of British executive salaries by international standards continues to make UK managers an attractive proposition especially those who are prepared to be reasonably flexible about working and living conditions. The typical American expatriate employee will often expect to take with him the standard of living associated with an executive lifestyle in the US. Consequently, more senior jobs are going to British or European personnel.

Engineers and technicians

This term covers many grades of expatriate worker, from truck drivers and road builders to site supervisors and project directors. Many overseas companies, especially airlines and construction companies, recruit directly in the UK by advertising in UK newspapers. Examine all such offers carefully. Many companies will arrange for technicians going abroad to meet compatriots on leave, who can answer their questions.

However, this is one area where opportunities are now very limited indeed. Workers from countries such as Korea, the Philippines and Pakistan now predominate at this end of the labour market.

At the top end of the scale, the Malla Technical Recruitment Consultancy at 173 175 Drummond Street, London NW1 3JD (tel: 0171 388 2284, fax: 0171 387 8312, e-mail: recruit@malla.com, web site: http://www.malla.com) has a register of international engineering experts on all subjects who are leased out on contract world-wide.

The professionally qualified

The professions and qualifications most in demand overseas are medicine, agriculture and food, process engineering, finance, civil engineering and construction. In general, positions in these areas can best be found through the companies themselves or through management consultants and head-hunters (executive search consultants). Many consultants specialise in particular professions such as accountancy.

Some are on a small, specialist scale. An example of an international, multi-purpose agency is International Training and Recruitment Link Ltd (ITRL, 56 High Street, Harston, Cambridge CB2 5PZ; tel: 01223 872747, fax: 01223 872212). ITRL recruit only for the Middle East, the Far East and North Africa. They are a major international training and recruitment agency specialising in executive, managerial, technical and scientific fields. They are particularly involved with construction, maintenance and operations, engineering, oil and petrochemicals, health care, hospitals, and general, financial and commercial management.

People with professional qualifications will obviously consult their appropriate professional association or trade union. In the medical profession, jobs are usually found through advertisements in the medical press. BMA members are advised to contact the International Department at the British Medical Association (BMA House, Tavistock Square, London WC1H 9JP; tel: 0171 383 6491, fax: 0171 383 6644) for information and advice on working abroad. Most intending emigrants would prefer to work in North America and Australasia, but opportunities are limited. Within the EU there is recognition of medical qualifications. Remuneration is highest in Germany and Denmark, followed by France, Belgium and Luxembourg, with the UK towards the bottom of the scale. But there is unlikely to be much of a brain drain to Europe since there is already a surplus of doctors in training and the profession is becoming particularly overcrowded in Italy and Scandinavia.

The developing countries, by contrast, are in urgent need of doctors and nurses. The average doctor/patient ratio in these countries is about 1:10,000 compared with 1:750 in the UK; in some areas it is as high as 1:80,000, rural areas being almost completely neglected. The International Health Exchange (8 10 Dryden Street, London WC2E 9NA; tel: 0171 836 5833, fax: 0171 379 1239 e-mail: info@ihe.org.uk) helps provide appropriately trained health personnel for programmes in countries in Africa, Asia, the Pacific, Eastern Europe, Latin America and other areas seeking assistance. It maintains a register of health workers for those actively seeking work in developing countries and areas requiring humanitarian aid.

Another useful publication is the CEPEC *Recruitment Guide*, which lists agencies and search consultants in the UK, including full details of their overseas work areas. CEPEC is itself a human resource consultancy and specialises in employee counselling, outplacement and career management. Further details from CEPEC, Lilly House, 13 Hanover Square, London W1R 9HD, tel: 0171 629 2266; fax: 0171 629 7066; e-mail: enquiries%focus@notesgw.compuserve.com.

In the UK the Department for Trade and Industry (DTI) provides information on the mutual recognition of professional qualifications at degree level and above and has overall responsibility for the operation of the UK Certificate of Experience Scheme, which is run by the British Chambers of Commerce on behalf of the DTI. The Department for Education and Employment (DfEE) provides advice on qualifications below degree level.

Further information can be obtained from DTI at Bay 212, Kingsgate House, 66 74 Victoria Street, London SW1E 6SW, tel: 0171 215 4648; fax: 0171 215 4489, and from DfEE at Room E4b, Moorfoot, Sheffield S1 4PQ, tel: 0114 259 4151; fax: 0114 259 4151; e-mail carol.rowlands@dfee.gov.uk, who can advise on international recognition of qualifications. Copies of the DTI/DfEE publication *Europe Open for Professions* are available from either organisation.

Information on the Certificate of Experience Scheme is available from the Certification Unit, British Chambers of Commerce, Westwood House, Westwood Business Park, Coventry CV4 8HS, tel: 01203 695688.

Finally, one can get a direct comparison between any UK qualifications and those recognised in any EU country via the

National Academic Recognition Information Centre. However, you can only do this from abroad to the local jobcentre equivalent by asking to contact the local NARIC representative.

Business schools

For high flyers, a possible route into the overseas job market is a course at one of the European business schools   either a short executive programme or a full-scale MBA. The latter course is in huge demand and is offered by a very large and ever-increasing number of schools world-wide, whether on a full, part-time or distant basis. The Internet is also being adopted as a learning medium. However, one should weigh up its worth with care, given the effort, time and expense involved. A book and directory of business schools approved by the Association of MBAs is the annual *AMBA Guide to Business Schools* (FT/Pitman).

Another possibility lies with the Open University Business School, which offers a range of 6-month courses on a distance-learning basis. OUBS Customer Relations Centre, PO Box 625, Milton Keynes MK1 1TY, tel: 01908 654321 (24 hrs).

The longest established European business school is INSEAD. Founded less than 40 years ago, in 1959, today the school is widely recognised as one of the most influential business schools in the world. Its global scope and multicultural diversity make it the model for international management education. Located in Fontainebleau, France, INSEAD runs an 11-month MBA programme, a PhD programme and shorter executive development courses with a focus on general management in an international environment. Holders of the MBA can find jobs through the INSEAD Career Management Service. The emphasis is on international business management. Each year several hundred companies find that INSEAD is an excellent source for recruiting talented, multilingual and geographically mobile managers with high potential. Over one-third of graduates go on to start their own business sometime in their career. Students come from more than 50 countries with no single nationality dominating.

The majority of MBA students come as non-sponsored individuals. Various scholarships and loans are available. INSEAD is clearly a good investment for your future if you have the right background. Courses are taught in English but a fair knowledge of French is required. A third language is required in order to graduate and courses in German and Spanish are available. For further information contact INSEAD, MBA Admissions, Boulevard de Constance, F-77305 Fountainebleau Cedex, tel: +33 1 60 72 40 05, fax: +33 1 60 74 33 00.

Department for International Development

The Department for International Development (DfID) manages Britain s programme of aid to developing countries. The range of skills required under the programme is vast and constantly changing. Workers are drawn from a large number of backgrounds and professions. Agriculture, architecture, education, engineering, finance, fisheries, forestry, health, management, social development and surveying are just some of the professional disciplines where experienced people may be needed.

The minimum requirement for most vacancies is usually a professional qualification and at least two to three year s relevant experience, including some in a developing country. A limited number of postgraduate study awards are also offered. Successful applicants are usually given assignments of up to two to three years as either a co-operation officer, employed by the DfID and on loan to the overseas client government, or as a supplemented officer, under contract to the relevant government on local salary, with a supplement provided by the DfID to equal UK pay level.

Where the DfID needs immediate expert advice, consultants are used on appointments lasting from a few days to several months. Such assignments are open to both employed and self-employed specialists. The DfID also provides assistance to the United Nations and its specialist agencies (eg International Labour Office) in recruitment to field programmes, as well as the Junior Professional Officers Scheme.

For further information please write, enclosing a CV, to the Service and Resource Development Group, Room AH304, Department for International Development, Abercrombie House, Eaglesham Road, East Kilbride, Glasgow G75 8EA (tel: 01355 844000, fax: 01355 844099).

The British Council

The British Council promotes Britain abroad. It provides access to British ideas, talents and experience through education and training, books and periodicals, the English language, the arts, science and technology.

It is represented in 109 countries, 209 libraries and information centres and over 118 English language schools and has offices in 228 towns and cities. The Council provides an unrivalled network of contacts with government departments, universities, embassies, professional bodies and business and industry in Britain and overseas.

The British Council is an independent and non-political organisation. In developing countries it has considerable responsibilities for the DfID in the field of educational aid, and in recent years it has become involved in the design and implementation of education projects funded by international lending agencies such as the World Bank.

The Council also acts as an agent for governments and other employers overseas in recruiting for contract teaching and educational advisory posts in ministries, universities, training colleges and secondary and primary schools. The Council usually guarantees the terms of such posts and sometimes subsidises them. In these appointments it works closely with the DfID. Teachers are also recruited on contract for the Council s network of English language schools.

Vacancies include teacher trainers, curriculum designers and British studies specialists for posts in projects or for direct placement with overseas institutions. Candidates must be professionally qualified and have appropriate experience.

Appointments are usually for one or two years initially and often renewable by agreement. Vacancies are advertised in *The Times Educational Supplement*, *The Guardian* and other journals as appropriate.

Teaching English as a foreign language

EFL teachers are in demand in both the private and public education sectors abroad. Public sector recruiting is usually done by the government concerned through the British Council; private recruitment varies from the highly reputable organisation (such as International House) to the distinctly dubious. Most EFL teachers have a degree and/or teaching qualification. An RSA/ Cambridge TEFLA qualification will also be required. A four-week RSA/Cambridge Certificate in TEFLA (Teaching English as a Foreign Language to Adults) is available at International House in London and Hastings, and at a number of other centres. The course may also be taken on a part-time basis. Experienced EFL teachers may gain a further qualification, the RSA/Cambridge Diploma in TEFLA (essential for more responsible posts). The University of Cambridge Local Examinations Syndicate (tel: 01223 553311) can provide comprehensive lists of the centres running courses leading to these awards, worldwide.

Apart from the checklist on page 120 (most of which does not apply), bear the following points in mind when applying for an EFL post abroad:

1. Will your travel expenses be paid? Some schools refund them on arrival or at the end of the contract.
2. Is accommodation provided? If so, is it free or is the rent deducted from your salary? Is your salary sufficient to meet the deduction? If you find your own accommodation, are you helped to find it, especially if your knowledge of the local language is modest? Does the school lend you money to help pay the accommodation agency s fee and deposit? If the accommodation is provided, does it include hard or soft furnishing, and what should you bring with you?
3. Contracts and work permits. Will you have a contract, how long for, and will the school obtain the permits to legalise your position in the country?
4. Salary. Are you paid by the hour, week or month? If you are paid by the hour, is there a guaranteed minimum amount of teaching available for you? Do ensure that you can survive financially in the face of cancelled classes, bank strikes and numerous public holidays. Are there cost of living adjustments in countries with alarming inflation rates?

   Salaries are generally geared to local rates, but do make sure they are adequate. In sterling terms, one may earn a very low salary (in Rabat, for instance) yet enjoy a higher standard of living than a teacher earning double in Italy, or three times as much in Singapore.

5. How many hours are you expected to teach? Be wary of employers who expect you to teach more than about 25 hours a week (remember you need additional time to prepare lessons). What paid leisure time do you expect? This is variable, but two weeks at both Easter and Christmas is fairly common.

6. What type of student will you be teaching? Children or adults, those learning general English or English for special purposes (ESP)?

7. What levels will you be teaching and what course books are used? Will there be a director of studies to help you over initial difficulties and provide some form of in-service training?

A knowledge of the local language is an asset; in some situations, it is absolutely essential. Without it, one s social contacts are restricted to the English-speaking community which, in some areas, is virtually non-existent.

Locating the vacancies

1. International House recruits teachers only for its own affiliated schools of which there are 100 in 26 countries. These schools abide by certain conditions:
   (a) There is a maximum of 25 hours teaching per week
   (b) Holidays are paid
   (c) Travel expenses are refunded
   (d) Medical insurance is arranged
   (e) There is usually a director of studies or senior teacher
   (f) Students are tested before the class starts so there are no mixed level classes.

   Vacancies elsewhere can be seen on the IH notice board in the Staffing Unit, 106 Piccadilly, London W1V 9FL (tel: 0171 491 2598, fax: 0171 491 2679, e-mail: 100645; 1547@compuserve.com).

2. Advertisements appear in publications such as *The Times Educational Supplement* (Fridays) and *The Guardian* (Tuesdays).

3. The British Council Central Management of Direct Teaching recruits EFL teachers for the British Council s Language Centres around the world. It can be contacted at 10 Spring Gardens, London SW1A 2BN (tel: 0171 389 4931, fax: 0171 389 4140). British Council vacancies are also advertised in the press. The British Council Overseas Appointments Services recruits for posts funded directly by overseas employers. It can be contacted at Medlock Street, Manchester M15 4AA, tel: 0161 957 7384; fax: 0161 957 7397.

4. The Centre for British Teachers, CfBT Education Services, 1 The Chambers, East Street, Reading RG1 4JD (tel: 0118 952 3900, fax: 0118 952 3924, e-mail: intrecruit@cfbt-hq.org.uk) recruits teachers for English language teaching projects in Brunei, Oman and Turkey and educational specialists for consultancies on donor funded projects in Eastern Europe, Africa, Asia and India.

5. The Central Bureau (c/o British Council, 10 Spring Gardens, London SW1A 2BN, tel: 0171 389 4929; fax: 0171 389 4426) compiles guides on a range of paid and voluntary work opportunities worldwide.

Opportunities for women

The Sex Discrimination Act makes it illegal to specify in an advertisement whether a British job is open to a man or woman, but no such restrictions apply to advertisements of overseas jobs. In practice, openings for career women in overseas countries are limited. Most European countries, theoretically at least, provide equal pay for equal work and apply the non-discrimination convention of the ILO. As in Britain, there is no discrimination in theory, but plenty in practice. It is difficult for women to get top-level jobs in industry and management in EU countries, though perhaps more usual in Sweden and in the USA. The number of women in senior business, managerial and technical positions is very small compared to the number of men in such positions. Many women do, however, work overseas as nurses, bilingual secretaries, interpreters, translators, teachers and nannies. Their salaries are usually above those paid in the UK and jobs are much sought after.

International demand for UK nurses has been reduced by world-wide recession and radical health service reforms in many countries, but opportunities still exist, particularly in the USA and the Middle East, for those with sound, post-registration experience and qualifications. The International Office of the Royal College of Nursing, 20 Cavendish Square, London W1M 0AB, tel: 0171 409 3333, provides overseas employment advice to its members, and overseas vacancies appear in weekly nursing journals such as *Nursing Standard*, on sale at newsagents.

In many developing countries, and in parts of the Middle East, it might be difficult, if not impossible, for a woman to take up paid work. A woman who gave up her own career to accompany her husband overseas might find it difficult to get a job in her own right unless she was exceptionally qualified, say as a doctor.

Many wives in developing countries club together to run a crÈche, nursery or kindergarten. As well as serving a useful purpose in themselves, such activities help to relieve the problem of boredom which is a frequent source of complaint among wives, particularly those whose children may be at school in the UK.

Secretarial jobs abroad are advertised in UK media and sometimes for English-speaking secretaries in foreign newspapers.

Au pairs

To be an au pair, you must be single and aged 18 27 ideally, with no dependants. Typically independent, resourceful and adaptable, au pairs also need to have a secure and sensible personality, as well as a sense of humour. Above all, a true fondness for children is essential.

The ideal relationship should be like that of a brother or sister. As well as looking after children, au pairs are normally expected to handle light housework, eg dusting, polishing, hoovering and ironing. Childcare can include preparing breakfast, providing an escort to school, looking after small children during the day, encouraging play, changing nappies and supervising bath time!

Hours vary from 25 30 hours per week for an au pair to 30 38 hours for an au pair +. On more formal lines, there is also the category of mother s help . Au pairs are provided with a pocket money allowance. The amount will vary according to hours. A private bedroom will be provided, and there should be two full days off per week. Use of a car can be an added benefit.

As a member of a family, au pairs are more able to become involved in the society and culture of the country they are visiting. There is the opportunity to learn a new language, which can enhance job prospects. Many au pairs develop close friendships with their host families that are maintained over the years.

The au pair is expected to make and pay for their own travel arrangements, although they should be met by the family on arrival. Any further in-country travel should be borne by the host. Length of stay can vary from two months to a year. With longer stays, it is not unusual for the family to pay the return air fare. Health insurance is a good idea, although possession of Form E111 can provide free or cheap medical care in some countries (mainly EU form available from DSS or local post offices). It is also wise to have a complete medical and dental check-up before departure. In addition to travel costs, enough money should be taken to meet sundry expenses like language classes, evening entertainment, etc. Food and household items should be provided in full by the host.

Although this all sounds very easy, equally, it is not difficult to find oneself in a very lonely situation, particularly if arrangements have been made privately. In this case, it is extremely important to make sure that all details are given in writing before travelling. It is often better to make use of an agency, who have established contacts with customer families and can make arrangements on your behalf, as well as providing support should you encounter difficulties.

Voluntary work

Those who are technically skilled or professionally qualified and who would like to share their skills with developing countries could apply to VSO (Voluntary Service Overseas).

VSO has over 1750 skilled people working in 58 countries: in Africa, Asia, the Caribbean, Eastern Europe and the Pacific. Placements are in education, health, natural resources, technical trades, engineering, business, communications and social development. Volunteers are aged from 20 to 70, usually 23 60, with no dependent children.

Accommodation and a modest living allowance is provided by the local employer. Flights, insurance and other allowances are provided by VSO. Posts are generally for two years, but many volunteers stay longer.

Working as a VSO volunteer is very much a two-way process; volunteers often feel that they learn more from the society and culture they are involved with than they can possibly contribute. For further information contact The Enquiries Unit, VSO, 317 Putney Bridge Road, London SW15 2PN, tel: 0181 780 7500, fax: 0181 780 7576, web site: http://www.oneworld.org/vso/.

Working on a kibbutz

Kibbutzim are communal societies in Israel which produce crops and light industrial goods. Founded in 1909, there are now 280 of them, each with its own cultural and social life. Matters of principle relating to the general running of the kibbutz are discussed and decided at a weekly meeting of all the members.

Arrangements to work on a kibbutz are made by agencies in different countries. Applicants should be between 18 and 32 years of age, physically and mentally fit; expectant mothers and one-parent families are not eligible. Volunteers buy their own return tickets, or must have adequate funds for the return journey. Minimum length of stay on a kibbutz is six weeks and the maximum as a working visitor is six months. Places in July and August are very limited and applications should be made at least two months in advance. There are no wages a small sum is paid to each member weekly as pocket money; toilet requisites, cigarettes and stationery are distributed regularly. Accommodation (two to four in a room), food, laundry, entertainment and medical care are all provided free.

Work starts early so that volunteers are mostly at leisure during the hottest part of the day; the working visitor is expected to put in eight hours daily, six days a week, in either agriculture, light industry or domestic service (dining room, laundry, kitchen). Sunday is a normal working day as the weekend starts at Friday lunch time. After four weeks there is a three-day free period. Kibbutzim arrange occasional excursions for their working volunteers.

Apply for information to: Kibbutz Representatives, 1a Accommodation Road, London NW11 8ED, tel: 0181 458 9235, fax: 0181 455 7930, e-mail: enquiries@kibbuttz.org.uk.

Learning the language

The traditional picture of the Englishman who expects all foreigners to speak English or hopes to get by with schoolboy French has disappeared. In the modern world of fast-moving communications, language proficiency is an essential tool. It is true that English is the world s leading language for business and commerce and is taught in most schools as the second language. But, in many countries, knowledge of the indigenous language is essential and often a prerequisite of employment. It is vital where a job involves contact with local people, particularly in administration or industry where orders and instructions have to be given and understood. Even where a job is technical and does not involve direct communication, it is an advantage to be able to join in conversation and be more fully integrated with local society.

Anybody working in the EU should be proficient in French and/or German. In Spain and Latin America, Spanish is essential (except in Brazil where Portuguese is spoken). In the Third World, and in the Middle East, knowledge of indigenous languages is not so essential but it is useful to speak Arabic or Swahili, particularly in remoter areas. So the best thing you can do if you are going to work overseas is to learn one or more languages or brush up your existing knowledge.

The increasing demand for languages is being met in a number of ways. There is the do-it-yourself approach which can include:

1. Learning at home, using Linguaphone courses or other self-study materials.
2. Hiring a private tutor: try to find a native speaker, who is prepared to conduct most of the lesson in the foreign lan-

guage rather than waste valuable time talking about the language in English.

3. Open learning courses at your local college of further education or university. Many have established drop in centres where you have access to a language laboratory, and possibly also computer-assisted learning, with back-up from a tutor when you need it. This form of learning can be very effective for those whose time is limited and who need a flexible programme of study.

You may prefer to attend a language class, and these are run by most local authority adult education institutes and colleges. However, learning on the basis of one or two sessions a week is not the most effective way of getting to grips with a foreign language you will make a lot more progress on a more intensive course.

Private language schools generally offer intensive or crash courses. Be careful to check the bona fides of a course before you enrol. An example of the type of tuition available is Berlitz (UK) Ltd (9 13 Grosvenor Street, London W1A 3BZ; tel: 0171 915 0909, fax: 0171 915 0222), which offers language programmes to suit the linguistic needs of all in both the business and non-business fields. Berlitz offer crash courses, private lessons and semi-private courses for two to three people in most languages. The full-time Total Immersion[fi] course lasts from one to six weeks for those wishing to improve their existing ability quickly. In-house courses for companies are also available.

Conrad Executive Language Training (15 King Street, London WC2E 8HN; tel: 0171 240 0855, fax: 0171 240 0715), founded in 1974, is specifically geared towards meeting the linguistic needs of business people. Tuition is structured to suit both the schedule of each client and specific language requirements. Classes can be held at Conrad s Covent Garden centre, in-company or privately, after a thorough language evaluation and needs analysis. Conrad is registered to ISO 9000 by BSI.

Courses available: The Crash Course (9 am 4 pm), suitable for all levels, is held over five days (not necessarily consecutively). The Extensive Course, also suitable for all levels, can be taken between 8 am and 8 pm; classes last at least one hour and are at times to suit the client. Conrad also offers cross-cultural training programmes for groups and individuals for all countries, and the Corporate Group Course (ideal for companies requiring language training for a small group of executives who have the same objectives and similar background knowledge).

The European Centre is a language consultancy helping individuals, companies and other organisations to communicate more effectively in international markets. Winner of two national awards in 1996, it specialises in the design, management and delivery of language training programmes for business and vocational purposes. All the programmes are designed to meet individual or corporate needs, based on a language assessment and training needs analysis. Further details from Jonathan Smith, The European Centre, Peter House, St Peter s Square, Manchester M1 5AN, tel: 0161 281 8844, fax: 0161 281 8822, e-mail: training@evcentre.co.uk.

Fees at language schools are high, but there is general agreement that it is a worthwhile investment. Administrators of language schools sometimes complain that too few companies attach real importance to language proficiency and often leave it too late for effective action.

The Association of Language Excellence Centres (ALEC) is a professional body for providers of language training and related services for business. It aims to establish and maintain quality

Further information and advice are available from CILT (the Centre for Information on Language Teaching and Research), 20 Bedfordbury, London WC2N 4LB; tel: 0171 379 5101, fax: 0171 379 5082. Written enquiries are preferred. At the same address is NATBLIS, the National Business Language Information Service (tel: 0171 379 5131, fax: 0171 379 5082), which provides information on business language training and on providers of business language services training, cultural briefing, interpreting, and translation.

2

Finding a Job Abroad

How do you set about trying to find a job abroad? The immediate and most effective answer will come as a surprise to some: you look in the UK papers, not only the nationals and the Sundays, but also the specialist press of your profession or occupation. Graduates can look in annual career directories, for details of overseas employers. It stands to reason that any employer wishing to recruit UK personnel will advertise in the UK press, but there is also another good reason why the overseas vacancies pages are worth scanning: they give a very good indication of going rates of salary and benefits in particular parts of the world. Indeed, even if you have been made an offer without having replied to an advertisement, it is worth looking closely at these pages over a few issues to make sure that the remuneration package being put to you is in line with market rates.

However, if you are actually looking for a job, do not just confine your reading to the ads. It is worth reading any news and features that relate to the countries you are interested in. Not only will news of general or specific developments a new type of industry opening up, for instance give you background information that might be very useful in an interview, but it might also in itself be a source of job leads. Indeed, if you can read the papers in the language of the country you would like to work in, so much the better. They will go into potential job-lead information in more depth, apart from the fact that they also contain job advertisements. How useful these are likely to be to the British job-seeker depends somewhat on the country in which the paper is published. In the Far East, for instance, employers would almost exclusively be looking for locals when advertising in a local paper. But in the EU, a response from a suitably qualified EU national might well produce a positive result. Indeed in some European countries, there is a trend towards taking on British people for overseas jobs. Quite a number of European countries are involved in projects in the Middle East and in other resource-rich countries where English is the dominant language. In those cases they are beginning to think in terms of putting some UK nationals on location as well as their own people.

Apart from the major newspapers, some countries have also developed their equivalent of career publications. Published every two weeks, *Overseas Jobs Express*, Premier House, Shoreham Airport, Sussex BN43 5FF (tel: 01273 440220, fax: 01273 440229, e-mail: editor@overseasjobs.com, web site: http://www.overseasjobs.com) carries international recruitment advertising and provides information and news about working abroad. This excellent paper costs £52 a year, or £18.95 for six issues. Overseas Jobs Express also publishes several other books including *Finding a Job in Canada* and *Finding a Job in Australia*, both £9.95, as well as a number of titles for young people wanting to live and work abroad.

There are also a number of news sheets which are advertised from time to time, but some of them, it must be said, are fly-by-night operations and you would be ill-advised to part with your money without seeing a sample copy or to subscribe for more than six months at a time.

Possible sources of job information are, of course, legion and they change constantly. Apart from keeping a close watch on the papers, as good a move as any is to get in touch with trade associations connected to the country in which you are interested or local chambers of commerce there. They will not be able to give you any job leads as such, unless you are very lucky, but they can usually give you lists of firms or other organisations which have a particularly close connection with the UK. Preliminary leads of this nature are essential if you are going to a country to look for a job on spec, though except in the EU you should never state this as your intention when entering a country. In most places now you need to have a job offer from a local employer in order to get a work permit, so you should always state that you are entering as a visitor, whatever your subsequent intention might be. It must be said, however, that some countries do not permit turning a visitor s visa into a work permit that is something you will have to check on, discreetly, before you go.

In general, however, going abroad on spec to find a job is not a good idea. Even in the EU, where it is permitted, some jobseekers have had unhappy experiences unless they are in hot areas such as electronics. By far the best plan is to get interviews lined up before you go or at least get some expressions of interest from potential employers they will probably not commit themselves to more than that from a distance, even if there is a job possibility. To do more might put them under an embarrassing moral obligation when you turn up on their doorstep, having spent a lot of time and money to get there.

British jobseekers now have greater access to vacancies in Europe with the introduction of the EURES (European Employment Services) computer network, providing jobseekers with free information and guidance on current opportunities throughout the European Union (EU). The database includes up-to-date information on living and working conditions in other member states. In Britain, anyone interested in working abroad can access the EURES database, and obtain advice from a Euroadviser, via their local Jobcentre. The Overseas Placing Unit of the Employment Service produces a useful information booklet *Working Abroad*, as well as a series of guides entitled *Working in* . . . , concerning specific countries. These deal with entry requirements, information sources, benefits, liabilities, taxation, state of the market and cultural notes. The OPU also holds information on work overseas in specific professions. Write with your details to Overseas Placing Unit, Level 2, Rockingham House, 123 West Street, Sheffield S1 4ER, tel: 0114 259 6051.

Further useful information on the EU and its members can also be accessed via Public Information Relays (PIR), European Documentation Centres (EDC) and Euro Info Centres (EIC) set up in libraries or at regional government offices or Business

Links. Contact your local library for details of your nearest source of EU information.

Writing on-spec letters to potential employers is a subject that is well covered elsewhere. In essence what you have to do is address yourself to something that you have identified as being the employer s need or possible need this is where researching the background and looking for job leads comes into play. For instance, if you have read in *Der Spiegel* or in *Frankfurter Allgemeine Zeitung* of a German firm being awarded a large contract in the Middle East, it is likely that they will respond in some way, provided your letter demonstrates that you have relevant experience. Even if they intend advertising the job, the fact that you have taken an intelligent interest in their activities will count in your favour. It is rarely worth while advertising in the situations wanted column though writing to headhunters is a good move, especially if you are qualified to work in one of the fields in current demand: electronic engineering, financial services and retailing. Letters should be kept short and your CV should not exceed two pages highlighting and quantifying achievements, rather than just listing posts you have held. With technical jobs you may have to show that your knowledge of the field is up to date with current developments, especially in areas where things are changing rapidly.

When a job is actually advertised, the interview will probably be in London, or your fares will be paid if you are called upon to travel abroad. Here again, the rules for replying to an advertisement are no different from those relating to UK employers: read the text carefully and frame your reply and organise your CV in such a way as to show you meet the essential requirements of the job. As one Canadian employer put it recently, paraphrasing, no doubt, John F Kennedy s much quoted presidential address, The question to ask is not what I can gain from moving to your company, but what your company (or organisation or school) can gain from me.

If you need to arrange your own travel, companies such as The Visaservice, 2 Northdown Street, London N1 9BG; tel: 0171 833 2709; 24-hour information line: 0891 343638 (50p at any time); fax: 0171 833 1857, web site: http//www. visaservice.co.uk specialise in processing applications for business, working holiday and tourism visas and passports on your behalf, which is particularly useful for those living outside London, where most embassies and consulates reside.

3

UK Taxation Aspects of Working Abroad

It is essential for anyone going to work abroad to seek advice on the tax implications of such a move. Your normal accountant or bank manager may not be sufficiently well versed in these matters, unless they have a good deal of experience in them, though most larger professional firms and bigger bank branches will be dealing with at least some expatriate clients. At the same time you should acquaint yourself at least with the basic principles of your tax position as an expatriate. Like most things concerned with tax, the concepts, although in some ways simple, are richly overlaid with confusion.

Range of taxes

First of all you should remember that the word tax embraces many different ways in which the UK tax man can put his hand in your pocket. For the expatriate it can include:

- Tax on income arising in the UK
- Tax on income arising overseas
- Capital gains tax
- Inheritance tax.

In addition, the expatriate needs to consider the tax laws of the country in which he has chosen to live.

You will usually be taxed on your overseas earnings in the country where you are working at that country s prevailing rate of tax and you may also be taxed in the UK. However, you should not have to pay tax on the same income twice under what are known as double taxation treaties.

Until the Spring 1998 Budget, anyone working abroad could escape paying tax in the UK (other than on income arising or earned in the UK) by spending 365 days out of the country. This could be any 365 day period and limited UK visits were allowed, and meant that any earnings from abroad escaped UK tax. This was known as the Foreign Earnings Deduction (FED).

Since the Budget and the abolition of the FED system the only way to escape UK tax is to become non-resident. This means that you must spend an entire tax year outside the UK to avoid UK tax on overseas earnings. Again, limited home-visits are allowed. The implications of this tax change are far reaching. Although famous rock bands have already received much publicity for changing their tour dates to escape UK tax, more humble workers may not find it so easy to change their contracts of employment. Those signing one year contracts to work overseas used to be able to escape UK tax on these earnings. They need to sign contracts that cover them for a full tax year or extend existing contracts to ensure they are working overseas for at least one tax year, for example from 6 April 1999 to April 2000. However, as many overseas workers   engineers, consultants, construction workers etc   are employed for the term of a project, this may not always be possible.

Anyone who had signed a contract to work overseas before the 17 March 1998 Budget and cannot change the term of their employment may now suffer 40 per cent tax on overseas earnings that they were expecting to earn tax free. If you are working for   or planning to work for   a UK multinational company that posts employees overseas, your employers will be aware of these tax implications and should be able to advise you on your position.

A handful of companies are planning to make up some of the losses employees will suffer as a result of the tax change but others will not. As a result you may find that working overseas is less financially attractive than in the past. The only group exempted from the abolition of FEDs are seafarers.

What is taxed in the UK

Regardless of whether your not your overseas earnings are free of UK tax, there are some items of income that cannot escape. Even if you are non-resident in the UK for tax purposes (you spend the entire tax year working or living overseas) all income arising in the UK is taxed here. So any interest on building society or bank savings, dividends, pensions or rents will be taxed in the UK. However, when calculating your tax liability the Inland Revenue will not add this UK income to your overseas earnings. As such you will probably escape higher rate tax. One way round this requirement is to move your investments off-shore. However, UK rental income will still be taxed and the Inland Revenue require agents (your letting agent or UK financial representative) to deduct tax before paying rents to overseas landlords. If you are resident for tax purposes in the UK (you spend less than the entire tax year working overseas) the Inland Revenue will tax you on your worldwide income.

Double taxation

As a result of the recent Budget changes you may find that your overseas earnings are taxed twice: once in the country where you are working and once in the UK.

You may also find that the country where you are working taxes you on your worldwide income as well as the Inland Revenue in the UK. To avoid being taxed twice you will usually be covered by a double taxation treaty (most countries have these and a list is available from your local tax office). The treaty will either say which country has the right to tax a particular source of income or will set out how you are able to set off the tax due or already paid in one country against the tax due or paid in another.

Non-residence

In using the innocuous word residence in the previous section we have touched on one of the key concepts in the whole business of the taxation of foreign earnings. To a large extent the amount of hold the tax man has over you depends in logic, as well as in justice and common sense, on where you are physically present during a tax year known as residence in the trade. The problem is how, having decided to leave this country for good or for a long period, do you establish that you are no longer resident here? The answer is simple, though buried in mumbo-jumbo.

If you work full time abroad for a period which includes at least one complete tax year (that is, one running from April 6 to April 5, not just any 12-month period) you will be regarded as no longer resident in this country. Provided your visits to the UK do not exceed 182 days in any one tax year nor an average of 90 days per annum over a four-year period, you will also be treated as non-resident. You can be non-resident on a yearly basis, so even if you do not meet the requirements one year, you may the next. You can also have dual residence for tax purposes in which case the double taxation treaty will apply. However, if you are in the armed forces or diplomatic service or another Crown employee, you will be taxed as if you worked in the UK and not as a non-resident. But any extra allowance paid for working abroad is not taxable. If you are in full-time employment abroad, the fact that you may maintain a house or flat here for your own use will not preclude you from being treated as non-resident.

So, what are the advantages of being non-resident? A non-resident is not liable to UK tax on any income arising outside the UK. This includes earnings from overseas employment even if those earnings are paid in the UK or sent back here. Any income arising in the UK such as profit from letting your UK home while you are away, investment income arising outside the UK or earnings from any duties (other than incidental duties) from an employment performed in the UK would potentially be subject to UK tax. However, a British subject who is not resident in the UK is still entitled to claim his full personal allowances which can be set against any income liable to UK tax.

Apart from the fact that once non-residence has been established your income outside the UK is no longer liable to UK tax, another benefit of your new-found status is that you may be able to get a tax rebate on some of the PAYE tax which you paid in the tax year in which you left. This is because you would probably not have had the full benefit of the personal allowances included in your PAYE tax code. The form on which you claim any repayment is a P85, which is also used to inform the Inland Revenue of your departure overseas.

Becoming a non-resident has other tax benefits. You may be able to escape capital gains tax   the tax paid on the profits or gains when you sell an asset. As a UK resident the first £6800 of gains in a tax year (the 1998-99 threshold) are exempt from tax. However, as a non-resident the entire amount of gains can escape this tax which is levied at your top rate of tax (up to 40 per cent).

In the past, overseas workers were able to escape the tax, provided they were non-resident for 36 months. So they could sell shares, second homes, businesses and any other investment or asset for vast profits free of tax. However, following the March 1998 Budget, if you sell a UK asset bought before you left the UK to be resident abroad, you will remain liable to UK capital gains tax unless you remain abroad for more than five complete tax years.

This means overseas workers can no longer sell assets while they are working abroad for short periods of time to escape tax. If you do not meet the five year rule your gains will be taxed in the UK in the year you resume residence. However, any capital gains on assets bought after you become resident abroad and before you return to the UK will still be exempt from capital gains tax provided they are held by a non-resident trust or non-resident company. As with income tax you should not be taxed twice under the double taxation treaty rules.

Failing to become non-resident

The situation becomes more difficult if you fail to become non-resident. This may happen because your employer abroad starts sending you to the UK for regular and frequent visits, or for some other reason you may spend too much time in the UK so that you break the 182-day and 90-day average rules.

Another more likely pitfall is this: supposing you take a tax-free job in a country and then decide to quit before you have completed a full tax year abroad and you return to the UK.

You would then be potentially liable for UK tax on your world-wide income including your earnings, even though these were advertised as being free of tax. In other words, such earnings are only tax free provided you stay long enough out of the UK tax network.

You might say, of course, that if your income is derived from overseas sources and you are effectively, if not technically, resident abroad, what can the tax man do if you break one of the conditions to be treated as not resident? The answer is: not a great deal until you eventually return to this country to live here. Then you will have to fill in a form about the purpose and length of your visits to the UK while you were living abroad and you would then be liable for arrears of tax found to be due.

Husbands and wives

The residence status of a husband and of a wife are determined quite separately and, with the advent of independent taxation, a wife is subject to tax on her own income. For this purpose money that you give or send to your wife is not treated as income in her hands. As such, if your husband/wife is still resident in the UK but you are not, you can transfer any unused married couple s allowance to the UK resident. This means he or she can earn more income before paying tax.

Miras

Tax relief on the interest on the first £30,000 of a qualifying mortgage is usually given under the MIRAS system. MIRAS stands for Mortgage Interest Relief At Source. Under MIRAS you get tax relief on these interest payments at 10 per cent, provided the property is your main or only home   known as your principal private residence. If your mortgage is not in MIRAS you will have to claim this tax relief

Curiously enough, expatriates, in certain limited circumstances, can also deduct the tax relief from their mortgage interest repayments on their main UK home even when they are not paying UK tax because they are not resident here. In effect, the

Exchequer is making eligible expatriates a present of the tax relief on their mortgage interest payments. However, the conditions for MIRAS as far as expatriates are concerned are quite narrow and it will only apply if you can tell the Inspector of Taxes that you intend to return to live in the mortgaged property within four years of the date of your original departure. However, the full implications of MIRAS are fairly technical and you should seek advice from your accountant or your building society about them.

Renting out your UK home

If you decide to rent out your UK home while you are abroad, you will be liable to tax on the net profit from the letting.

Under a new rule brought in to coincide with the introduction of Self Assessment, rents payable to landlords living abroad are subject to deduction of tax at source. Either the tenant if he pays rent directly to the landlord or a letting agent who collects the rents for the landlord must deduct basic rate tax from the rent and pay it to the Inland Revenue each quarter. This can only be avoided if the landlord applies for exemption from tax withholding by completing a form NRL1 for the Inland Revenue. This form includes an undertaking that the landlord will submit a tax return at the end of each year and will fully meet all obligations concerning UK tax.

Dealing with the Inland Revenue

Under the new Self Assessment rules there are fixed interest and penalties imposed on anyone who is late in submitting a tax return or paying any tax due. You should therefore ensure that your tax affairs are up to date before you go abroad and, if you have any continuing UK income, that you have made the necessary arrangements to complete tax returns and pay any tax due promptly while you are away.

If you are sent a tax return you must fill it in and return it by the deadline, which is 31 January   nine months after the end of the tax year. The new Self Assessment tax returns have a section on non-residence which needs to be filled in so the Inland

Revenue can decide whether or not you should be taxed on your worldwide income or just your UK income.

The Inland Revenue has a range of free help sheets which you may find useful. These include:

IR20 Residents and non-residents
IR58 Going to work abroad?
IR300 Non-residents and investment income
IR302 Dual residents

The March 1998 Budget put a new onus on taxpayers to notify the Inland Revenue of adjustments to foreign tax paid, so if you have had or receive a tax rebate from an overseas tax authority after claiming tax relief in the UK you can no longer keep this extra cash.

Pension arrangements

An important consideration when going to work overseas is the impact that this may have on your pension arrangements. If you are sent abroad by your UK employer, you may continue to participate in your employer s pension scheme without regard to your residence status, provided the Inland Revenue agree.

If you have your own personal pension plan the contributions you can make are a fixed percentage of what the tax man calls net relevant earnings. If you are not resident and exempt from tax on your overseas earnings, these will not be classed as relevant earnings and it may well be that you would not be able to make any contributions.

It may be that you can join the pension plan of your overseas employer and, provided you are not resident in the UK, there would be no UK tax implications on contributions into that plan. You should, however, bear in mind that 90 per cent of the pension deriving from such funds is taxed when you return to the UK. In other words, it is treated slightly more favourably than UK-based pension schemes.

Pension arrangements are complicated and you are strongly advised to take advice before entering into any arrangements.

Overseas workers planning to use personal portfolio bonds to help finance their retirement should note that tax relief on these is now being withdrawn with the Government planning to tax them. These bonds allow overseas workers to build up an investment tax-free and only pay tax once the bonds are cashed in. This tax change will lose investors £30 million a year. The advent of the single currency in Europe may also affect off-shore tax havens in future years.

Returning to the UK

As well as seeking advice when you go to work abroad, it is also necessary when you are planning to return here. Along with the weather, the tax man will be there to extend his doubtful welcome because once you return to the UK permanently, you become resident and ordinarily resident from the date of your arrival.

The only aspect of this situation which falls into the category of good news is the fact that a full year s personal allowances and reliefs will be granted, even though you may have been resident in the UK for only part of that year. The obvious implication of this is that the timing of your return is important: if you arrive at the beginning of the tax year the concession will be worthless; if you arrive too late in the tax year you may not have enough UK income to set your allowances off against. Somewhere in the middle of the tax year would be ideal if you can arrange it that way.

A non-resident is not liable to tax on income from abroad but it is sometimes difficult to determine what is regarded as income derived from abroad. For example, earnings for a period when you are regarded as not resident in the UK are exempt from tax. However, the Inland Revenue has recently changed its practice regarding the tax treatment of what it calls terminal leave pay . This would be pay from your overseas employment which continues after the date you return permanently to the UK.

In the Revenue s view, pay for the period from the date you resume residence here is taxable so the obvious way to avoid this potential problem is to delay your return by taking a holiday abroad. Alternatively, it may be possible to terminate your overseas employment before you return by encashing any outstanding leave. On the other hand, if you have already paid foreign tax on this terminal leave pay it is likely that the tax credit for this foreign tax will more than cover any UK tax which may be charged.

You will also have to watch the position on UK bank deposit and building society accounts. You can as a non-resident claim to have interest on these accounts paid gross instead of having tax deducted at source. If you do so, however, you should remember that in the year you return to the UK the exemption from tax withholding will be withdrawn from the date you become resident and the tax man will calculate the tax due on the interest paid gross up to that date. The way to prevent this is to close the UK account in the tax year before you return and place the money in an offshore bank account which pays interest gross. If the offshore account is then closed shortly before you return to the UK, the interest earned on that account would be tax free.

If you have any assets which are showing a potential capital gain you should consider disposing of them during a period when you are exempt from capital gains tax. If the asset is showing a loss, however, it may be better to dispose of it when you are subject to capital gains tax so that you can have the credit for that loss. You will be subject to capital gains tax in the tax year of your return to the UK, including the period before your arrival here, if the period overseas is less than three years.

Very often the problem for returning expatriates is that they are not sure whether they are going to stay permanently in the UK. It may depend on whether they manage to get a satisfactory job here, or they may have acquired a taste for the expatriate life and have come back for a trial period to see whether that taste is irreversible. It should, therefore, be noted that the treatment of temporary visitors (six months or less) is more favourable than that extended to those who have decided to become resident and ordinarily resident here. If you are unclear about your future plans you should make this fact plain to your financial consultant so that he can advise you on how best to mitigate and avoid your UK tax burden.

Domicile

At the start of this chapter reference is made to inheritance tax. For the purpose of inheritance tax, it is not the residence status of the individual which determines liability, but the person s domicile. Although ordinary English usage indicates otherwise, in tax terminology those two words residence and domicile do not mean the same thing.

Inheritance tax, the tax that replaced capital transfer tax, is in some ways similar to the old concept of death duties in that a charge is made on the transfer of assets at death up to a maximum of 40 per cent. On the other hand, no charge is made on the transfer of assets between individuals provided these have been made more than seven years before death. In effect, it is a penalty on hanging on to one s assets for too long!

The liability to inheritance tax continues unless you are not only resident but also domiciled abroad. This means, in effect, that you have made a permanent home there and demonstrated the fact by, for instance, taking out citizenship, building up business or sending your children to school there while at the same time severing your ties with the UK. Once domicile is established in another country you would still have to wait three years before you can forget about inheritance tax. Even then it will continue to remain operative on assets you own in the UK.

There have been a number of cases in recent years Kuwait is the most notable example where expatriates have had to pull out of a country for political reasons. This can have disastrous consequences for your tax position in the UK because, as we have stated earlier, you have to stay abroad for at least a year for your tax-free salary to be regarded as such by the Inland Revenue in the UK.

4

Financial Planning and the Expatriate

For most people, working abroad means a rise in income. For those in countries with a low rate of income tax, or, as is the case in some countries in the Middle East, without income tax, it may be the first chance they have had to accumulate a substantial amount of money, and this may indeed be the whole object of the exercise. Expatriates are therefore an obvious target for firms and individuals offering financial advice on such matters as tax, mortgages, insurance schemes, school fee funding, income building plans and stock and alternative investments. Most of them are honest, but some are better than others, either in choosing investments wisely or in finding schemes that are most appropriate to the needs and circumstances of their client, or both. At any rate the expatriate with money to spend is nowadays faced with a wide variety of choices, ranging from enterprising local traders, proffering allegedly valuable antiques, and fly-by-night operators, selling real estate in inaccessible tropical swamps, to serious financial advisers and consultants. Assuming that you will have the sense to avoid the former, how do you choose independent financial consultants, what advice are they likely to give you and how do you evaluate it?

The selection of an adviser

Nowadays consultants travel widely and it should not be too difficult to make contact with them through advertisements, through one s own company s financial staff or, best of all, by word of mouth through friends of long standing. When the consultant meets you, he (we assume here that he will be male, though a number of women are moving into this field as well) will have to know a great deal about your financial circumstances to be able to produce a package that suits you. It is therefore important to spend some time before you meet resolving such questions as whether you are looking for income or capital appreciation, whether or not you plan to settle ultimately in the UK, whether you plan to retire early and so on.

Anderson Sinclair, a firm of consultants with long experience in advising expatriates, have devised a questionnaire which they go through with prospective clients and which helps to define the investment mix which would be right for them. Some of its salient points are:

(a) In what currency the salary is paid
(b) Dates of departure from the UK and any visits there within the last three years
(c) When expecting to return permanently to the UK
(d) Mortgage commitments in the UK
(e) Whether intending to buy UK property
(f) Existing investment/life assurance/pension arrangements
(g) School fees provisions if/when not paid by employer
(h) Amount available for investment annually or as a lump sum
(i) Client s attitude to investment: interested, don t want to bother with it personally, speculative, conservative.

You should also be prepared to fire a few questions at your prospective adviser. Obviously you will want to know how much he is going to charge. You should also check on his experience, track record and whether he is authorised to carry out his consultancy by the UK regulatory authorities under the Financial Services Act. Financial advisers who are located outside the UK are not bound by this Act. Nevertheless, the fact that they have chosen not to be authorised might be interpreted as carrying a health, or wealth, warning. In the case of investment advice, a past performance sheet of his recommendations over a three-year period should be requested. The results may not be conclusive   anybody can make money in a boom or lose

it in a recession but if you ask him to compare his performance with the *Financial Times* share index, this will at least give you some indication.

An extremely important development was the passing of the Financial Services Act. This laid down strict rules for a variety of UK-based providers of financial services. They are now required to explain the full facts about any investment they recommend and also to make sure that it is appropriate to the client s financial circumstances. They are required, for instance, to show that in the light of the client s circumstances, it is the most suitable buy available. They also have to keep much more detailed records than was the case in the past.

However, the Act does not cover firms which carry out their activities outside British jurisdiction. It follows, therefore, that those who do not want to comply with the laws will work from somewhere offshore. All the more reason to beware of some of the more exotic locations from which investments are sometimes marketed but it should be noted that not even such respectable places as Frankfurt or Z rich will provide investor protection under the Act. In the absence of its safeguards there are one or two key questions which are worth asking anybody who approaches you with the offer of investment advice:

(a) Where is his company and/or the funds he represents principally based? Offices in unregulated tax havens like Andorra or Liechtenstein are often a bad sign. Connection with a reputable UK company is best.

(b) How often will you get a valuation of your holdings? It should be every six months.

(c) What are the charges and how are they arrived at?

(d) Assuming it is a limited company, not a sole trader or a partnership, when did the organisation the salesman represents last file a set of accounts? You do not have to be able to read accounts, but if they have not filed any within the last couple of years that could be a bad sign.

(e) Does his organisation carry professional indemnity insurance? Note, however, this only protects you against negligence or criminal action not against bad advice!

Twenty heads are better than one

Where a choice of currency can make a difference, offering twenty can make a very real difference, eliminating the inconvenience of exchange and, perhaps more importantly, the expense.

That is why we offer plans denominated in any of twenty currencies and funds managed in as many as ten.

This flexible approach brings investors a great deal more financial freedom and exemplifies the innovation and understanding which has helped to establish Hansard International as a leader amongst Offshore Companies.

Call or write today for more information.

HANSARD INTERNATIONAL
The OFFSHORE COMPANY

Hansard International Limited, P.O. Box 192, Anglo International House, Bank Hill, North Quay,
Douglas, Isle of Man, IM99 1QL. Telephone: 01624 688000 Fax 01624 688008

Policies can be denominated in: UK Sterling, USA, Canadian, Hong Kong, Australian & New Zealand Dollars;
Swiss, French & Belgian Francs; Deutsche Mark, Swedish Krona, Norwegian Krone; Danish Krone; Spanish
Pesetas; Italian Lire; Dutch Guilders; Irish Punts; Portuguese Escudos; Japanese Yen; Botswana Pula and ECUs.

You should ask for written confirmation of anything you are told. That might not have a lot of legal force with a representative of a foreign-based company, but it should deter the most blatant rogues. However, the passage of the Financial Services Act does mean that buying British is safest, if not necessarily best.

Investment

There are really only three types of objectives in investment: growth, income and growth with income. The choice of one main objective usually involves some sacrifice in regard to the other. A high degree of capital appreciation generally implies a lower level of income and vice versa. Growth with income is an ideal, but generally it means some growth with some income, not a maximisation of both. Ultimately, the objective is the preservation of capital in bad times and the increase of wealth in good ones, but your adviser cannot perform miracles. If he is lucky enough to catch the market in an upward phase he may be able to show quick results, but normally investment is a process that pays off over a longer period and through the course of varying market cycles.

Investment strategy

Following his preliminary meetings with you, your consultant should be able to formulate an investment strategy for you, based on your particular circumstances and such factors as the degree of risk that can be taken. The scheme he is most likely to recommend is that the bulk of your funds should be invested in an offshore fund . Offshore funds are variants of the unit trust and are registered with the government s blessing in tax havens. They are usually managed from well-known financial centres such as New York, Hong Kong or London. They are particularly suitable for expatriates because the income is tax free and because they are outside foreign exchange controls. Though the latter have been suspended by the present government, there is no guarantee that they will not be reintroduced at some future date.

There are other reasons for considering offshore funds as a way of investing your money:

1. The spread of investments is worldwide, thus protecting you in some measure from the fluctuations of individual national economies.
2. Their management is of high quality.
3. They follow closely the investment policy of institutions (ie pension fund managers, insurance companies and major financial consultants) which now dominate stock markets and whose decisions therefore affect price movements.
4. Portfolio managers do a better job than private investors, who have a tendency to hold on to problem shares in the hope that they will pick up.

Investment possibilities through managed funds

There are many investment opportunities in the offshore fund markets, from specialised funds in individual countries to international ones spread across many industries. There are equally many ways of investing: regular investments, lump-sum purchase of units, periodic and irregular investments. It is also possible to invest in commodity markets and there are specialists trading in gold, silver, diamonds, sapphires and metals generally. Another innovation is the currency fund, which regulates holdings of foreign exchange and aims to predict fluctuations in exchange rates.

Your consultant should be able not only to inform you of the various schemes available, but also to advise on the degree of risk, the quality of management available and the combination of investments most likely to achieve your aims.

For those who prefer the safety of banks or building society deposits, there is now a concession to non-residents interest is paid without tax being deducted at source. However, you will have to inform your bank about your non-resident status. A building society may also require you to open a separate, non-resident account.

You may still be assessed for income tax on any interest earned in the year of your return to the UK. For this reason, there are a number of advantages in taking up the facilities that UK banks offer non-residents to open an account in one of the established tax havens, notably the Channel Islands and the Isle of Man.

In all cases, though, there are important tax considerations before you return to the UK. You should discuss these with your adviser at least six months before then, so that the necessary plans can be drawn up.

Life assurance

Life assurance is also a form of investment in the sense that it provides financial protection for yourself and your family. As with other forms of investment, there are numerous possible options, many of them difficult for the layman to follow, and the temptation is to throw one s hand in and fall, metaphorically speaking, for the first smooth-talking young sales-person arriving on the doorstep with just the policy for you . If you do, you are quite likely to end up paying more than you should for the wrong type of policy. Even if the representative comes from a reputable company, this is by no means a guarantee that what you are being offered is a good buy. The difference in rates and profits between insurance companies is larger than you might think.

The right way to buy life assurance is through an independent professional adviser, outlining to him what you feel your needs are. In fact, even if you already have a policy, either on your own account or through your employer, there are a number of points you should check:

1. You should advise the company issuing the policy of a change of residence status.
2. You should check that your policy has no restrictions about overseas living.
3. You must ensure that you have set up a suitable system for paying premiums in your absence (eg via a banker s order).

Assuming, however, that you do not already have adequate life assurance, your adviser is likely to come up with one of four basic life assurance schemes:

1. Term assurance: this pays a fixed sum if you die within a specified time (eg before the age of 55).
2. Whole life: this pays a fixed sum irrespective of when you die.

3. Endowment: this gives you a sum of money at a fixed date, and is not only related to death. It is often used as a way of insuring mortgage payments; the mortgage is paid off when the policy matures.
4. Family income benefit: this gives an income after death and would usually be used to provide for your spouse and children. As a rule this would be taken out to give cover until all your children reach maturity.

All these policies may be taken out for a fixed sum and can be with or without profits. There may also be other variants, the most common of which is the facility to turn term assurance into an endowment policy. Your main concern, however, may be the degree of cover you require and this depends on the level of commitments that would be incurred by your family in the event of your death. A rule of thumb in most cases is that the capital sum provided should be five times the individual s annual income, combined with cover of between a half and three-quarters of annual salary until the children in the family reach maturity. You need not necessarily take out an insurance policy in sterling. There are foreign currency policies and, even though they are more expensive than sterling ones, for long-term expatriates in certain tax situations these may have aspects to recommend them. Again you will need professional advice in assessing your particular circumstances and choosing a scheme.

A recent development to the market is the advent of Critical Illness Cover. This type of cover is becoming much more commonplace in the UK and is now becoming available for those working abroad. The plan can cover *inter alia* cancer, heart attack, stroke, permanent disability and terminal illness, and pays a lump sum. This kind of arrangement can prove valuable financial compensation even though one s ability to work may not be affected through some of the insured contingencies.

School fees planning

There are many schemes available for school fees planning. These schemes aim to provide you with a tax-free income at a specified date for a predetermined length of time. They need not necessarily be used for educational purposes, and some readers may feel that if the employer is paying school fees, as is often the case, there is no need to take out such a policy. However, parents should bear in mind that it is highly advisable not to interrupt children s education, and taking out such a policy would obviously be a good way of ensuring that your child could go on with his education at the same school, even if your employment with that employer ended.

Pensions

One of the most important aspects of financial planning for expatriates relates to pensions. Most people will have been members of a UK scheme and will have been either contracted in to or contracted out of the government pension provisions. If your employer has contracted out that is, made his own arrangements for you within the guidelines laid down by the government you will normally retain the full benefits of the scheme, even if you are not resident in the UK. If he has contracted in, you will lose your right to the benefits once your contribution ceases. Private, contracted out schemes usually include a lump-sum death benefit as well as provision for benefits for disability.

This assumes that you are going to work abroad for a UK employer. If this is not the case, you will have to make your own arrangements with the help of your adviser, unless your employer abroad has a scheme of his own. Most multinationals do have such schemes, but they may have set up a pension fund in the country of residence and that country may have rules of its own and be subject to local legislation. Therefore, even if your employer is providing a scheme, you should ask for your adviser s comments on it.

People working overseas can now take a Jersey pension linked to a UK tax-exempt pension fund. The contract is linked to the With Profit Fund of a select number of life offices. Termination benefits can be taken wholly in cash and free of any tax deduction in Jersey. Benefits can be taken at any age, and there is no limit imposed on contribution. The scheme is essentially for the benefit of those expatriates not planning to return and take up residence in the UK.

Returning to the UK

All aspects of pension and investment planning need to be reviewed if you are returning to the UK, or you may leave yourself open to tax problems that could easily have been avoided with good advice. You should therefore notify your financial consultant at least 12 months before the tax year of your return so that he can make arrangements to mitigate tax liabilities. The subject of tax is dealt with in more depth in Chapter 3.

Short-term contracts

Someone going abroad on a short-term contract of two years or less is in a somewhat different investment position from those who have committed themselves to longer spells or intend to remain working abroad. Certainly you should be very careful about taking on investment or pension plan schemes which require regular payments over periods longer than your contract. For instance, there was the case of a doctor in the Gulf on a two-year contract who was persuaded to invest £1500 a month in a unit-linked life assurance scheme with a 10-year duration. Clearly, on what he could reasonably expect to earn back in the UK, he had no hope of keeping up payments on that scale   yet to extricate himself from that commitment, once this became clear to him, cost six months premiums: £9000!

In the opinion of some investment consultants, non-resident expatriates on short-term contracts might be best advised to put their savings deposit into a Channel Islands bank account. As not ordinarily resident non-residents they would not have to pay income tax on the interest up to the tax year of their return. Speculative investments tend to be risky on a short-term profit basis. When looking for longer-term profits, expatriates on two-year contracts or less are liable to be caught within the UK capital gains tax network unless they are able to realise their profits in the tax year before they return. If they endeavour to do so having regained UK resident status, they would be liable for CGT, even though the investment had initially been made when they were non-resident and not ordinarily resident.

Offshore insurance policies

The legislation relating to these has become increasingly complicated. Tax-mitigating benefits available through offshore insurance policies to those working abroad, but intending to return to the UK, have gradually been eroded by the Chancellor in his Finance Acts.

Since February 1988, the removal of certain technical tax-avoidance devices available to expatriates no longer makes it possible for them to draw a tax-free income from life policies. These can, however, be encashed free of tax and financial advisers suggest taking out a large number of single policies (rather than one large one) and encashing them separately and in small numbers. This effectively creates a tax-free income.

There are also some other tax-mitigating schemes related to offshore insurance policies. These are technically very complex. They are also subject to change as the Inland Revenue and financial experts play their cat and mouse game with tax loopholes. You should therefore check the latest position with an independent UK adviser before undertaking any offshore insurance commitment.

Offshore broker bond

A fairly recent development is the offshore broker bond whose asset is a fund. This is administered in a tax haven by a subsidiary of one of the major UK life offices, who appoints an independent financial adviser to manage the underlying assets. The adviser in this case will be wearing two hats, both as fund manager and broker, so he needs to have good reasons for recommending his own fund.

The advantages of the broker bond are in the tax treatment and its efficient route to the stock and bond markets. All the investment decisions are made for you. Broker fund managers have the time and resources, not always available to the individual investor, to select investments to make the best use of your capital. When located in remote areas, it is impossible to monitor one s investments regularly, which is important in today s volatile markets.

5

Working Abroad and National Insurance

The desire to earn more money   and to pay less of it in tax and other deductions   looms large for many as a motive for going to work abroad. People who take this step are often temperamentally inclined to be strongly individualistic and self-reliant and as such many feel that they would rather fend for themselves when circumstances get difficult than rely on what they regard as state hand-outs . Whatever the virtues of this attitude of mind may be, those who have it are more to be commended for their sense of independence than their common sense. The fact is that during your working life in the UK you will have made compulsory National Insurance contributions and you are therefore eligible for benefits in the same way as if you had paid premiums into a private insurance scheme; drawing a state benefit you are entitled to is no more taking a hand-out than making an insurance claim.

National Insurance has another feature in common with private insurance: you lose your entitlement to benefit if you fail to keep up your contributions, though the circumstances under which this would happen are different from, and more gradual than in, the private sector. Furthermore, you cannot immediately reactivate your eligibility for benefits in full if, your payments having lapsed for a period of time, you return to this country and once again become liable to make contributions. For instance, in order to qualify in full for a UK retirement pension you must have paid the minimum contribution for each year for at least 90 per cent of your working life. In the case of other benefits too, in order to qualify to get them, there must be a record of your having made a certain level of contributions in the two tax years governing that in which benefits are being claimed.

DSS Agencies

National Insurance provisions are handled by Executive Agencies of the Department of Social Security. The Contributions Agency deals with all contributions and insurability matters, while the Benefits Agency deals with all matters relating to social security benefits.

NI contribution matters for persons working abroad are handled by the Contributions Agency s International Services, Longbenton, Newcastle upon Tyne NE98 1YX; tel: 0191 225 4811. Matters relating to benefits are handled by the Benefit Agency s Pensions and Overseas Benefits Directorate at Newcastle upon Tyne NE98 1BA.

Leaflet NI 38, or for European Economic Area countries leaflet SA29, available from either Agency at Newcastle, or from a local social security office, sets out the basic conditions relating to National Insurance and benefits abroad.

Liability for contributions while abroad

If your employer in the UK sends you to work in another European Economic Area country or in a country with whom the UK has a reciprocal agreement (these are listed in leaflet NI 38) for a period not expected to exceed that which is specified in the EC regulations *or* the reciprocal agreement (RA) involved, you will normally continue to be subject to the UK social security scheme for that period and you will be required to pay Class 1 contributions as though you were in the UK. (The specified period can vary between one year where the EC regulations apply and up to five years depending upon the reciprocal agreement involved.) If your employment unexpectedly lasts longer than the specified period , then for certain countries you may remain insured under the UK scheme with the agreement of the authorities in the country in which you are working. Your employer will obtain a certificate for you from the Contributions Agency, International Services, at Newcastle upon Tyne confirming your continued liability under the UK scheme, which you should present to the foreign authorities if required to confirm your non-liability under their scheme.

If you are sent by your UK employer to an EU member state or to a country with which there is a reciprocal agreement in circumstances other than the above, eg for an initial period expected to exceed 12 months or for a period of indefinite duration, then normally you will cease to be liable to pay UK contributions from the date you are posted and will instead become liable to pay into the scheme of the country you are working in. Leaflet SA29 tells you about the European Community (EC) Regulations on social security and their effect on EU nationals. If you would like a copy of leaflet SA29 or would like more information, you can telephone or write to International Services. Alternatively you can get a copy of leaflet SA29 from your local social security office.

If you are sent by your employer to a country other than those in the EU or with which there is a reciprocal agreement you will be liable to pay Class 1 contributions for the first 52 weeks of your posting **provided** your employer has a place of business in the UK, you were resident in the UK immediately before you took up employment abroad, you remain ordinarily resident in the UK while you are abroad and you are under UK retirement age (currently 60 for women and 65 for men).

Making voluntary contributions

For non-EU and non-RA countries when your period of liability for Class 1 contributions ends, you may wish to pay voluntary Class 3 contributions to the UK scheme in order to protect your UK retirement/widow s pension entitlement. We will deal with the mechanics of this later, but at this stage it should be pointed out that if you are going abroad for a British-based firm you will be liable to make the same contributions as if you were employed in this country up to a maximum earnings level of £485 per week (1998/99 tax year). Your proportion of this contribution will be deducted from your salary, as if you were still working in the UK. Payment of these contributions for the first 52 weeks of your employment abroad will make you eligible to receive incapacity or unemployment benefit and, in the case of a woman, maternity allowance, under the usual conditions applicable to those benefits, on your return to the UK even though this may be some years later because Class 1 contributions will be deemed to have been paid in the tax year(s) relevant to your claim. This is subject to the proviso that you remained ordinarily resident in the UK during your absence. If you did not intend to sever your connection with the UK when you went abroad, continuing ordinary residence will usually be accepted. To establish ordinary residence you may need to show that you maintained a home or accommodation in the UK or stored your furniture in the UK during your absence. To maintain entitlement to UK retirement pension or widow s benefits, however, it will usually be necessary to pay Class 3 contributions after the Class 1 period has expired although this may not be necessary for the balance of the year April to April in which Class 1 liability ceased. The Contributions Agency, International Services, at Newcastle upon Tyne can advise you about this. Remember always to quote your National Insurance number when you write and the country involved.

Class 1 contributions are not payable at all in respect of employment abroad if your employer has no place of business in the UK. However, if you work for an overseas government or an international agency such as the UN, you will be able to pay your share of the Class 1 contribution for the first 52 weeks of your employment abroad and so qualify on return to the UK for the benefits named in the previous paragraph.

You may, of course, have been a self-employed person paying the Class 2 rate of £6.35 a week for the 1998/99 tax year. These contributions also cover a more limited range of benefits Jobseeker s Allowance (previously unemployment benefit) and injury or death caused by an industrial accident or prescribed disease are excluded but like Class 3 contributions, they can also be paid voluntarily if you go to work in an EU country or countries with which the UK has an RA agreement, provided you are gainfully occupied there. However, you *need not* pay

Class 2 contributions just because you were self-employed before you went abroad. You can go to the voluntary Class 3 rate, but if you want to qualify for incapacity benefit when you return to the UK, provided you were employed abroad you can switch back to Class 2 payments for the two tax years governing the benefit year in which you are due to return. Thus, for the sake of 10 pence a week, you may feel it is not worth switching to the Class 3 rate if you intend to come back to this country in a year or two.

These rates and conditions apply, of course, as much to women as to men. The right of married women to pay reduced rate contributions has been phased out. If you get married while working abroad you should write to International Services for leaflet CA 13 which explains in more detail your National Insurance position as a married woman. A married woman may consider paying contributions in her own right (eg for retirement pension purposes). See leaflet NI 38.

Leaflet NI 38 contains a form at the back (CF 83) which should be filled in when you want to start making voluntary payments. You can pay by annual lump sum, by arranging for someone in the UK to make regular payments for you, or through direct debit if you have a bank or building society in the UK or Channel Islands.

Class 2 and Class 3 contributions can be paid before the end of the sixth tax year following the one in which they were due. However, although you have six years in which to pay there is a limited period in which to pay at the relevant year s contribution rates. International Services can advise you about this. Whatever method you choose it is important that your contributions are paid on time. For further information see leaflet CA07 *Unpaid and late paid contributions*.

Getting NI benefits abroad

Thus far we have only mentioned the range of benefits available to you once you return to the UK. But is there any way you can become eligible for benefits while still abroad? Generally, the answer is that you can only receive retirement pensions and widows benefits, but there are important exceptions in the case of EU countries and some others a full list is given in leaflet

NI 38   with which the UK has reciprocal agreements. How those agreements affect you varies somewhat from country to country, but in essence they mean that the contributions you have paid in the UK count, for benefit purposes, as if you had paid them in the reciprocal agreement country, and vice versa. This is usually advantageous if you do become eligible for benefit while abroad because in relation to the cost of living   or even in absolute terms   UK benefits are lower than many foreign ones. You will, in general, have to pay contributions to the scheme of the country you are working in, so by the same token if you are going to a country with which the UK has a reciprocal agreement, you will have to decide if you want to pay voluntary contributions to the UK in order to maintain UK pension entitlement when you return here. The Contributions Agency can advise you on this. If you have not yet come under the scheme of a foreign country and are paying Class 1, 2 or 3 contributions to the UK while working abroad then, if you think you are eligible for benefit, you should write to the Benefits Agency, Pensions and Overseas Benefits Directorate immediately the contingency governing your claim arises. One important point to bear in mind in this case, though, is that if benefit can be paid, you will only get paid at the UK rate, not that of similar welfare schemes of the country in which you are living. In many cases the latter may be much more generous than UK rates; furthermore, UK rates may bear very little relationship to the cost of living abroad.

In this connection it is also worth pointing out that the UK is by no means the top of the world league table when it comes to the percentage of the pay packet taken up by contributions to social services. In many of the EU countries, in particular, it is significantly higher. This is an important detail to discuss with a prospective employer, because the social wage and what you have to put in to get it obviously has a bearing on the real value of the remuneration package you are being offered.

Working abroad and the NHS

In one important instance UK benefits are actually more generous than those of many other countries. We refer here to the

UK National Health Service. But medical expenses incurred abroad are definitely not refunded by the NHS, which is only available to people living in this country; so, contrary to popular belief, you will no longer be able to get free NHS treatment in this country once you become permanently resident abroad. Many overseas countries do have reciprocal health agreements with the UK once again a list is given in leaflet NI 38 but the services they provide are not exactly comparable with those of the British NHS. Form E111, available from the DSS or post offices, is an essential document in being able to access this reciprocal care. See also leaflet T5 *Health Advice for Travellers Anywhere in the World.* The range of treatment provided free of charge varies considerably and it is advisable to take out private health insurance to cover eventualities where free medical attention is not, or is only partially, available. Leaflets giving information on the procedures you need to observe, both in the case of temporary spells and permanent residence abroad, are listed in leaflet NI 38, available from the Contributions Agency s International Services.

Child benefit while working abroad

There are various situations which, in different ways, affect your entitlement to receive child benefit while working abroad:

1. If you go abroad permanently, taking your children with you, your child benefits cease from the date of your departure. When you arrive in the new country you can only rely on that country s family benefit.
2. If you go to work in another EU country you will generally be insured under its social security legislation and so entitled to the local family allowances. If you are insured under another EU scheme but leave your children behind in Great Britain, you may still be entitled to family allowances from the EU country in which you are insured. If you remain insured under the Great Britain scheme, child benefit may still be payable whether your children are in Great Britain or with you. If your children are not with you, you would have to maintain them by at least the weekly rate of child benefit after the first 56 days. If your children live with you but

your spouse or partner is insured under another EU scheme, you will be entitled to local family allowances. However, you may be paid a supplement equal to the difference between the local rate and the Great Britain rate of benefit if the Great Britain rate is higher.

3. If you have been sent abroad to work temporarily, for a period of not more than eight weeks, and you return within that time, benefit will continue to be paid whether or not you take your children with you. Child benefit orders cannot be cashed outside Great Britain, but you will be able to cash them when you return, provided each order is cashed within three months of the date stamped on it. After eight weeks of temporary absence, your eligibility for Great Britain child benefit ceases unless you happen to be in one of the reciprocal agreement countries.

4. You can also continue to be eligible for Great Britain child benefit, even after eight weeks of absence, if in the relevant tax year at least half your earnings from the employment which took you abroad are liable to United Kingdom income tax. However, in this case your entitlement cannot be decided until your tax liability has been assessed.

5. If a child is born abroad within eight weeks of the mother s departure from Great Britain and she is abroad only temporarily, child benefit may be paid from then until the end of the eight-week period of absence. If you wish to claim in these circumstances you should write to the DSS, Child Benefit Centre (Washington), PO Box 1, Newcastle upon Tyne NE88 1AA, quoting your child benefit number if you are already getting child benefit for another child.

6. Special rules exist in respect of serving members of the forces and civil servants; persons falling into these categories should consult their paying officer or Establishments Division.

Full details of these schemes, including the form CH 181(TO) which you have to fill in before your departure, are set out in leaflet CH 6, available from your local DSS office. Alternatively, you can get a copy by writing to DSS Information Division, Leaflet Unit, Block 4, Government Buildings, Honeypot Lane, Stanmore, Middlesex HA7 1AY.

Unemployment benefits for overseas job hunters

Under EU law you can go job-seeking for up to three months in most EU countries, provided you have been registered as unemployed in the UK for four weeks before departure. You are entitled to receive Jobseeker s Allowance on the day of departure and you actually register for work in the new country. While you are in the other country, you can continue drawing UK Jobseeker s Allowance via the employment services of the country you are in provided you follow their control procedures.

You should inform your local unemployment benefit office *in person* of your intention well in advance of your departure, and obtain from them leaflet UBL 22. The Pensions and Overseas Benefits Directorate of the Benefits Agency will then issue the authorisation form E303 to you if you are going to France, Greece, Portugal, Spain, Germany or Italy and there is enough time before your departure. Otherwise, it will be sent to your address there. If you are going to another EU country, the form will be sent to a liaison office in the country concerned. Regardless of which country you are going to, ask your local unemployment benefits office to issue you with a letter of introduction. You should give this and form E303 if you have it to the employment services when registering for work in another EU country.

In practice, many EU countries have blocked this progressive move by putting obstacles in the way over such matters as residence permits France is particularly bad in this respect because the UK is not alone among European Union countries in having an unemployment problem. The good news is that if you do succeed in getting a job in an EU country, in some states not only are wages and salaries higher but so also are unemployment benefits. If you are unlucky enough to lose your new job after being insurably employed under the social security scheme of an EU country, your previous UK insurance may be taken into account to help you become eligible for unemployment benefits which are very much higher than those in the UK.

All Jobcentres now handle vacancies in the EU and can give further details on relevant legislation and social welfare provisions. The Employment Service issues a useful leaflet on these matters, called *Working Abroad*, as well as others detailing conditions in individual countries.

UK pension schemes and the expatriate

UK pension schemes have been affected by changes in the state provisions introduced in July 1988. Many pension experts think that employees of companies contracted in to the state scheme, known as SERPS, might be better advised to set up a personal pension scheme which the new legislation now allows them to do, on an individual basis. The value of such a step would depend on a wide variety of circumstances, such as age, whether the expatriate has taxable income in the UK, and if the employer has a contracted out pension scheme, just how good its benefits are. The issues are very complicated and you should seek advice from a reputable financial management firm with experience of expatriate problems.

6

Expatriate Medical Insurance

Most of the countries that expatriates go to do not operate a national health service like that of the UK. It comes as something of a shock to find oneself paying £50 or more for a routine visit to a doctor or dentist and the costs of hospitalisation can be such as to wipe out the savings of months, or even years. In places like the EU, South Africa, Australia or other developed Commonwealth countries there are established local methods of medical insurance, and in many cases the cost of this is included in the remuneration package. If not, it is certainly a matter which should be clarified while you are negotiating the job offer.

As far as OPEC and similar resource-rich economies are concerned, some of these countries do have state medical schemes, and as a matter of fact their hospitals are, in many cases, better equipped than our increasingly run-down institutions. They are, however, established primarily for the benefit of local nationals, which means that the customs and culture of medical care are different from those which most westerners are used to. For this reason, most expatriates in those countries arrange for attention in private hospitals which, needless to say, tends to be very expensive indeed. Medical insurance for anyone going to these places is therefore essential and a number of plans have now been developed specifically for expatriates. The table on pages 73 6 provides a comparison of these schemes as of 1997 and, as can be seen, there are some that are apparently better than others.

A survey of current expatriate medical schemes

Benefits	PPP healthcare International Health Plan (Prestige Option)	BUPA International Lifeline (Gold)
Overall maximum	£750,000	£500,000
Hospital accommodation	Full refund	Full refund
Home nursing	Full refund up to 14 days	£600
Surgeon s and anaesthetists fees	Full refund	Full refund
Operating theatre fees	Full refund	Full refund
Hospital (non-surgical) treatment	Full refund (£2,000 limit on outpatient, with £20 excess visit)	Full refund (outpatients £2000)
GP treatment	Full refund within £2,000 outpatient limit. £20 excess per visit	£600
Maternity care	Complications only: as benefits above. Normal childbirth - no benefits	Complications only
Emergency dental treatment	Accidental damage within £2,000 outpatient limit. £20 excess per visit.	£400 per person per annum
Emergency evacuation/ repatriation	Full refund	Optional Under 21: £23 Over 21: £69

General Aspects

Exeter Friendly Society Interplan (European level 3)	Goodhealth Worldwide Ltd Falcon Healthcare Plan
£100,000	£500,000 per person, per year
Up to £30,000 per condition per year	Full refund
Up to 14 days per year	Full refund up to 8 weeks, per condition
Full refund	Full refund
As above	As above
As above	As above
£100 per year	As above
Excluded	Limited to £3000 per pregnancy
Excluded	Accidental damage to £2500 per insured. Routine and surgical cover also provided up to £250 per annum.
Optional	Full refund

A survey of current expatriate medical schemes (contd)

Benefits	PPP healthcare International Health Plan (Comprehensive Option)	BUPA International Lifeline (Gold)
Premium	Varies according to age and area[1] (PPP healthcare) operate a series of five-year bands).	Varies according to age[2].
		Lifeline Gold[1]
	Europe[2]	Under 21: £299
	Adult 40 44: £718.20	21 24: £437
	Child: £262.20	25 29: £584
		30 34: £634
		35 39: £685
	World excl.	40 44: £782
	North America	45 49: £918
	Adult 40 44: £883.50	50 54: £1024
	Child: £329.50	55 59: £1247
		60 64: £1625
		65 69: £2357
		70 74: £2826
		75 79: £3210
		80+: £3663
	1. Higher premiums apply for the USA and Canada. Rates quoted are for individuals. Company paid groups are lower.	1. Individual cover only.
	2. Ten per cent discount for annual payment by direct debit or credit card. Further 5 per cent if subscriber is a member of a recognised trade or professional group.	2. Higher premiums apply for USA and Canada.

Exeter Friendly Society Interplan (European level 3)	*Goodhealth Worldwide Ltd Falcon Healthcare*		
Age related on joining only[1,2]	Varies by age and area. Many options.		
Age 21: £278	0 18:	1 £193.57	2 £226.35
30: £358		3 £424.77	4 £234.60
40: £492	18 35:	1 £475.09	2 £555.45
50: £708		3 £865.54	4 £469.20
60: £1060	36 50:	1 £571.87	2 £710.98
70: £1696		3 £1266.27	4 £569.77
74: £2139	51 64:	1 £738.99	2 £864.00
Dependent children		3 £1570.80	4 £713.00
up to 18 years: £70	65+	1 £1099.75	2 £1285.75
		3 £1755.16	4 £1189.73

1: Middle East
2: Africa
3: Central and South America, Caribbean
4: Europe and rest of the world

* (Renewals only)

1. Discounts available for voluntary excess payments on sliding scale.

2. Five per cent discount if paying annually in advance by direct debit.

However, the insurance business is fiercely competitive and it is quite likely that at any given point in the year the pattern of advantage will change. If you are paying your own insurance it is vital to ask your broker for a complete list of all the plans that are available, so that you can make a comparison between them. You will need to establish whether quoted premiums include or exclude insurance premium tax for an accurate comparison. It is also worth finding out how long they take to settle claims.

It is important to be sure that the scheme covers medical attention irrespective of the circumstances which caused it to be necessary. A case has been reported where an expatriate was seriously injured by an assault while at home, only to discover that his medical insurance did not cover injuries sustained outside his workplace. Another point to watch, though it does not strictly speaking come under medical insurance, is personal accident cover and consequential loss of earnings. It is worth checking whether your cover extends to that eventuality.

It is also necessary, when it comes to making claims   and particularly when requesting repatriation for urgent treatment that the local practitioner should be credible from the point of view of the insurers. It is a good idea to make yourself known to him at an early stage after your arrival and to notify your insurers about his identity. You should also carry the name of your insurers with you or at least keep it in some convenient place. Goodhealth Worldwide and PPP healthcare issue a card which provides a convenient *aide-mØmoire*. Both carry the policy number and also emergency contact numbers. PPP healthcare also operate a 24-hour health information service to members and their families, which is proving extremely popular.

Another firm which issues its clients with a card is International SOS Assistance, whose medical and security schemes enable the holder, or those looking after him or her, to call for medical assistance at six main centres throughout the world. They specialise in emergency medical evacuation to the nearest high-quality medical facility, repatriation and return of mortal remains. PPP, BUPA, Goodhealth Worldwide, Expacare, IPH, William Russell, Carecard International and other private insurers use these services. As they point out, it is only of limited use to have cover for repatriation unless it can be implemented easily. GESA Assistance provides a similar service to, among others, Falcon Healthcare.

Catering particularly for the retired expatriate, the Exeter Friendly Society does not automatically increase premium rates with advancing age, making their policies a good buy for the over-50s.

John Wason (Insurance Brokers) Ltd, founded by a former expatriate, offers a specialist Overseas Personal Insurance scheme, which includes optional medical and personal accident/sickness cover world-wide. Levels of cover accord with units purchased.

Refer to pages 365 7 for contact details of these organisations.

Finally, there is the possibility of free, or subsidised, local medical care courtesy of a reciprocal agreement with the UK health authorities. EU and many other countries have such agreements, but the terms do vary. Form E111 is the required paperwork and is available from post offices or the DSS. However, this scheme is no substitute for a good insurance policy.

Checklist

1. Does the scheme cover all eventualities?
2. Are the scheme s benefits realistic in the light of local costs?
3. Can you make claims immediately or is there an initial indemnity period during which claims are disallowed? (Some insurers insist on this to protect themselves from claims caused by pre-existing medical conditions .)
4. Is there a clause providing for emergency repatriation by air, or air ambulance, if suitable treatment is not available locally? If so, who decides what constitutes an emergency and/or adequate local treatment?
5. Is the insurer s nearest office accessible personally or by telephone? (For instance, it is very difficult to get in touch with London if you are in Indonesia.)
6. What is the length of the insurer s settlement period for claims?

7. Is there a discount for members of professional or other associations?
8. Does the policy continue to apply, partly or fully, while you are back in the UK?
9. Note comments on AIDS and HIV testing in the Preface, pages xxi xxii.

7

Letting and Insuring Your Home While Abroad

Most home owners going to live abroad for a limited period will be looking for a tenant to live in their house or flat while they are away. There is, of course, an obvious alternative, which is to sell, but then there is the question of storage of your effects the average storage charge for the contents of a typical three-bedroomed house will be £50 £60 per week and, more to the point, the fact that when you do return to this country you will have no place of your own to go to. Even if you do not intend to return to the house you lived in when you come back, it may be advisable to retain ownership because your house represents a fairly inflation-indexed asset.

The case for letting, as opposed to leaving your home empty hardly needs to be put today when crime and vandalism are constantly in the headlines. The government, recognising the difficulties for owners leaving their homes and wishing to encourage the private landlord, have recently introduced the 1996 Housing Act which came into force on 27 February 1997. This Act created two new types of tenancies Assured and Assured Shorthold, and simplified the many provisions of the various Rent and Housing Acts from 1965 to 1988, thus making letting safer and easier. The Assured Tenancy offers much comfort for security of tenure to a tenant while the Assured Shorthold guarantees possession to a landlord at the end of a tenancy. It is not possible here to define the various differences between these two forms of tenancy, but there are specific aspects of which the owner-occupier needs to be aware. However, lettings to large companies where the occupier is a genuine employee being housed by the company temporarily are excluded from the Act. It should be noted that a letting to a member of the Diplomatic Corps who has immunity is inadvisable, as the individual would be outside the jurisdiction of British courts. It is essential, therefore, for the owner to obtain proper advice before deciding which form of tenancy to choose. All new tenancies are automatically Assured Shorthold tenancies unless parties agree otherwise.

Assured shorthold tenancies

1. These can be for any length of time if both parties agree. However, the landlord will not be able to seek a court order for possession before the end of six months unless there has been a breach of the tenancy agreement.
2. The tenant may apply to the Rent Assessment Committee during the period of the tenancy to fix the rental at a market figure during the first six months. However, on the expiry of the original term, the owner is entitled to require the tenant to pay a higher rental and the tenant is not entitled to go back to the Rent Assessment Committee. It is therefore preferable to have relatively short lease periods.
3. Two months notice has to be served that the landlord requires possession before or on the day the fixed term comes to an end and, if the tenant refuses to leave, the Courts must grant possession, after the expiry of the notice.

The benefits of an assured tenancy are as follows: there is very little rent control; there is no restriction on the initial rent; premiums can be taken (although this is unlikely to be a marketable facility); rents can be increased during the tenancy, provided there is a term in the agreement; and even where not so provided the landlord may serve notice under the Act to increase the rent. In this latter instance, the tenant may go to the Rent Assessment Committee who must fix the rent at a market figure, not at the previous imposition of what was perhaps unfortunately called a fair rent.

Possession of the property can still be obtained by virtue of former owner-occupation and the service of the appropriate notice on the tenant before the commencement of the tenancy. Additional provisions for a mandatory possession order have been included in the new Act, such as two months arrears of rent, and there are a number of discretionary grounds on which possession can be granted, even if the owner does not wish to return to the house. However, there is one specific disadvantage with the Act if the owner is unfortunate enough to have a tenant who refuses to leave when he wishes to reoccupy. This is the provision under the Act where the owner is obliged to serve two months notice advising the tenant that he requires possession and on what ground(s) prior to any proceedings being commenced. This undoubtedly will extend the period needed before a possession order is granted by the Court and owners would be well advised to take out one of the various insurance policies now available to cover hotel costs, legal fees, etc and as a minimum to make sure that either alternative accommodation is temporarily available in the event of a return home earlier than expected or the tenancy is terminated well before the projected date of return.

Assured tenancies

1. An assured tenancy may be for a fixed term or periodic, ie month to month.
2. The tenant must be an individual, not a limited company.
3. The tenant must occupy the house or flat as his only or principal home.
4. There are various terms which should be provided in the agreement and in particular a provision for the rent to be increased by notice in writing.

As must now be obvious to the reader, the rules do nothing to encourage the owner to attempt to let the property or manage his home himself while away, and the need for an experienced property management firm becomes even more important than in the past. A solicitor might be an alternative but, although possibly more versed in the legal technicalities than a managing agent, he will not be in a position to market the house to the best advantage (if at all) and solicitors practices do not usually have staff experienced in property management, able to carry out inspections, deal with repairs, arrange inventories and to handle the many and various problems that often arise.

Having obtained advice to ensure that you have the correct form of tenancy, you now need to find an experienced and reliable estate agent (ideally, he should be a member of the Royal Institution of Chartered Surveyors, the Incorporated Society of Valuers and Auctioneers, the Association of Residential Letting Agents or the National Association of Estate Agents) specialising in property management who will be well versed in both the legal and financial aspects of the property market.

Property management

Property management is a rather specialised branch of estate agency and you should check carefully that the agent you go to can give you the service you need, that he is not just an accommodation broker, and that he is equipped to handle the letting, collection of rental and management of your property, as well as the more common kinds of agency work. Your solicitor should be able to advise you here, but to some extent you will have to rely on your own judgement of how ready and satisfactory the agent s answers are to the sort of questions you are going to want to ask him. There are several specialised firms well equipped to deal with your affairs. One such firm is Anderton & Son with offices in Croydon, Beckenham, Addiscombe, and Cheam, which supplied much of the information upon which this chapter is based. They deal with the southern commuting area serving London, from Ewell eastwards to Chislehurst, and also with country properties as far out as Sevenoaks and westwards to Dorking.

In the first place the agent you instruct should have a clear idea of the kind of tenant you can expect for your property, and preferably be able to show you that he does have people on his books who are looking for rented accommodation of this kind. Obviously the rental and the tenant you can expect will vary with what you have to offer. A normal family house in a good area should attract someone like the executive of a multinational company who is in a similar, but reverse, position to your own: that is, a man working here on a contract basis for a limited period of time who may well provide a stable tenancy for the whole or a substantial part of your absence. A smaller house or flat would be more likely to attract a younger person who only wants the property for a limited period or who, at any rate, might be reluctant to accept a long-term commitment because of the possibility of a change in professional circumstances or marital status. Equally, if you are only going to be away for a shortish period like 6 to 12 months, you are going to be rather lucky to find a tenant whose needs exactly overlap with your absence. You would probably have to accept a slightly shorter period than your exact stay abroad.

For your part you should bear in mind that tenants, unlike house purchasers, are usually only interested in a property with almost immediate possession, but you should give the agent, wherever possible, at least two or three months warning of your departure in order that interest may be built up by advertising, mailing out details, etc over a period of time.

Rent

How much rent you can expect will also vary with what you have to offer and where it is, but the point to bear in mind is that rents are not usually subject to bargaining like a house price. Bargaining, if there is to be any, is more likely to occur over the terms of the lease which are set out below. Do not, therefore, ask for an unrealistically high figure in the expectation that the tenant will regard this as a starting point for negotiation.

Your agent, if he knows his job, will be able to advise you on the rental you should ask, though if you have not had previous dealings with him it might be advisable to have your solicitor check out his figures or to ask the agent to give you some instances of rentals being charged for similar accommodation. On the other hand, an offer which is a bit less than you had hoped for, but from a good tenant, might be worth taking in preference to a better one from somebody who, for various reasons, looks more doubtful.

Terms of agreement

A property management agent should have, or be able to produce fairly quickly, a draft agreement to cover the specific situation of the overseas landlord. You should show this to your solicitor and how well it is drafted will again be a pointer to how effective the agent concerned is likely to be. The document should cover at least the following points:

1. The intervals of payment   monthly or quarterly   and the length of lease.
2. A prohibition from assigning the lease without your express permission; likewise from keeping animals on the premises or using them for other than residential purposes.
3. An undertaking by the tenant to make good any damage, other than fair wear and tear, to fixtures, fittings and furniture and to maintain the garden.
4. An undertaking by the tenant to pay for telephone and other services from the commencement of the lease, including Council Tax.
5. An undertaking to allow the landlord, or his agent, regular access to the property for inspection and repair; and two months before the expiry of the lease to allow him to take other prospective tenants or purchasers round the property.
6. A clause stating that the lease is terminated if any of the other clauses are broken although the wording has to be carefully drafted to avoid invalidating the agreement.
7. What you, as landlord, are responsible for in the way of repairs: usually the maintenance of the structure and furnishings of the property together with anything left in the property (eg the central heating boiler). You can exclude some items, such as the television, from your responsibility, but generally the tenant is only liable for specific damage to items left in the house and not for their general maintenance.

The Government has recently tightened up safety laws in respect of gas appliances. In November 1994 the Gas Safety (Installation & Use) Regulations 1994 were introduced, forcing Landlords to take greater responsibility for the safety of their tenants by regularly servicing and repairing any gas appliances through a British Gas or Corgi registered company. Heavy penalties will be enforced for failing to comply.

8. Any special restrictions you want to impose: if, for example, your house is full of valuable antiques you may wish to specify no small children .

9. The conditions under which the tenancy can be terminated prior to its full period having run and without any breach having taken place.

10. If this is to be an Assured tenancy, notice must be served under Schedule 2, Grounds 1 and 2 of the Housing Act 1988 which notifies the tenant that you are an owner-occupier within the meaning of the Housing Act. This gives the landlord and those members of his family who occupied the house before it was let the right to reoccupy it when the lease expires or is terminated, and protects the mortgage.

11. Notice under Sections 47 and 48 of the Landlord and Tenant Act 1987. The former should be on all rent demands; the latter, notifying the tenant of an address in England and Wales at which notices can be served on the landlord, need only be served once on a tenant at the beginning of a tenancy.

Although the agreement is probably the central document in the transactions involved in letting your house, it does not bring to an end all the things you have to think about. For instance, there is the important matter of the contents insurance. Letting your home to a third party is probably not covered in your policy and you will have to notify your insurers (and the people who hold your mortgage) that this is what you are doing. In many instances, insurance companies will not insure the contents if the property is to be let and you will need to check carefully that you have cover and can switch to another company if it becomes necessary. This is covered in greater detail on page 90, under Insurance. At the same time you would be wise to check that the contents insurance covers the full value of what you have left in the house. This check could be combined with making a proper inventory of the contents which is in any case essential before tenants move into a furnished property. Making an exact inventory is quite a time-consuming business and you should bear in mind that it will also have to be checked at the end of the lease, when you may not be there. There are several firms that provide a specialist inventory service at both ends of the lease, covering dilapidations as well as items actually missing, for quite a modest charge which, incidentally, is deductible from the tax due from the letting. Any good property management agent should be able to put you on to one of them.

It is also essential that landlords are aware of important fire regulations that have recently come into force concerning the supply of furniture and furnishings when letting out accommodation. The Furniture (Fire) (Safety) Regulations 1988, introduced for all landlords on 1 January 1997, make it an offence to supply furniture which does not comply with the regulations concerning fire resistance. Essentially, it covers all upholstery and upholstered furnishings, including loose fittings and permanent or loose covers. These must comply with the following three tests, each of which measures the flame-retardant properties of the furnishings: Cigarette Test; Match Test; Ignitability Test. Heavy penalties will be enforced for failing to comply.

Your managing agent should be able to provide details of exactly what furniture should be replaced and when.

Finding the tenant and getting his signature on the agreement marks the beginning rather than the end of the property management firm s responsibilities. Broadly, these fall under two headings: the collection of rental and the management of the property. The rent is collected from the tenant, usually on a standing order basis, under the terms   monthly or quarterly as set out in the agreement; and, in the event of persistent non-payment, the agent will instruct solicitors on your behalf to issue a county court summons, or if you have taken out rental or legal insurance, the agent will contact the insurance company.

What can you expect from the agent?
Management is a more complex subject but an experienced property management agent should be able to supply you with a list of the services that he can undertake. It is, therefore, also a checklist of the kind of eventualities that may crop up in your

absence which, broadly speaking, relate to the collection of rent, the payment of charges such as service charges and insurance, arrangements for repairs to the fabric of the building and its contents, garden maintenance or when forwarding mail.

Thus, apart from the basic business of collecting the rent, the agent can also pay, on your behalf, any charges on the property (eg ground rent, water rates and insurance) that your contract with the tenant does not specify should be paid by him. There may also be annual maintenance agreements to pay in respect of items like central heating plant and the washing machine.

Then there is the question of what to do about repairs. As we have indicated earlier, whatever you manage to get the tenant to agree to take care of under the terms of the lease, there are certain responsibilities for maintenance and repair that you have to accept by virtue of your status as a landlord. If repairs are necessary, you will simply have to trust the agent to obtain fair prices for you.

On the other hand, except in the case of essential repairs which affect the tenant s legal rights of enjoyment of the property, you can ask your agent to provide estimates for having the work carried out, so that your approval must be obtained before the job is put in hand. Bear in mind, though, that in certain parts of the world the postal system may not be all that reliable. You may, therefore, find it a good idea to put a clause in the management contract giving the agent freedom to proceed with the best estimate if he does not hear from you within a specified period. For the same reason it is also wise to ask the agent to send you a formal acknowledgement of receipt of any special or new instructions you have given him. An example of this might be an instruction to inspect the property at regular intervals.

Depending on how many concessions you have to make to the tenant to get him to sign the lease, there may be other articles for which repair and maintenance remain your responsibility. These may include washing machines, TV and the deep freeze. Such responsibilities should be set out in the management contract and you should give the agent the details of any guarantees or maintenance contracts relating to them and photocopies of the actual documents for reference. If no such arrangements apply, you should list the manufacturers names and the model number and age of each item so that the agent can get the manufacturer to send the repair people along equipped with the right spares.

It is very important that a third party, other than you and the tenant, should be in possession of all this information, particularly when there is likely to be more than one tenancy during your absence; and it is a competent management agent, rather than friends, relatives or even a solicitor, who will be best equipped in this case to find new tenants, to check their references, to draw up new agreements and supervise the hand-over of the tenancy.

Costs and tax

The costs of all these services vary according to the nature of the package you need. The professional societies already mentioned recommend charges, which would be applicable in most circumstances. For example, letting and collection is usually 10 per cent of annual rental. In the case of management services, expect to find additional charges made (usually 5 to 7 per cent of the annual rent). These are reasonable fees for the quite considerable headaches involved. We have shown enough of them here to indicate that not only is it virtually impossible to administer a tenancy yourself from a distance, but also that these are not matters to be left to an amateur friend or relative however well intentioned. In real terms the agent s charges may be reduced because they are deductible against the tax levied in the UK against rental income.

Expatriates letting their houses also derive a further benefit in respect of capital gains tax. Generally, if you let your principal residence, when you come to sell it you can claim exemption from CGT only for those years in which you lived in it yourself. However, if you let it because you are absent abroad this does not apply, provided you come back to live in the house before you sell it.

Finally, in this context, it is worth pointing out that some building societies are now prepared to consider giving mortgages to expatriates for the purchase of a property in the UK *and* to allow them to lease that property for the period of their stay overseas. Up to 90 per cent of the purchase price is available at normal building society rates of interest.

This is an attractive proposition for expatriates, particularly for young executives and professional people who have not yet bought a home in the UK but are earning a substantial income in, say, the Middle East, and for older expatriates perhaps thinking of a retirement home in the UK.

Some agencies supply details of the building societies offering this facility, or you could approach a society directly and explain your position. Should you buy a house as an expatriate and then let it until you return, the earlier recommendation that you leave the management of the property to an experienced and competent agent still applies.

You should check that if a UK property is bought purely as an investment, you would have to time its sale carefully to avoid liability to CGT see Chapter 3.

Taxation is too complex a subject and varies considerably in its effects on the individual, preventing any practical advice being offered other than to state the importance of employing the services of an accountant in your absence, but it must be stressed that rent received in the UK is considered unearned income, and is subject to UK tax laws. A new scheme now operates whereby letting agents, or where there are no letting agents, tenants of a non-resident landlord must deduct tax at the basic rate from the rental income, and pay tax quarterly to the Inland Revenue. These landlords who wish to receive their income with no tax deducted can apply to FICO for approval. Forms are available from: FICO (non-residents), St John s House, Merton Road, Bootle, Merseyside L69 9BB; tel: 0151 472 6208/6209.

Insurance

One important point that is often overlooked by people who let their house or flat is the necessity of notifying the insurers that a change of occupancy has taken place. Insurance policies only cover occupancy by the insured, not his tenants, though it can be extended to do so on payment of what is usually only a small premium. As many insurance companies will not cover properties that are or will be let, notifying the company concerned becomes essential.

What worries insurance companies much more is if the house is left unoccupied for any length of time. If you look at your policy you will see that it lapses if you leave your house empty for more than 30 days or so   a point that is sometimes forgotten by people who go away on extended holidays. If you are going abroad and leave the house empty   maybe because you have not yet succeeded in finding a tenant   the insurers will usually insist that you turn off the main services and that the premises are inspected regularly by a qualified person. That means someone like a letting agent, not a relative or friend. Even if you have let the house without an agent, it may still be advisable to get one to look after the place. A situation could easily occur where the tenant moves out, leaving the place empty and without satisfactory steps having been taken from an insurance point of view. Furthermore, if the worst happens and the house is broken into or damaged, it is imperative that the insurers are notified right away. The effects of damage can be made worse unless they are rapidly attended to, and insurers do not hold themselves responsible for anything that happens between the time the insured eventuality occurs and the time they are notified of it. For instance, if your house is broken into and, a few days later, vandals get in through a broken point of entry and cause further damage, you would not be covered for that second incident unless the insurers had been notified of the first break-in.

Valuable contents are best put into storage and insured there: Pickfords, for instance, charge a premium of 12‰ per cent of the storage charge, inclusive of insurance premium tax. For contents worth more than £25,000, a reduction may be possible. For very high value items, safe deposit boxes are becoming popular, but from an everyday point of view, the important thing is to make sure you are insured for full values. If you insure contents for £15,000 and the insurer s assessors value them at £20,000 you will only get three-quarters of your claim. To keep insured values in line with rising costs, an index-linked policy would be the best buy for anyone contemplating a long stay abroad. A policy specially written for expatriates is available from Europea-IMG Ltd: the Weavers Homeowners Policy. They also offer expatriate motor insurance on private cars being used overseas. All insurance premiums are now subject to insurance premium tax (IPT).

Insuring at full value, incidentally, is equally important when it comes to insuring contents and personal belongings in your residence abroad. Many items will cost much more locally if you have to replace them than they did at the time they were originally bought. There are a few such policies available in the UK, or it may be possible to insure in the country concerned.

Finally, but most important, you should insure against legal and hotel costs when letting your house. Although in principle the legal instruments for quick repossession exist, events have shown that a bloody-minded tenant with a committed lawyer can spin things out to his or her advantage for almost an indefinite period. Premiums, which can be offset against rental income, are in the region of £85 a year.

Also recently introduced, rental protection policies have become available, some providing limited cover at a relatively low premium, others covering the higher rental amounts, which are naturally more expensive. In addition, these policies will normally cover legal and other costs. However, due to wide cover, the insurance companies usually insist on their own credit check and the employment of a managing agent, as well as the usual references.

The same companies will add, as an extra, buildings and/or contents cover when the property is let, often at rates which are competitive to the premiums charged when the property was owner-occupied.

Only selected agents with a professional background offer policies which protect rent, so the choice of a managing agent becomes even more important than before if you want to protect your rental income.

8

Moving Out, Settling In and Coming Home

What to take

Whatever agonising variables you feed into your mental computer about what and what not to take, you will certainly find that in the end you are left with two basic choices   either to take very little other than clothes, books, favourite possessions and whatever small items you and your family need to feel at home, or to take virtually everything.

It clearly depends on where you are going, how long you are going for, and who you are going to work for. If you are taking up an appointment in a sophisticated European capital or in North America, obviously you will not need the same kind of things as you would in a developing country, say in Africa or Asia, where everything tends to be scarce and expensive. If you are going to a tropical country, or the Middle East, clothes and equipment will be very different from what you will need in a temperate or northern area.

As a rule, travelling reasonably light is the best course of action. Even if you are going to be away for a long time, it seldom pays to take large items of household equipment, such as sofas, beds or wardrobes; the cost of shipping bulky items is very high. In any case, it can take quite a long time to clear them through customs when they arrive, so you will either have to send them ahead or find yourself arriving in a new place without any furniture.

Such situations are apt to be inconvenient and will probably result in your having to buy some things simply to tide you over. Clothes, bedlinen, crockery, kitchen equipment and so forth are cheap to transport   shipping companies usually convey some baggage free of charge   and usually expensive to replace at the other end. Furthermore, these items lend themselves to being sent ahead, and you can usually make do, or borrow, in the meantime.

Antiques are always worth taking, since they are vastly expensive in most places outside the UK, but remember that old furniture and pictures can be sensitive to climatic change. Such problems may also exist with electric equipment, and your CD player or food mixer may have to go through costly adaptations to fit in with foreign voltages. Records, tapes and musical instruments deteriorate in hot climates. There can also be problems over import controls, though most authorities have special dispensations for personal possessions.

As far as household equipment is concerned, much depends on the terms of your contract. Most commercial firms in developing countries will provide a fully furnished house or apartment (possibly also a car). Fully furnished means that everything, down to the last lampshade, is provided and you only need your personal effects. National governments and public corporations usually supply hard furnished accommodation. Hard furnished is what it implies. Only the bare necessities such as tables and chairs and a bed are provided, and you will need to supply curtains, cushions, linen, loose covers, cutlery, crockery and kitchen gear. Often you can buy these things from an outgoing tenant or returning expatriate, but you have to be on the spot for this.

It is strongly recommended that where a married couple are going out to a developing country the husband should travel out alone in advance, unless furnished accommodation is assured, and only send for the family when this has been fixed up. It may mean staying in a hotel or hostel for a time, but it is worth the inconvenience to be able to learn the ropes at first hand and decide what will be needed from home. Some companies arrange for both husband and wife to go out in advance for a reconnaissance visit.

In some cases, especially if the contract is a short-term one, in a difficult country, it is recommended that the husband should go out alone, leaving his wife and family in the UK. This may sound heartless, but it does minimise the upheaval and avoids disrupting the children s education.

If you are going to a tropical country where conditions are difficult, you may not be able to buy such items as a deep freeze, food mixer, sewing machine, hairdryer and electric iron except in the main centres. A portable electric fan is useful if the house is not air conditioned. An electric kettle is a must and so is a torch. There may be power cuts, so stock up with candles.

If you have very young children with you, take pram, carrycot, pushchair and plenty of toys. Camping equipment, eg tents and sleeping bags, may be useful, and so may gardening tools, as many houses have quite large gardens. Take golf clubs, tennis rackets, photographic equipment, etc, since these leisure and luxury goods may be unobtainable or very expensive overseas, though this will again depend very much on where you go.

Stock up with cosmetics and toiletries, drugs and medicines since everything in this line is expensive and difficult to obtain. Find out the voltage and type of electric plug in use and, before you go if possible, check with the appliance manufacturer about any adaptations.

Don t rely on somebody sending you something from home. Postage can be exorbitant, mails are slow and the contents liable to be pilfered. It may be possible to get your children, or your neighbour s children, to bring things out when they come on leave from school.

Removal

The best way to handle the question of actual removal is to consult one of the big removal firms. Overseas removal is not a job you should take on yourself, nor is it a good thing on which to try to save money. Moving abroad is a very different proposition from moving in this country and, in choosing your remover, it is better to ask for a good name than a good quote. The bigger removers are well informed about living conditions in overseas countries check, though, that any printed literature they give you is fully up to date.

Removers are knowledgeable about what you can and should take with you, and most have agents at ports of entry who can help with the sometimes interminable business of clearing your belongings through customs. Another advantage of a name remover is that they can generally get a better insurance deal than a smaller firm. You should, incidentally, increase your insurance to cover replacement costs at the other end. If you cannot get any specific information about this, an increase of 50 to 80 per cent over UK values will serve as a rough guideline.

An alternative to using one of the big names is to contact one of the specialist consortia of overseas removal companies. These are made up of hand-picked, privately owned companies specialising in overseas removals. As a team, members provide the strength and capacity of a large international concern; individually they are able to provide a local, personal service that many customers prefer.

All members conform to standards of service which are the same all over the world. So a remover operating out of the UK will provide the same level of service as his counterparts in Italy, for instance. Using the consortium method is rather like using a removal company with branch offices all over the world.

In the past there has been extensive publicity over the sudden demise of overseas removal companies, which having received payment in advance have left their customers belongings either in the warehouse or, worse still, languishing in an overseas country. This usually resulted in families having to pay twice over for their household effects to be delivered, and many who could not afford to pay again had to abandon their belongings altogether.

Protection against this sort of disaster is now available through the Advance Payments Guarantee Scheme operated by the Overseas Group of the British Association of Removers. The Scheme provides that customers who have paid removal charges in advance to a firm participating in the Scheme are guaranteed that, in the event of the removal company ceasing to trade, their belongings will either be delivered at no further cost, or they will be refunded the cost of the removal charges.

It should not be assumed that all removers are in the Scheme. The safeguard provided by the Scheme is available only through members of the BAR Overseas Group. The guarantee is underwritten by a mutual insurance company set up by the industry.

The British Association of Removers itself will be happy to supply readers with leaflets giving advice on moving abroad and brochures on the Advance Payments Guarantee Scheme. The Association also provides a list of companies participating in the Scheme. Readers should send a 9 in 4 in sae to the British Association of Removers, 3 Churchill Court, 58 Station Road, North Harrow HA2 7SA (tel: 0181 861 3331, fax: 0181 861 3332).

Removal costs vary according to the distance to be covered, the method of transportation (land, sea or air), the terms of the arrangement (delivery to port or home, packed or unpacked) and a range of other factors. Customers should obtain *written* estimates from several companies. Beware of firms which quote on the basis of approximate measures. Be specific, understand exactly the terms of the arrangement and obtain a written agreement, so that you have what amounts to a contract with which to resist surcharges imposed at the point of disembarkation.

Some people like to pack their own things. If so, it is best to use custom-made cardboard boxes, which are stout, light and can be banded to withstand rough handling and exposure. These generally come with movers details, logo and grids in which details of the contents, origin and whether fragile or not, can be entered. It is essential to make a list of contents and advisable to see that your cases or boxes are readily identifiable for when you collect them at the other end. Smaller goods can be taken with you, up to the 20 kg allowable limit. Some things may be carried as hand luggage, depending on how full the plane is. But on all these points, be guided by the experts.

Pets often pose a problem. Some shipping companies and airlines require a bill of health from a veterinary surgeon. In all cases, before leaving the UK you should first obtain an export health certificate from the Ministry of Agriculture, Fisheries and Food. There are a number of specialist animal shipping services available. You will need to apply in good time beforehand to MAFF for an information pack so that you can make the necessary arrangements. When you return to the UK your pet will have to be placed in quarantine.

Choice of removers checklist

1. The remover should provide a free estimate and a written quote.
2. Does the quote specify *professional* packing under your general supervision?
3. How will fragile items, furniture and articles be packed?
4. What insurance cover is offered? If there is any excess (ie a minimum figure below which you will not be reimbursed) what is it?
5. Can the removers immediately provide the name and address of the port agents at your destination?
6. Will they deliver to your residence at the other end, or will you have to arrange clearance yourself? Check that the quotation specifies whether the goods will be delivered to residence or to port only.
7. What proportion of their current business is in overseas removals?

VAT

You will almost certainly find that some of the things you want are cheaper to buy here, even allowing for shipping charges. You should make sure that you take full advantage of the various VAT export schemes under which a UK resident going abroad can escape having to pay UK VAT altogether.

There are two schemes, one for motor vehicles and one for other goods.

Motor vehicles

If you will be living outside the EU
You have to purchase your new vehicle from a dealer who operates the Personal Export Scheme. He will give you VAT Form 410 to fill in, which will require you to fulfil certain conditions. The relevant notes are found in VAT Notice 705. Motor cycles and motor caravans are also covered by this scheme.

- You must personally take delivery of the vehicle, and it must be used only by you, or someone else who is also leaving the EU and has your permission to use it.
- You have to take the vehicle abroad within six months of delivery, or within 12 months if you have lived outside the EU for more than 365 days in the previous two years, or more than 1095 days in the previous six years.
- You and the car must remain outside the EU for at least six consecutive months.

Alternatively, the supplier can deliver the car directly to your destination, free of VAT. See VAT Notice 703.

If you will be living within the EU
You must complete Form VAT 411, supplied by the motor dealer.

- The vehicle must be new, and you must take it to your destination within two months of delivery. Cars must not have been driven for more than 1864 miles in this time.
- You must declare the vehicle to the member state s fiscal authority.

After you have had the vehicle abroad for at least 12 months you may re-import it without paying VAT, provided you are either a diplomat, a member of an officially recognised international organisation, a member of NATO or returning UK Forces Personnel or you can prove that the duty and tax have been paid. Otherwise you will have to pay VAT on the value of the vehicle at the time of reimportation. If you return to the UK within six months of the date of export, the full amount of VAT on the sale must be paid. If the vehicle is found to be in the UK after the date for its export shown on the registration document (ie six months from purchase date if you are leaving the EU, or two months otherwise), you will have to pay VAT in full and it will also be liable to forfeiture. This applies even if failure to export the vehicle is due to circumstances beyond your control (eg theft or destruction). Therefore, while the car is still in the UK, before export, it is essential to insure it for its full value, including potential VAT. Obviously, it is important to license, register and insure the vehicle if you will be using it in the UK before departure.

Other goods
If you have been in the EU for more than 365 days in the previous two years and are going to a final destination outside the EU for at least 12 consecutive months, you may buy goods using the Retail Export Scheme. At participating retailers, you must ask to complete VAT Form 435 at the time of purchase. To receive a refund equal to the amount of VAT you must get this form certified by a Customs authority when the goods are exported   the goods must be delivered to your shipper or freight forwarder at your final point of departure from the EU. You cannot take delivery of them in this country. The refund is then paid by the retailer, not Customs and Excise. See VAT Notices 704 and 704/1. As there is a lot of documentation involved, you may find this procedure is not worth your while unless you are making fairly large purchases and only in one or two shops.

Taking a car abroad

British people tend to prefer right-hand drive and will therefore consider buying their car here and taking it with them. First check at the embassy of the country you propose to live in that private car imports are permitted.

Probably the best way to plan this is to make a list of what you will want your car to do. The road surfaces may be worse than those you are used to, so you may consider taking a good second-hand car rather than a brand new one. You will not then be so worried about driving through very narrow streets. In some places drivers actually park by shunting the cars ahead and behind!

If you buy a new car in the UK before going abroad, you can use it here for six months, run it in and have your first service before you take it overseas. Check the servicing facilities in the area where you plan to live. It would be unwise to take a car abroad if the nearest dealer service is 70 miles away. This factor may well limit your choice.

A big car will be expensive with petrol and difficult to park. If you will be living in an apartment and there is no garage, the car will usually be left in the street and possibly for long periods at that. Consider carefully the security of your car and what you may have in it. Choose a model with locking wheel nuts and high quality locks so that it is hard to get into without smashing the windows. Radio thefts are prevalent in some countries; therefore you may wish to consider a demountable radio.

Should you decide to take a small car to a hot country, always buy one with a sun roof because the smaller cars tend not to carry air conditioning.

People moving to Spain, for example, will often choose diesel cars because the fuel is half the price of petrol and easily available. Lead-free petrol is now available in many countries and you should check whether your engine will take this quality. Some engines need minor adaptation.

The other possibility is to hire a car in the UK. First check whether the hire company is happy with your destination and route. Restrictions depend on insurance cover for more out-of-the-way locations. You should also have the hirer provide you with proof of ownership   in this case form VE103a. Hirers are more than happy to do business with expatriates because of the length of hire and the fact that most are credit- and trustworthy. With regard to this latter point, it will be essential to pay by credit card.

Taking your existing car abroad

If you take the car you own at present abroad for longer than 12 months, this is regarded as a permanent export and the procedure is described in leaflet V526, obtainable from your local Vehicle Registration Office.

The following procedure applies to exports from England, Scotland, Wales and the Isles of Scilly only, not to Northern Ireland, the Isle of Man or the Channel Islands, where cars are registered separately.

Complete section 2 on the back of the Vehicle Registration Document, entering the proposed date of export, and send the document to your local Vehicle Registration Office or to the Driver and Vehicle Licensing Centre. This should be done well in advance of your departure.

You will receive back a Certificate of Export (V561) which in effect confirms your vehicle registration and replaces the vehicle registration document (V5). Some countries, however, are failing to recognise this certificate as a registration document, which can cause problems when you wish to re-register your vehicle in another country.

A different procedure applies in Northern Ireland, the Isle of Man and the Channel Islands, where vehicles are registered locally; it is necessary to register and license a car taken *to* these places for over 12 months as soon as the current British tax disc expires, if not before. The Certificate of Export mentioned above will still be necessary, although these authorities may accept the vehicle registration document for re-registration purposes.

Motoring services in Europe

The Alliance Internationale de Tourisme (AIT) has its headquarters in Geneva, and motoring clubs throughout Europe are affiliated to it, including the Royal Automobile Club and the Automobile Association. There is also the Federation Internationale de l Automobile, based in Paris, of which the RAC is a member. These clubs provide a wide range of services to each other s members travelling abroad, so membership of one is worthwhile.

Customs

Regulations and procedures vary. Most customs authorities allow you to take in used things for your personal use and often let people, eg newly married couples, bring in new things duty free. Wherever possible keep receipts to show to the customs officials.

In most places, you are allowed to take in household and used personal effects , including refrigerators, radios, TV receivers and minor electrical appliances, but duties on new items of this kind are usually fairly steep. There are bans everywhere on guns, plants and drugs. Many Middle East and North African countries operate a boycott list, so do not take anything without checking the situation. Duty free wines, spirits and tobacco up to a certain amount   check with the airline   are normally allowed, except in most Middle East countries.

Removal checklist

Don t forget to tell the following organisations that you are moving abroad:

Your bank.

Income Tax Office. Notify the Inland Revenue giving the exact date of departure.

Contributions Agency, International Services (for information on National Insurance Contributions and related health cover), Longbenton, Newcastle upon Tyne, NE98 1YX, or *The Benefits Agency, Pensions and Overseas Benefits Directorate* (for advice on benefits and related health cover), at Tyneview Park, Newcastle upon Tyne NE98 1BA. Include your full name, date of birth and UK NI or pension number, together with details of the country to which you are moving and the duration of your stay.

Vehicle licence. If you are taking your vehicle abroad for longer than a year this is regarded as a permanent export . In this case you should return your existing (new style) registration document to the Driver and Vehicle Licensing Centre, Swansea SA99 1AB, filling in the permanent export section. Alternatively, you can apply to your local Vehicle Registration Office for the necessary forms.

Driving licence. You will probably want to retain your British driving licence. Some countries recognise it as valid and a list of those which do not is available from the RAC and the AA.

International Driving Permit. An International Driving Permit is obtainable from the RAC or AA (even if you are not a member) and is valid for one year. The licence is not valid in the country where it is issued so you must obtain it before leaving the UK. Most countries require residents to hold a local driving licence so check whether this is the case on taking up your new residence. Contact RAC Travel Services, PO Box 1500, Bristol BS99 2LH. (telephone 0800 550055 for information), or any Automobile Association shop.

Motor insurance. Notify your insurers of the date of your departure   your insurance should be cancelled from that date and you should obtain a refund for the rest of the insurance period. Ask your insurance company for a letter outlining your no-claims record to show to your new insurer.

Life and other insurances. Notify the companies concerned or your insurance broker if you use one.

Council tax. Notify the town hall.

Dentist and optician. Let them know you are moving, as a matter of courtesy. It will save posting useless check-up reminders.

Private health insurance. Notify subscriber records department.

Gas. If you use it, notify your local gas showroom giving at least *48 hours* notice. They will give you a standard form to fill in with details of the move and any current hire-purchase agreements. If appliances are to be removed they require as much notice as possible to arrange an appointment; there is a disconnection charge.

Electricity. Notify your local district office or showroom at least *48 hours* before moving. Arrangements are much the same as for gas.

Water. The local water board should also be notified at least *48 hours* before the move. Drain tanks and pipes if the house is to remain empty in winter.

Telephone. Notify your local telephone sales office as shown in the front of your directory at least *seven days* before the move.

Libraries. Return books and give in tickets to be cancelled.

Professional advisers such as solicitors, accountants, stockbrokers, insurance brokers, etc. Make sure they have a forwarding address.

Stocks and shares. Write to the company registrar at the address on the last annual report or share certificates.

Organisations and clubs any business, civic, social, cultural, sports or automobile club of which you are a member. For the AA write to Membership Subscriptions and Records, PO Box 50, Basingstoke, Hampshire RG21 2ED and for the RAC write to Membership Enquiries, PO Box 1500, Bristol BS99 2LH.

Credit card companies. Advise them that you are leaving the country.

Hire purchase and rental companies. Notify the office where repayments are made. You will need to settle your account.

Local business accounts department stores, newsagents, dairy, baker, chemist, dry cleaner, laundry, motor service station.

Publications. Cancel postal subscriptions to newspapers, magazines, professional and trade journals, book and record clubs, etc.

National Health Service. Return your NHS card to the Family Health Services Authority for your area, giving your date of departure, or hand it in to the immigration officer at your point of departure.

Pension schemes. If you have a frozen or paid-up pension from a previous employer notify the pension trust of your new address.

TV. If you have a rented set, make arrangements to return it.

Post Office. Notify day of departure and UK contact address.

Personal Giro. The Post Office have a special sae for this.

Premium Bonds anything rather than join the sad list of unclaimed prizes! Contact Premium Bonds, National Savings, Blackpool FY3 9XR to check the current position, because in a few countries, Premium Bond holdings may contravene lottery laws.

Save As You Earn and National Savings Certificates. It is important to notify any permanent change of address. Advise the Savings and Certificates and SAYE Office, Durham DH99 1NS, quoting the contract number(s).

National Savings Bank. Notify at Glasgow G58 1SB.

National Savings Income Bonds. Notify Income Bonds, Blackpool FY3 9YP.

Your landlord. If you are a tenant, give the appropriate notice to quit.

Your tenants. If you are a landlord, that UK address you ve organised will be needed.

Your employer. Give new address details, or a contact address, in writing.

Schools. Try to give your children s schools a term s notice that they will be leaving. If you wish your children s education to be continued in Britain, contact your local education authority or the Department for Education and Employment, Sanctuary Buildings, Great Smith Street, London SW1P 3BT, for advice, and see Chapter 9.

Make sure your *removers* have any temporary contact address and phone numbers for you, both in the UK and abroad, so that they can get in touch with you when the need arises. It is also useful for them if you can tell them when you expect to arrive in your new country.

Before you go

There are certain things you must see about before you actually leave. There are obvious chores, like cancelling milk and papers, etc. Have a thorough medical check for yourself and your family before you go, including teeth and eyes. Some jobs, of course, depend on physical fitness. Make sure you have the necessary vaccination certificates and check the requirements. Most tropical countries need certificates against smallpox and possibly cholera and yellow fever; other vaccinations may be advisable. If you are going to the tropics you should contact your GP about anti-malarial precautions. For the most up-to-date advice on malaria in the region where you are going, you should contact the Malaria Reference Laboratory at the London School of Hygiene and Tropical Medicine.

In many countries it is advisable to include a rabies injection in your schedule of jabs for yourself and members of your family. You should also warn children of the perils of cuddling strange animals which may harbour other diseases in addition to the rabies threat.

Check that you have all your documents to hand up-to-date passport, visas, cheque book, permits, health certificates, letter of appointment. Take spare passport photos it is probably best for husband and wife to have separate passports and all your diplomas and references, even birth and marriage certificates. The appetite for documents is well-nigh insatiable in some countries!

Melancholy though it may sound, you should also make some provision for the unthinkable: instructions in the case of death, disablement or catastrophe while you are abroad. Contact your financial adviser or insurance company for more information.

If you have a reliable solicitor, you might also consider the possibility of giving him or her power of attorney. This is a simple legal transaction which essentially means that the person having that power can act in your stead. If you need a large sum of money to be sent out to you in a hurry, it is very useful to have a responsible person in the UK whom you can fax or telex for it and who can raise the money from your bank. Likewise, if you have left your house in the hands of managing agents who are not doing their stuff, you need someone on the spot who can sort things out. Giving someone power of attorney obviously implies a high degree of trust, but there are occasions when it could save you the cost of a return fare home.

Keeping your vote while living abroad

On moving abroad, you retain your right to vote in UK and European parliamentary elections; however, there are a number of conditions of which you should be aware. To be eligible you must be a British citizen and satisfy *either* of two sets of conditions:

Set 1
- you have previously been on the electoral register for an address in the UK;
- you were living there on the qualifying date;*
- there are no more than 20 years between the qualifying dates for that register and the one on which you now wish to appear.

Set 2
- you last lived in the UK less than 20 years before the qualifying date for the register on which you wish to appear;
- you were too young to be on the electoral register which was based on the last qualifying date before you left;
- a parent or guardian was on the electoral register, for the address where you were living on that date;
- you are at least 18 years old, or will become 18 when the register comes into force.

You have to register every year on or before the qualifying date and you may continue to register while overseas for 20 years from the qualifying date for the last electoral register on which you appeared as a UK resident.

How to register
To register you must fill in an Overseas Elector s Declaration form RPF 37 which you can get from the nearest British consular or diplomatic mission. The following information will be required: your full name and overseas address, the UK address

---

* The qualifying date in England, Scotland and Wales is 10 October each year and in Northern Ireland, 15 September. This is for the electoral register which comes into force on 16 February of the following year and remains in force for 12 months from that date.

where you were last registered and the date you left the UK. The first-time overseas elector will have to find someone to support the declaration who is aged 18 or over, has a British passport and is a British citizen, is not living in the UK and who knows you but is not a close relative. First-time overseas electors who left the UK before they were old enough to register will also have to provide a copy of their full birth certificate and information about the parent or guardian on whose registration they are relying.

How to vote and remain registered

You do not have a postal vote. Instead you must appoint a proxy who will vote on your behalf. He or she must be a citizen of Britain, the Commonwealth or the Republic of Ireland, a UK resident, and willing and legally able to vote on your behalf. The application form for appointing a proxy is attached to the Overseas Elector s Declaration form. Your declaration, proxy application and, if required, birth certificate should be returned to the electoral registration officer for the area where you were last registered. The electoral registration officer will write to tell you whether you qualify as an overseas elector and will be included on the register: if you do not, he or she will explain why. You will be sent a reminder each year, and another declaration form will be enclosed with this.

Settling in

You arrive, with or without your family, and may find you are not met at the airport. This is the first of many irritations which people going out to work for overseas governments may encounter. It does not usually happen with companies. You may have to stay in a hotel or hostel for a considerable time, so make sure in advance who is going to foot the bill. You will need money to meet such contingencies and to pay for telephones and taxis to and from the airport.

Even if you are lucky enough to move into a house or apartment, you will find a bare larder. This is where any tins or packet foods you brought with you will come in useful. (In Jamaica, the Corona Worldwide branch will provide a loan of a basket of essentials for people waiting for their baggage to be unloaded.)

One early need will be to fix up domestic help, if you want it. It is usually best to engage a house steward and/or any other servants on the personal recommendation of the previous occupant (you may inherit their staff) or a neighbour. Find out from the local labour office what the going rate is and negotiate accordingly, making it quite clear from the start what duties the staff will be expected to perform, eg in the kitchen, washing and housework. Living quarters are usually provided, but find out beforehand whether your steward plans to bring all his family and relatives to stay with him!

Both for insurance purposes and your own peace of mind, make proper security arrangements. Some people, either individually or in groups, employ night-watchmen; others rely on dogs, or on special locks. The extent of pilfering and burglary in many African countries has grown alarmingly in recent years, so make sure your precautions are fully adequate. John Wason (Insurance Brokers) Ltd, founded by a former expatriate, offers a specialist Overseas Personal Insurance scheme, which includes home contents, belongings, money and personal liability, as well as optional medical and accident/sickness cover. It is claimed to be the only such policy available on a stand-alone basis, and as such would be useful for those in rented or company property.

At an early stage it is a good idea to see to all your requirements for banking and for obtaining work and residence permits, income tax coding, and the driving licence and test requirements where necessary. Find out also about health products and medical facilities, contributions to provident funds and subscriptions to clubs. Many employers pay for these.

Finally, keep a close eye on the health of young children, particularly on persistent tummy upsets and fevers. It is advisable always to use water you have sterilised yourself, not bottled water of unknown provenance.

Briefing

There is also the question of preparation, other than physical, for your move. Do you know what the country you are going to is like? What facilities are there for shopping, leisure and entertainment? What is the climate like and what clothes will you need? Are there any pitfalls you should know about or any special behavioural dos and don ts? Nowadays, overseas countries are very sensitive about foreigners understanding that their new patterns of government and economic development are not just pale imitations of the West.

The importance of getting properly briefed beforehand cannot be overestimated. This will not only save you from possible embarrassing situations   for example, if you don t know the rules about drinking in the Middle East   but will help you to decide what you need to take with you and give you some idea of the atmosphere in which you will work and live.

Many commercial firms and recruitment agencies try to ensure that staff are briefed before they are posted overseas, but for some people it may be their first long stay abroad (apart from their annual holiday) and they will be starting from scratch. Others may be old hands who feel more at home in a foreign country than in the UK. But for everyone, wherever they go, getting up-to-date information about conditions will be time well spent. The Centre for International Briefing (Farnham Castle, Farnham GU9 0AG; tel: 01252 721194, fax: 01252 719277) provides intensive residential courses on various countries throughout Africa, the Middle East, the USA, Canada, Latin America, the Caribbean, Asia, the Pacific and Europe (see page 156) and also intensive residential language tuition. The Centre has also introduced one-day business-focused briefings for business travellers and those home-based managers with country or regional responsibility. Monthly scheduled programmes are available for the Middle East and Japan. Customised programmes are available for most major destinations.

Another organisation which you will find helpful is Corona Worldwide, (formerly the Women s Corona Society) c/o The Commonwealth Institute, Kensington High Street, London W8 6NQ (tel: 0171 610 4407). Corona s *Notes for Newcomers* series on over 100 countries contains all the practical and day-to-day information needed for the preparation for a move, what is available on arrival, medical services, education, recreation facilities and a great deal more (approx £5 per set). Pamphlets on Culture Shock, Chinese Etiquette and Customs and Living in a Muslim Country are further aids to adjusting and understanding a different culture and customs. Living Overseas one-day briefings are held in London and tailored to the individual client s circumstances. They also produce a leaflet on Returning to Britain. The Society s 32 branches overseas, affiliated societies and personal contacts in many countries provide a welcoming link for newcomers.

Employment Conditions Abroad Ltd (Anchor House, 15 Britten Street, London SW3 3TY; tel: 0171 351 5000, fax: 0171 351 9396, e-mail: eca@ecaltd.com) has all the answers to your questions about living costs, working conditions, salaries, taxes, etc. It does not, however, provide individuals with information or answer personal enquiries apart from the sale of *Country Outlines for Expatriates,* available for 80 countries. ECA serves over 700 member companies (which include nearly all the major British companies and corporations which employ personnel overseas). These services include detailed reports on the cost of living in 170 countries and employment information with salary comparisons and personal tax for some 75 different countries, although its information base is virtually worldwide.

Going Places Expatriate Briefing, 84 Coombe Road, New Malden, Surrey KT3 4QS, tel: 0181 949 8811, provide tailored briefings to individuals or groups, in-house or in the home. Briefings last from three hours to a full day and cover preparation, living in-country, working in-country, coming home. Expertise is available on over 50 countries for both the working and accompanying partner.

Going through diplomatic channels

Expatriates who work for British companies or those from other western countries in the developing or newly industrialised world can usually expect their employers to come to their aid in case of a political upheaval, or even if they get into personal difficulties deserved or otherwise. Furthermore, they can expect their contracts of employment to be clear-cut and to conform to western norms. Neither of these things is necessarily true if you work for a local employer, as is increasingly the case. The money is often better, but the risk is greater.

Some guidance on points to watch out for in taking up an appointment with a local employer in a developing country is given in the Employment Conditions Checklist in Chapter 11. Ultimately, though, you have no protection other than your own vigilance and UK diplomatic channels in the country concerned. They are generally very much criticised by expatriates as being ineffectual or indifferent, but the Foreign and Commonwealth Office claim this is because their role is not understood. For a start, they cannot intervene in contractual disputes, *unless* a British subject is being discriminated against in comparison with other employees. They can, however, recommend you to a local lawyer who may be able to help you and they maintain carefully vetted lists of reliable legal firms. Best of all, they say, is to write to the British embassy or consulate nearest to your location before you leave the UK and ask them to put you in touch with someone who can give you a line on your prospective employer. Though UK diplomatic sources do keep track of known bad hats among employers, in the main they prefer such information to go through non-diplomatic channels, for obvious reasons.

The consular service of the Foreign Office is now very sensitive about the criticisms that have been made of it. If you fail to get an answer from the embassy or consulate you have contacted, or you are not satisfied with the service provided at a British embassy, high commission or consulate, you should write to: Head of Consular Division, Foreign & Commonwealth Office, 1 Palace Street, London SW1E 5HE, tel: 0171 238 4586, fax: 0171 238 4509.

Primarily, of course, the role of British diplomats is to protect British subjects from the consequences of political upheavals. For instance, they got them and their dependants out of Iran, Lebanon, and, more recently, Malaysia, though there seems to have been some, perhaps understandable, disarray in the advice given to expatriates in Kuwait following the Iraqi invasion in August 1990. They were less successful, also, in protecting expatriates from the reprisal arrests in Libya, but any expatriate who goes to a notoriously high-risk place like that must take into account the circumstances there before deciding to accept an appointment. They are also not able to protect you from the consequences if you break the law of the land you are in. At most they can visit you in prison, arrange for you to be properly represented legally and intercede discreetly for an amnesty for you. A UK or multinational company would, in such cases, arrange for you to be flown out on the first available plane, usually with the connivance of the authorities.

Whatever your feelings about the efficacy or otherwise of British diplomatic protection, you should register with the embassy or consulate as soon as possible after you arrive to work in any developing country. This means they can contact you if a sudden emergency arises, whether personal or political. It cannot do any harm; and if you wake up one morning to the sound of gunfire, as has happened to many an expatriate, you may be very glad that you took that precaution.

Foreign & Commonwealth Travel Advice is designed to help British travellers avoid trouble by providing succint and up-to-date information on threats to personal safety arising from political unrest, lawlessness, violence, natural disasters and epidemics. Some 650 notices are issued each year covering more than 130 countries. Notices are constantly renewed on the basis of information from our posts overseas. The full range of notices is available on BBC2 Ceefax pages 470 onwards, and on the FCO s web site, along with a range of Consular Division publicity material, http://www.fco.gov.uk. The public can contact the Travel Advice Unit direct between 9.30 am and 4.00 pm Monday to Friday on 0171 238 4503/4504.

Other Consular Services information leaflets, including Checklist for Travellers , Backpackers and Independent Travellers and British Consular Services Abroad are widely distributed through travel agents, shipping and airlines, public libraries, Citizens Advice Bureaux and the UK Passport Agency, and can be obtained by faxing the Distribution Centre on 01444 246620.

Personal security

There are overseas countries where crimes against persons, either for gain or to make political points, are a serious hazard.

Countries where Islamic fundamentalism is on the increase are a case in point. Other places, notably in Africa and Latin America, qualify as high-risk locations in terms of personal safety, eg Colombia, Brazilian cities and Johannesburg. There are also corporate or national connections which may be the target of terrorists:

- Anything to do with Israel. It is still advisable to carry a separate passport if you have a visa for Israel but also travel to the Middle East.
- Employees of companies associated with pollution, nuclear waste and animal experiments.
- Nationals of countries which have recently been, or are currently, in serious dispute with countries in which an expatriate is living or even its allies.

According to the international security consultants, Control Risks, resident expatriates tend to be more at risk in these circumstances than visiting businessmen and, in an interview with the author, they spelled out some security precautions that people living in exposed locations should take:

1. Avoid daily routines, like taking the same route to work every day at fixed times.
2. Remove bushes and thick vegetation around the entrance to your house or place of work they could make a hiding place for criminals and people tend to be least vigilant as they approach familiar places.
3. If you think you are being followed, head immediately for a place where there are as many other people around as possible. Criminals prefer not to strike when there are witnesses about.
4. Report suspicious incidents to the police and encourage your family to be alert for them; for instance, students coming to your door to make unlikely sounding surveys. If you get threatening telephone calls, report these to the police also and try to remember any peculiarities of voice or accent, or any background noise that might give a hint as to where the call was made from.
5. Watch out for abandoned cars in the vicinity. These are sometimes dumped by criminals to test police vigilance.

6. Avoid conspicuous displays of affluence.
7. Try to have a room in your house to which you and your family can retreat if serious danger threatens. It should have good doors with stout locks, and windows which can be secured from the inside but which do not bar escape routes. If possible get professional advice on how to prepare what is called a keep in your house.
8. Using firearms as a form of self-defence is fraught with danger. You will nearly always be faced with more than one assailant and you have to be prepared to shoot to kill. That in itself is much less easy than it is made to look in the movies; furthermore, in some countries foreigners are always in the wrong in such circumstances.
9. The best form of defence and survival is to rehearse a plan of action in your mind in case you are attacked or in danger and to stick to it if you can. The thing to avoid above all is panic, because that way you lose control of the situation.

In addition to these general points, it is worth considering a rather more sinister statistic: at least 560 people were killed by terrorist bombs in 1995. There were at least 300 attacks, many of which were not picked up by the international press. Countries concerned ranged from Austria to the US. Many security consultants, as well as the Foreign Office, can provide general advice on these matters. However, it is worth remembering that the chances of winning the lottery jackpot are rather higher than that of being anywhere near a terrorist attack.

Reading matter

You may never have been much of a book buyer while living in the UK, but many expatriates report that not being able to get hold of books when they want them is an unexpected deprivation, especially in postings where other forms of entertainment, at any rate in English, are hard to come by.

Many places do, of course, have bookshops which stock some English titles, but the selection is often very limited (children s books are particularly hard to get) and prices are always much higher than the UK price shown tantalisingly on the jacket. You can, however, import your own books at standard London prices through the admirable Good Book Guide (24 Seward Street, London EC1V 3GB; 24-hour tel: 0171 490 9905, fax: 0171 490 9908, e-mail: enquiries@good-book-guide.co.uk) or order books on the Internet from Amazon.com. They are a mail order book service with a substantial trade among expatriates all over the world. You can choose your books from their monthly guide, for which there is a modest annual subscription, but they can also get any book in print for you, including paperbacks. There are also regular video and audio listings offering a wealth of entertainment: drama, documentary, comedy and children s programmes.

The choices in the guide are accompanied by brief, helpful notes written by outside experts (eg Chris Bonington on travel) and the selection of titles is broad, covering both high-brow literature and commercial best sellers, all chosen on merit alone. The subject areas are broad too, ranging through all kinds of interests. However, the Good Book Guide is not a book club there is no obligation to buy. A free trial issue can be requested.

Payment is on a cash with order basis or by credit card and clear instructions are given with each issue of the guide on how to pay from anywhere in the world.

Home comforts

Sending for goods through mail order catalogues can make up for deficiencies in local shops when working abroad. Although many companies that provide goods by mail order confine their activities to the UK and will not send goods abroad (no doubt because of potential payment problems), there is nothing to stop you making arrangements to get catalogues through UK friends or relatives and ordering through them. Expatriates with young children are reported to find the Mothercare catalogue very useful. Harrods and Fortnum & Mason will send goods anywhere in the world and you can pay by credit card. Harrods also operate worldwide accounts.

Coming home

Coming back to live in the UK may seem straightforward compared with the complexities of moving out to a job abroad, but if you are to reap the full benefit of a spell as a non-UK resident, planning for your return also requires forethought and preparation.

Take the matter of bringing back personal possessions. Price differentials between countries are no longer as great as they used to be, but there are still quite a number of places where, even taking freight into account, it is worth buying things like electronic or audio-visual equipment even cars locally and shipping them back home. In countries which operate exchange controls this may also be a possible way of taking out assets in the form of goods. But beware of the catch: unless you can show that an article has been used and owned for six months, you are liable for import duty and VAT on top of that. It is no use asking an obliging vendor to provide backdated invoices, because if you are unlucky enough to come under investigation, customs officials check serial numbers as well as documents. Another thing to be aware of is that once your personal possessions, including cars, are imported without payment of import duty and VAT, they cannot be sold or disposed of within 12 months, or they become liable for both these taxes.

Even with well-used goods, you can be in for unforeseen costs unless you get your timing right. The problem is that possessions shipped back to the UK will not be released until their owner arrives home. You can get a relative to clear them on your behalf, but that person would be liable for provisional duty on their value which is only repaid when you yourself get back. It takes about a fortnight to clear goods through customs anyway, so you will need expert advice at the other end if you are to steer the difficult course between paying warehouse charges in the UK because the goods have arrived too soon, or finding yourself without the basic necessities of life because you have sent them off too late.

The most important thing, though, is that they should actually arrive. The cheapest form of shipping may not be the best. The right course of action is to find a local firm that has a reputable agent in the UK, and to make sure you get door-to-door insurance cover.

You should also notify the letting agents who are looking after your UK property at least three months before your return, so that they can give due notice to tenants.

However, unless you have been sent out by a UK employer, the biggest problem in returning home can be in finding another job. Well before that point you should be sending your CV round to headhunters who are always on the lookout for those with specialist qualifications. If you feel that you may have difficulty placing yourself on the job market on grounds of age or lack of specific skills, it may be worth consulting a career counsellor. They cannot find you a job and you should be wary of those who imply otherwise, but their advice, though not cheap, has been found to be a good investment by many mid-career job-seekers.

9

Your Children s Education

Susan Jackson, BA, PGCE, MA

General considerations

For those contemplating a job abroad, the issue of schooling cannot be taken lightly. Not only can an unsatisfactory educational solution prejudice a child s chance of achieving academic success, it can also create tensions which have an adverse effect on the home and working environment. In some cases it may lead to the premature termination of overseas contracts.

Educational options certainly demand careful thought and planning. Among the possibilities to be considered are:

1. A boarding school in the UK.
2. A day school in the UK (with guardianships/relatives).
3. An expatriate school abroad.
4. A company-sponsored school abroad.
5. A local national school abroad.
6. Home teaching abroad.

The ultimate choice will be determined by the age, ability and personality of your child, together with the quality of education available abroad and the expected duration of a contract. It will

Susan Jackson trained as a teacher and worked in bilingual and international schools both in the UK and overseas, before becoming the headmistress of a girls public school in the UK and the principal of a large independent bilingual girls school in Buenos Aires, Argentina. In recent years she has been engaged as an educational consultant to the European Council of International Schools, the Church Schools Company and the National Development Centre for Education and Management Policy at the University of Bristol. In 1992, on behalf of ECIS, she was responsible for setting up a new international school in northern Spain for a major multinational company.

also be based on personal financial considerations and on the education support policy of the employer.

School fees (all, or a substantial part) may be paid by major international companies and organisations, and in some cases by governmental agencies. Whether such an allowance is used to contribute towards education at a UK boarding school or at a local fee-paying school will depend on local availability and the employer s policy. Some of these organisations employ trained staff to offer advice and support. They may also cover travelling expenses to and from the school in the UK, including air fares.

Smaller British companies may indicate that the salary they offer includes an unspecified sum towards the cost of schooling. Locally owned companies, particularly in developing countries, rarely provide an educational allowance.

One factor which must be considered at the outset is that few organisations can be relied upon to give any help with school fees once the assignment abroad has been completed. On return to the UK many parents may find it difficult to finance boarding school fees from a lower, and often more heavily taxed, personal income. However, it can be disruptive to move your children from one school to another and particularly inadvisable at a sensitive stage in their schooling when they have begun a GCSE or A-level course. On the other hand, if you have chosen a school abroad with a curriculum which bears little or no resemblance to that followed in the UK, your child may find it hard to cover lost ground. When selecting a school it is crucial

to look ahead and to make plans which will serve your child s best interest when your overseas contract comes to an end.

Schools in the UK

The independent system

Children have individual talents and develop at different stages in a variety of ways, so it is important that they are placed in a school which is well suited to their needs and is able to encourage the development of their particular skills. However, the breadth of choice offered by the independent sector can be bewildering for those parents who have had no previous experience. As a first step parents will need to become acquainted with the structure of the independent system. Briefly, it is as follows:

Ages 5 7/8: Pupils attend an independent pre-preparatory school (pre-prep), or the pre-prep department of a preparatory school. This corresponds to the infants section in local authority schools.

Ages 7/8 11/13: Children attend an independent preparatory school (or prep school). Some senior schools have their own prep schools. Many prep schools, though independently run, have established close links with several senior schools, to which the majority of their pupils move. Traditionally, senior girls and boys day schools and senior girls boarding schools have accepted pupils at 11. Senior boys boarding schools commonly take pupils at 13.

Many prep schools work towards the Common Entrance Examination.

Ages 11/13 16: Pupils attend a senior school, commonly known as public schools, where the heads may be members of the Headmasters and Headmistresses Conference (HMC) or the Girls Schools Association (GSA), and are usually prepared for the General Certificate of Secondary Education (GCSE) examinations. GCSE courses normally cover a two-year period and the examinations are taken at 15 or 16. At this stage the curriculum is generally organised to allow pupils to take the widest possible spread of GCSE subjects.

Apart from providing a child with the basic requirement for subsequent study at Advanced (A) level and entry into the sixth form, GCSEs are required for entry to professions and higher education. For example, most universities set two entrance requirements:

1. The general requirement for admission, which is usually stated as a certain number of GCSE passes at grade C or above and a minimum number of A-level passes (ie grades A E), and
2. The course requirement in which candidates may be asked to offer GCSE passes and A-level passes in named subjects.

Ages 16 18: Students are prepared for A-levels over a two-year period. This is an exacting course, which commonly involves studying three subjects in depth. The grades to be aimed for will be stipulated by professional organisations or universities.

Advanced Supplementary (AS) levels are also offered as an alternative to A-levels by some schools. Two AS levels are equivalent to one A-level and pupils can opt to replace one or more A-levels with AS levels, either to broaden or to enhance their specialisation (eg a language with sciences).

In recent years, while A-levels have been subject to government review, a new emphasis has been given to vocation-based General National Vocational Qualifications (GNVQs). The advanced level GNVQ is comparable to two A-levels and fulfils the minimum entry requirement for a university place.

GCSE and A-level examinations are set by independent examining boards. It is important for parents to note that syllabuses and set books vary between the boards, as do the subjects which are provided.

In many independent schools in Scotland pupils study for the Scottish Certificate of Education (SCE). The Standard Grade is taken at 15 and approximates to the GCSE. The Higher Grade is taken the following year, in five or six subjects. The Scottish Certificate of Sixth Year Studies (SCSYS) offers pupils a further qualification after Higher Grade. The Scottish public examinations are recognised for entry to all UK universities. Just as Scottish universities accept A-levels, English universities accept Scottish Highers but their offer of a place is frequently dependent upon the candidate obtaining specified grades in SCSYS.

General Aspects

All-age schools: Some parents prefer to send their children to schools (especially girls schools) which run from 5 to 18. In this way they seek to guarantee the continuity of educational provision, although in many schools examinations are required for entrance to the senior school.

Boarding schools

Many parents find it difficult to decide whether to send their child to a day or boarding school. For parents who are working overseas boarding is an obvious choice. Indeed, some parents may opt for a job abroad in order to finance their children s education at a boarding school.

How to find a boarding school

Selecting the most appropriate school for your child can be a time-consuming and confusing process, but there are several organisations to help you make your choice.

The Independent Schools Information Service (ISIS), 56 Buckingham Gate, London SW1E 6AG (tel: 0171 630 8793, fax: 0171 630 5013), produces a number of helpful publications including *Choosing Your Independent School* (£9.50 plus postage). They also offer a comprehensive placement service (£350 + VAT) and a consultancy service, which consists of an interview at the London office (£100 + VAT). A clearing house service is available to provide a shortlist of suitable schools, at a charge of £30 + VAT.

Advice is also available free of charge from Gabbitas Educational Consultants Ltd, Carrington House, 126 130 Regent Street, London W1R 6EE; tel: 0171 734 0161 or 0171 439 2071, fax: 0171 437 1764. Gabbitas invites parents to tell them as much as possible about their child, their circumstances and the type of school they are looking for. On the basis of this information they are able to recommend a selection of suitable schools from a wide range of independent boarding and day schools. Shortlisted schools are asked to send parents a prospectus. It is then up to the parents to visit the schools personally. There is no charge for this service. Gabbitas also offers detailed guidance on education at all levels (a fee of £130 + VAT per hour is charged for such consultations). Experienced consultants deal with a range of educational issues, including options at 16+ and planning for higher education and career opportunities.

How to choose a boarding school

Having shortlisted several schools, either with or without the guidance of a professional organisation, parents are well advised to read the prospectus through carefully, and to prepare a checklist of questions in readiness for a visit to a school.

Many of the factors governing choice are self-evident and conclusions will be arrived at quickly. Access to an international airport, proximity to relatives, religious denomination, co-educational or single-sex, the academic aims of the school and the scale of fees are points which all parents will need to consider. Also important are:

1. *The academic record of the school.* Parents should ask to see recent public examination results (ideally for the previous three to five years, department by department) if a list is not included with the prospectus material. What is the percentage pass rate as a reflection of all the pupils in the examination year? How many pupils gained grades A or B?

   It is important to determine which subjects are taught at GCSE and A-level; some schools may have achieved good examination results by concentrating on a narrow curriculum, and restricting examination entries to the more able pupils. How many GCSE subjects do the pupils normally take and are they all done at the same time? Can a combination of science and humanities subjects be taken at A-level?

   How does the school's curriculum compare with the National Curriculum? Independent schools are not required to follow the National Curriculum. In practice, they generally aim to offer more not less.

   How well is the school educating the children it admits? You should find out where pupils go when they leave the school. Which schools do prep school-leavers enter? Do any win scholarships? How many sixth-form pupils go on to university?

Check the school s ranking in the academic league tables. Two versions of the public exams taken by secondary pupils are published annually: one in late summer by the Independent Schools Information Service (ISIS) and one in November by the DfEE. The ISIS version includes the GCSE and A-level results for independent schools and the academically strong state schools. The Government s version includes the GCSE and A-level results of *all* schools and colleges on a region by region basis.

2. *The qualifications and approach of the teaching staff.* Schools should provide a staff list. It is recommended that parents visit a school in term time so that they can see lessons in progress and assess the relationship between staff and pupils. Are children lively and attentive? If a visit on a normal working day overlaps the mid-morning break so much the better; parents will learn far more about the values of the school at this time than from a mission statement in the prospectus. Do the staff seem to know the pupils? Is warmth and respect demonstrated between staff and pupils?

How often do teachers meet to discuss the children s work? How well does the head seem to know the children, and how well liked does he/she appear to be?

3. *The staff/pupil ratio.* Large classes inhibit individual progress, but classes can also be too small to be stimulating. Most schools divide pupils into sets for core subjects such as mathematics and foreign languages. Many schools now allocate personal tutors to monitor individual progress. Are arrangements made to help slow learners or to accelerate quick ones?

4. *The physical environment.* As the school will be your child s home for a major part of the year the buildings should be clean, cheerful and adequately heated. Ask to visit the dormitories/bedrooms and washing facilities. Find out which facilities are available to boarders at weekends, eg, the sports hall or IT facilities.

5. *The attitude to discipline.* Parents should ask to see a copy of the school rules, together with the normal sanctions and punishments. To what extent is reliance placed on pupils to

maintain discipline? Is positive behaviour rewarded? Try to establish whether discipline in the school strikes the right balance. Does it teach children about self-responsibility? How would the school expect to deal with serious offenders, particularly in the areas of drugs, alcohol and smoking?

6. *The quality of sports education.* How much emphasis is placed on sporting activities? Are competitive games encouraged?

7. *The range of information technology.* Ask whether the school is networked and how much information can be obtained electronically by individual pupils. Check that the school has a rolling programme for bringing staff up to date with technological developments and that information technology is being used across the curriculum. You should expect to find each department using available technology in the way that is most appropriate to their needs.

8. *The range of extra-curricular activities.* How will your child be occupied outside study hours? Is a colourful programme of weekend events available? What activities will be arranged for your child over an exeat weekend when other children are spending time with their parents? Is there an involvement with the local community?

9. *The quality of pastoral care.* What are the arrangements for supervising boarders? You should meet prospective house staff. Will your child be cared for as an individual? What arrangements will be made if your child is ill?

10. *Costs.* The costs of boarding schools vary but you should expect to pay between £2500 and £3500 per term at a prep school, and between £3500 and £4800 per term at a girls or boys senior school. In some schools extras can prove to be a heavy additional commitment.

11. *The numbers in the sixth form.* Do pupils choose to stay at the school after GCSE? Compare the size of the fifth form with the first year sixth. Is there a sizeable fall in numbers, and if so why?

12. *The quality of careers counselling.* How successful is the school in guiding progress towards higher education? What proportion of sixth form pupils go on to university? Does the school rely on a member of the teaching staff to run the careers department, or employ a qualified careers adviser?

Are children assisted in making GCSE and A-level choices with university and career intentions in mind?

13. *Contact with parents.* How are parents kept informed about their child s progress? What opportunities exist for parents to meet and communicate with the staff?

14. *The house system.* Most schools are subdivided into houses which provide a focus and a sense of identity for the children. Is the house allocated or chosen? How many children are there in each house? How is the house run? What checks are imposed on a child s freedom of movement? Parents should be taken to meet house staff who will be concerned with their child s welfare. They may wish to enquire how long the present house master or mistress is likely to remain in post.

15. *School publications.* School magazines often reveal more about the life and ethos of a school than a formal prospectus. Parents should ask to see the most recent copy. Many heads also write an annual school report, listing recent corporate and individual achievements. This too should be available on request. The School Development Plan will reveal the plans that the head and governors have to ensure that the school remains viable; it may also be available on request.

16. *References.* Many schools are willing to supply names, addresses and telephone numbers of existing parents. They can often be an informal source of useful information about the school. The heads of preparatory schools are also a useful source of information about senior schools as they tend to receive regular feedback from former pupils and parents.

Entrance examination

To be admitted to an independent secondary school your child will normally be required to pass the school s entrance test or the Common Entrance examination, which is set for candidates of 11+, 12+ and 13+ (the appropriate examination is normally determined by the child s age on 1 September in the year of entry).

At 11+ the subjects examined are English, mathematics, science and reasoning. Examinations take place in January and November.

At 12+ candidates sit papers in English, mathematics, science and French (written and oral). Latin may be offered as an optional paper. Examinations take place in February/March and November.

At 13+ the papers are English, mathematics, science, French (written and oral), history, geography and religious studies. English as an additional language, German, Spanish, Latin and Greek may be offered as optional papers. Examinations take place in February/March, June (for most candidates) and November. Candidates for boys schools most commonly take the 13+ examination.

Each senior school sets its own entrance standards and is responsible for the assessment of papers. Some schools require candidates to sit their own independent examinations in addition, or as an alternative, to Common Entrance. The examinations are normally taken at the candidate s own school.

Children applying to boarding schools from abroad or from state schools will be in direct competition with those who have been tutored for the entrance examinations at UK prep schools. Many schools will take this fact into consideration when making their assessments. However, in some cases it may be necessary to arrange individual coaching in advance of the examination. Consultancy and assessment, as well as tuition, are available from members of the Association of Tutors, Sunnycroft, 63 King Edward Road, Northampton NN1 5LY; tel: 01604 624171. Supportive tuition or complete coverage can be provided for primary and secondary work, as well as some university-level work. Some services are available on a distance basis, and some as intensive, holiday-period schemes. Examination advice and preparation for particular exams, like the Common Entrance, is a particular expertise.

The syllabuses for each subject, and the examination papers, are set by the Independent Schools Examinations Board. Copies of syllabuses, past papers and information are available from: The Independent Schools Examinations Board, Jordan House, Christchurch Road, New Milton, Hants BH25 6QJ; tel: 01425 621111, fax: 01425 620044.

Scholarships

Many independent schools offer entrance scholarships to children of outstanding ability or potential. These may be based either on general academic standard or on particular strengths, notably musical, sporting or artistic. Individual schools will supply details on request.

A number of schools offer bursaries for means-tested families. Others make specific awards to the children of clergy and service families.

ISIS runs an advisory service on scholarships and bursaries for parents seeking general advice.

Insurance and financial planning

A growing number of financial service groups and independent financial advisers are able to offer school fee plans, with obvious benefits for those who are able to plan and save well in advance. For those with a more immediate requirement, loan schemes, both equity and non-equity based, are available. ISIS produce a useful leaflet called *School Fees*.

Many schools co-operate with insurance companies in schemes for the remission of school fees during unavoidable absence through illness. Other policies are available which guarantee the continued payment of fees in the event of a parent s death, disablement or redundancy before the completion of schooling.

Maintained boarding schools

Some local authorities run their own boarding schools or offer boarding facilities alongside day schools. Eighteen of these maintained schools have opted out and are now grant maintained (grant maintained schools will be given a new status under government plans but this should not affect the education provided). Although any child with a legal right to attend school in Britain may seek entry to any maintained school, some authorities give priority to local children, even for boarding places. As tuition is free at these schools and parents pay only for boarding, the overall costs are approximately one-half to two-thirds of the cost of an independent school. Many pupils are from service families, or have parents who work for banks or government agencies abroad.

The Directory of Maintained Boarding Schools provides details of 38 schools which have boarding places. Copies may be obtained from The Boarding Schools Association, Ysgol Nant,

Valley Road, Llanfairfechan, Gwynedd LL33 0ES, tel/fax: 01248 680542 or from the DfEE Publications Centre, PO Box 5050, Sudbury, Suffolk CO10 6ZQ, tel: 084560 22260, fax: 0845 6033360.

Local authority grants
Some education authorities are prepared to give grants to assist with boarding school fees when both parents are abroad and there are no places available in a state boarding school. Application should be made to the director of education or chief education officer for the area in the UK in which the family is normally resident.

Arrangements for your child
A boarding school accepts responsibility for the day-to-day welfare of its pupils in term-time, but overseas parents will naturally want assurance that their child is being cared for at all times, including short holiday periods and occasions when they may be in transit between school and home. There are a number of organisations which care for children in these circumstances.

Child supervision
Some boarding schools are able to send a school bus or driver to collect children from, and deliver them to, the nearest airport. Where this service is not available parents may wish to use a commercial escort service. These can be provided by:

- Universal Aunts Ltd, PO Box 304, London SW4 0NN (tel: 0171 498 8200, fax: 0171 622 1914) can arrange for children to be taken to and from school according to parents instructions. They try to allot the same aunt to a child so that a warm relationship is established. When required to do so they can also arrange for children to be accommodated for the night in the home of one of the aunts. Holiday accommodation is also available. Fees for meetings are based on the length of working time, and the time of day they take place. Between 8.00 am and 6.00 pm the charge for escorting up to three children is £45.00 for four hours or less, exclusive of unaccompanied travelling time and fares. Public transport is at cost, car travel is 24 pence per mile. Overnight accommodation including breakfast is £18.00 per child.

- Corona Worldwide, c/o The Commonwealth Institute, Kensington High Street, London W8 6NQ (tel/fax: 0171 610 4407) provide a dependants (adults and children) escort service for members at the charge of £35.00 per person, per single journey of six hours or less and £55 per return journey. Other rates on application. Overnight accommodation may also be arranged if necessary, for children only. Membership of the parents Corona Society is £10 per year.

Finding a guardian

Most boarding schools require parents to appoint a local guardian for their child. Several organisations are able to offer a guardianship service for parents who do not wish to impose upon relations or family friends.

Guardianship schemes have developed in response to demands from parents and schools to cover welfare, education and finance. Some, or all, of the following services may be offered:

- identifying a suitable guardian family;
- travel arrangements including booking and purchasing airline tickets;
- passport and visa formalities;
- payment of school fees;
- purchasing school uniform and equipment;
- management of pocket money;
- arranging insurance and medical care;
- periodic visits to the school to monitor progress;
- help with subject selection for GCSE and A-level;
- assistance with higher education placement;
- organisation of holiday courses and visits;
- arranging accommodation for exeats, weekends and holidays;
- escorting children to and from school;
- personal liaison between school and parents;
- attendance at parent/teacher meetings and other school functions.

Guardianship services are provided by, for example, the following organisations:

- Clarendon International Education, 41 Clarendon Square, Royal Leamington Spa, Warwickshire CV32 5Q2 (tel: 01926 316793, fax: 01926 883278) can offer three levels of service the comprehensive Prestige Guardianship at the rate of £1000 + VAT per term; Mini Guardianship at £600 + VAT per term; and a flexible Help and Advice service at £150 + VAT per term. They can also organise professional consultancy and take care of special arrangements such as airport meetings at individual rates.

- Guardians and Tutors, 131 Pomphlett Road, Plymstock, Plymouth PL6 7BU (tel: 01752 401942) provide a versatile service. They charge £500 + VAT per year for guardianship plus £500 + VAT deposit per year, and from £15 + VAT per day for accommodation.

- Gabbitas Educational Consultants Ltd (address on page 124) run a comprehensive guardianship service which takes care of all aspects of education, welfare and finance. They will find a guardian family living near to the school, who will be sympathetic towards your child and provide a secure and warm environment. Their fees are £800 plus VAT per term in the first year, £700 plus VAT per term thereafter, plus an initial registration fee of £80 plus VAT.

- Joanella Slattery Associates (JSA), Gilpin, Station Road, Withyham, Hartfield, East Sussex TN7 4BT, tel: 01892 770585/0850 943106; fax: 01892 770120, e-mail: joanella@sol.com offer free educational advice as well as a comprehensive guardianship service. Guardian families living near the school provide a home to overseas students. The standard guardianship service is £850 plus VAT per child per annum; there is a deluxe service at £900 plus VAT per child per year. Added to this is a registration fee of £117.50 + VAT per child and allowances and expenses payable to guardian families which vary from £300 to £500 per term.

- GJW Education Services, Southcote, Coreway, Sidmouth EX10 9SD; tel: 01395 512300; fax: 01395 577271, e-mail: gjweaver@netcomuk.co.uk offer a complete service to overseas parents whose children attend independent boarding schools · in England and Wales. Guardianship fees are £150 £250 + VAT per term. The initial registration fee is £35 + VAT. Temporary accommodation during school holidays and an escort service are also available.

Day schools

If you feel that your child is unsuited to boarding school life, or that it would be too disruptive to move schools for example, during the GCSE years you may wish to consider a day place. Where relatives and friends are available to care for your child this arrangement can work smoothly, particularly when a child continues at his or her present school. Many older children are reluctant to leave their friends and interests behind, and are able to respond positively to a new degree of independence.

In some cases, where there are no relatives or friends to rely on and parents wish to avoid placing their child in lodgings, mothers stay behind with their children. Although this offers the child continuity it can cause strains in the marital relationship and may offset the financial benefits of the posting.

Few employers offer more than a token allowance for lodging if your child remains at a day school in the UK.

Schools abroad

Expatriate schools

Unlike other nations such as France, Germany, Japan or Switzerland, Britain provides no financial assistance for the creation and management of schools for British expatriates. This means that British parents moving abroad must expect to pay substantial school fees unless they choose to send their children to local national schools.

British schools

So-called British schools abroad use English as the language of instruction and aim to follow a curriculum which corresponds to the National Curriculum. This is an advantage for children who will return to the UK system. The extent to which the schools are genuinely British in outlook will depend on the background of the staff and headteacher, and the influence of the local British community. Although a high percentage of British pupils usually attend these schools, they are open to pupils of different nationalities.

Most British schools are not government approved. However, a group of 26 schools in the EU are members of the Council of British Independent Schools in the European Communities (COBISEC), which is recognised by the Department for Education and Employment (DfEE). Like UK state schools, COBISEC schools receive regular inspections from the Office for Standards in Education (OFSTED). Advice is available from the COBISEC Secretariat, c/o Mrs S. Melchers, Lucy s, Lucy s Hill, Hythe, Kent CT21 5ES, tel: 01303 260857.

A number of British schools are affiliated to UK professional educational associations, such as the Headmasters and Headmistresses Conference (HMC) and the Girls Schools Association (GSA). Such links enable schools to keep abreast of educational developments taking place in the UK, and to share the benefits of staff development courses.

The European schools
The nine official European schools were set up by agreement among the member states of the EU to provide a multinational education almost exclusively for the children of staff employed in the institutions of the EU. The schools are situated in Brussels (2), Luxembourg, Mol, Belgium, Varese, Italy, Munich and Karlsruhe, Germany, Bergen, Holland and Culham, Oxfordshire, UK. The European schools are day schools with a 4 to 19 age range. Pupils are organised in separate language sections and follow a common curriculum leading in the secondary school to the European Baccalaureate, the schools own leaving examination. A tenth school is under construction in Brussels and should open in September 1999. Information about the schools is available from the European Schools Team at the DfEE (tel: 0171 925 5000).

American schools
American schools offer an American curriculum, but may be an option for British children because the language of instruction

is English. It is important to remember that the educational approach will be quite different and that pupils will be prepared for American examinations at college entry level, such as the Standard Achievement Tests (SATs). To graduate from an American school a certain number of credits are required. Credit courses in the final two years of schooling may include Honours and Advanced Placement Sections which provide able students with special challenges. British universities are familiar with the entrance requirements of leading American universities and set similar entry requirements for applicants from American-style schools.

International schools

International schools are established in most capital cities of the world. They may be distinguished by the fact that they are independent of any state system and aim to educate children from a variety of nationalities.

Many are outstanding schools, offering intellectual pluralism and exceptional cultural variety typically 50 to 60 different nationalities are represented in the student body. Some are members of international associations such as the United World Colleges and the European Council of International Schools (ECIS), others have headteachers in membership of the (British-based) Headmasters and Headmistresses Conference or the Girls Schools Association.

In many respects they are as varied as their locations large or small, monolingual, bilingual (using a foreign language as a medium of instruction for some subjects) or even multilingual (using more than one foreign language as a medium of instruction), traditional or emphatically modern. Some are subsidised by local governments, others are among the most costly schools in the world. Almost all are co-educational, and in the majority the language of instruction is English.

International schools may follow a standard US college preparatory programme or a standard GCSE or International GCSE (IGCSE) programme, or a combination of these. Although a number of schools also work towards national examinations such as the German Abitur or the Spanish Bachillerato, at sixth-form level many are now preparing for the diploma of the International Baccalaureate Organisation (IBO).

The International Baccalaureate (IB) is based on a two-year curriculum which maintains a balance between the sciences, the arts and languages. The programme is broader than A-levels as all students must offer one subject from each of six groups:

- Language A (first language)
- Language B (second language)
- Individuals and societies
- Experimental sciences
- Mathematics
- Electives (including art, music, IT).

Of the six subjects studied, three are taken at Higher level, and three at Standard level. This represents a deliberate compromise between the European emphasis on breadth and the British tradition of rigorous specialisation. In effect students offer three subjects to A-level equivalent standard and three subjects to a standard somewhat above GCSE. To be eligible for the award of the Diploma candidates must score a minimum of points and meet three additional requirements: submission of an extended essay; satisfactory completion of a Theory of Knowledge Course; and compulsory participation in a CAS programme (Creativity, Action, Service).

Students holding the IB Diploma have entered more than 700 universities throughout the world. All UK universities accept the IB as satisfying their general requirement for entrance. For further information contact: The International Baccalaureate Organisation, Curriculum and Assessment Centre, Peterson House, Fortran Road, St Mellons, Cardiff CF3 0LT; tel: 01222 774 000, fax: 01222 774 001.

Another worldwide school-leaving certificate, which has been available to English-medium schools throughout the world since 1986, is the Advanced Intermediate Certificate of Education (AICE). AICE is a group certificate which is awarded on the basis of a broad and balanced curriculum of five full-credit courses or their equivalent. All candidates must take at least one course from three subject groups: mathematics and sciences; languages; and arts and humanities. The AICE curriculum, which is designed to be of worldwide relevance, offers a high degree of flexibility. As there are no compulsory subjects, student programmes may range from the highly specialised to the general. Most UK universities now accept AICE as an alternative to A-levels. AICE is administered by the University of Cambridge Local Examinations Syndicate (UCLES), 1 Hills Road, Cambridge CB1 2EU, tel: 01223 553311, fax: 01223 460278.

How to find an overseas school
Help and advice on the selection of an overseas school can be provided by World-wide Education Service (WES) Ltd, Canada House, 272 Field End Road, Eastcote HA4 9NA, tel: 0181 582 0317/0318, fax: 0181 429 4838.

For detailed information about the 400 international schools in membership of ECIS and brief details on 400 non-member schools, including enrolment, curriculum, fees, school premises, extracurricular activities, staff details and school ownership, see *The International Schools Directory* (£35), which is available from John Catt, Great Glenham, Saxmundham, Suffolk IP17 2DH, tel: 01728 663666. The on-line version of the Directory can be found on the ECIS web site on http://www.ecis.org.

How to choose a school abroad
When selecting a school abroad it may prove useful to consider the points raised earlier on choosing a UK boarding school. However, there are several additional factors which should be considered when evaluating overseas schools:

1. Many employers pay for families to visit the country before their projected move. This gives them the opportunity to visit the available schools (it is useful to obtain prospectuses beforehand) in person, and to consider the alternatives with existing expatriate parents and organised parents groups which are attached to the schools. However, it is important to remember that other people may have standards which do not correspond to your own.

    In many instances expatriate schools become both a community and a social centre for expatriate families. This can be a great help for incoming families.

2. It is advisable to link house-hunting with the choice of school so that transportation problems can be considered in advance.

3. A rapid turnover of pupils can be expected in many schools as a reflection of the frequent movement of personnel by companies. However, this should not be the case with the majority of staff. As children may take time to adjust to new teaching styles it is important that there is continuity in the classroom.

4. It is important to establish how schools overseas are controlled. Many schools are run by boards composed of leading figures from the local community, including representatives from the parent body and the organisations which use the school. The latter may be relied upon to ensure that the facilities available to their employees are of a high standard.

5. Every effort should be made to meet the headteacher, who is responsible for the quality and organisation of the school. He or she will be able to tell you whether there is a waiting list for admission to the school and when you need to register your child. In some instances the waiting time for admission can be a full academic year. Other schools may be ready to accept pupils at almost any time.

6. Take time to consider the curriculum. How far does it correspond to the National Curriculum in the UK? How straightforward will it be for your child to transfer back to the UK? Try to establish how much support, both pastoral and academic, is provided for individual children, to enable them to cope with the process of transition.

7. It is important to consider the type of report and record-keeping system which is in operation in the school. How much information will be available as a record of your child's achievement at the school? Pupil profiles are particularly essential for children who move from school to school frequently.

8. The language of instruction will be of key importance to your child. Find out what kind of English is used whether it is American, British or non-mother tongue English. How many children and staff do not have English as a first language? Are they likely to hinder your child's progress?

9. Expatriate schools are geared to accept pupils at any stage during the school year. However, the process of transition is generally easier when pupils begin school at the start of a new term.

10. If your company is not offering an educational allowance, do take account of costs. ECIS reports that in Paris full day fees can range from $10,000 in a junior school to $15,000 in a secondary school. In New York comparable figures are $10,000 at elementary level and $18,000 at secondary level, in Hong Kong from $7,000 to $10,000 and in Brazil from $10,000 to $16,000. In addition, some schools may require parents to pay a substantial registration fee.

Company sponsored schools

Where difficulties arise in finding a suitable local school, companies may decide to open their own site-based school. The success of such enterprises will depend to a large extent on the quality of the teaching staff and the existence of educational support. Schools may be very small, and a group of children of different ages and ability will be taught in one class by a single teacher. In remote areas it can be difficult to attract suitably qualified staff and the spouses of on-site employees may be encouraged to take responsibility for classes.

Without external monitoring, company schools may lose touch with educational developments and offer a rather limited education. Regular contact with an outside source ensures that satisfactory educational standards are maintained.

Home School Teaching can set up and monitor small schools in isolated overseas locations, often with less than 20 pupils, for international companies or groups of parents. They also recruit teachers. Private family tutors can be arranged for a fee which is negotiated on an individual basis. Home School Teaching, Blagrove House, Blagrove Street, Reading RG1 1QA, tel: 0118 958 9993, fax: 0118 958 9994, e-mail: office@creshome.demon. co.uk, web site: www.creshome.demon.co. uk.

Local national schools

Within Europe there are significant advantages to be gained in sending your child to a local national school, not least an opportunity to acquire proficiency in another language and to absorb a new culture. Although the standard of educational provision may vary there is no doubt that in some countries, such as France and Germany, it is excellent. However, a complete immersion in another language and culture is demanding and it will depend very much on the age and ability of the children as to how successfully they can adapt.

Learning the full range of school subjects in a new language can be exacting, particularly where no provision is made for extra language tuition. Parents who do not speak the necessary language themselves must remember that they will be able to offer little advice and assistance to their child, who may feel isolated as a result.

For those on short-term contracts it is important to consider how well such a schooling will prepare children for the next stage in a UK education. Certainly, a child working towards GCSE examinations could expect to be disadvantaged. The experience may also pose difficulties for younger children returning to the UK.

Transfer into and out of school systems in other parts of the world can also pose problems. Traditional teaching methods which rely on rote learning are still applied in many developing countries, where schools are frequently ill-equipped and crowded. As education is so highly prized as a route out of poverty, expatriates will not be encouraged to supplant a local child. However, where no alternative exists, parents may need to compensate for a restricted curriculum by providing supplementary lessons at home.

Differences in attitudes to schooling are particularly marked in countries where religious and political beliefs have shaped the curriculum. Even in other parts of the English-speaking world there are fundamental differences in approach. For example, in Australia formal schooling starts at 6 and secondary education at 12.

Special needs

Parents of a child with a learning disability will find that they have a very restricted choice of educational alternatives. Only a handful of boarding schools in the UK are equipped to deal with children with special needs and even fewer overseas schools, although some do make provision for children who are behind because they have changed schools frequently.

The World-wide Education Service (WES) Home Service (address p.138) employs a consultant educational psychologist, highly experienced in assessing children with emotional or learning difficulties. Appointments can be arranged, to fit in with home leave, for a modest fee.

Advice on the provision of dyslexia units within schools may be provided by the Dyslexia Institute, 133 Gresham Road, Staines, Middlesex TW18 2AJ, tel: 01784 463851, or the British Dyslexia Association, 98 London Road, Reading RG1 5AU, tel: 01734 668271.

Home teaching

Occasionally parents are faced with the prospect of teaching their children themselves because no school is available locally. This is a demanding activity but can be very rewarding, especially for spouses who find that they are prevented by local laws from taking up employment.

An advantage of lessons given at home is that they can be designed to provide educational continuity, particularly where instruction follows a plan provided by your child s previous school or a recognised UK-based commercial home school service . Home school requires the strong commitment and active participation of a parent, but offers continuous support with teaching difficulties as they arise.

The World-wide Education Service (WES), (address p.140), has been concerned with home teaching in the UK and overseas for over 100 years. It provides full courses, books, materials, teacher notes, lesson plans, timetables and monitoring procedures to enable parents to teach children aged 3 to 13 years, and to be involved in the assessment process. Each family is assigned a tutor who provides regular guidance and advice and can be contacted at any time. Specialist questions are referred to a team of WES Home School advisers. Tutors are available for personal interviews for example, during home leave.

The WES Home School curriculum includes all core and foundation subjects specified by the National Curriculum so that children are able to fit back into a UK school with relative ease. At the same time, parent-teachers are strongly encouraged to relate their child s learning to the local environment. The benefit to the child of living in another country is stressed throughout the programmes. Although children educated at home can miss the social contact with their peers and a competitive school environment, WES Home School claims that they are often in advance of their contemporaries when they return to schools in Britain.

The fees for the Nursery Course for 3 to 4 year-olds are £410. A Reception course for 4 to 5 year-olds costs £925. A full year s course for children from 5 to 12 is £1456. Charges are also made per subject, for parents who wish to supplement a school course overseas which does not correspond to the National Curriculum. Books and international postage are not included in the above fees.

Increasing numbers of parents choose to teach older children at home. Structured correspondence courses, which require relatively little parental guidance, are available from Mercers College, 14 Baldock Street, Ware SG12 9DN; tel: 01920 465926, fax: 01920 484909. The needs of children of all ages are catered for, and courses aim to follow the National Curriculum. Programmes include reading and numeracy schemes for young children and preparation for the Common Entrance Examinations.

A broad range of courses is also offered which leads to the General Certificate of Secondary Education (GCSE) and the International General Certificate of Secondary Education (IGCSE). The IGCSE is a single-subject examination, but students can take the group examination, the International Certificate of Education (ICE), sitting seven subjects from six subject groups. Both examinations are administered by the University of Cambridge Local Examinations Syndicate (UCLES).

Many students also continue to take GCE O-levels; it is still possible to sit these overseas and they are a good introduction to A-level work. The college offers A-levels.

Fees per term range from £295 for under 7s to £650 up to 16 years. Fees for part-time courses are £215 for each subject at GCSE level, and £275 for one subject at A-level.

The National Extension College, 18 Brooklands Avenue, Cambridge CB2 2HN, tel: 01223 316644, fax: 01223 313586, also offers correspondence courses leading to GCSE/IGCSE and A-level. Fees for one GCSE/IGCSE subject are £225, and for each additional GCSE/IGCSE on the same enrolment £190. For one A-level subject the charge is £265; each additional A-level on the same enrolment is £215.

Support, advice and information for families contemplating home-based education as an alternative to schooling is available from Education Otherwise, PO Box 120, Leamington Spa CV32 7ER.

Higher education

Applying to universities

The Universities and Colleges Admissions Service (UCAS), Fulton House, Jessop Avenue, Cheltenham, Gloucestershire GL50 3SH, tel: 01242 227788, is the central agency which acts on behalf of all UK universities (except the Open University) and most colleges of higher education to process applications for entry to first degree, diploma and HND courses. All applications for entry, except for transfers, must be made through UCAS. The *UCAS Handbook*, which is free of charge, lists the courses which are available and provides the information required to complete the UCAS application form. The *Handbook* should be read in conjunction with the prospectuses of individual universities.

Prospective students may also use ECCTIS, which is a government-supported, computerised information service covering 100,000 course opportunities. ECCTIS works closely with UCAS, and the contents of the UCAS Handbook are available on the database. There are 5500 ECCTIS access points in the UK and in British Council offices worldwide.

The application cycle is clearly outlined in the *UCAS Handbook*. All application forms should reach UCAS between 1 September and 15 December preceding the year of entry.

Applicants to Oxford and Cambridge must make a direct application to these universities, in addition to completing the UCAS form.

The decision about whether an individual applicant can be admitted to a university is entirely at the discretion of the university concerned. Institutions normally set minimum requirements which are listed in the UCAS annual *University and College Entrance; the official guide* (available from bookshops or by post from Sheed and Ward Ltd, 14 Coopers Row, London EC3N 2BH, tel: 0171 702 9799. Price £19.95 plus £3 p&p). Enquiries about the suitability of qualifications should be addressed to the university admissions officer of the university concerned.

Student finance

Students who have not already received a grant for higher education and are ordinarily resident in England, Wales or Northern Ireland are eligible to receive a grant from their Local Education Authority (that is from the area in which they normally live), or, in the case of Scottish students, from the Student Awards Agency for Scotland. The amount of an individual grant, which is designed to cover university fees and living expenses, is determined by parental income. Applications to Local Education Authorities should be made in the January preceding the September entry.

To qualify for home student status in respect of grants and university fees a family must reside in the UK for three years prior to the start of higher education. Provided that they are able to satisfy conditions that are similar to those set for UK students, European Union (EU) nationals also receive a free or virtually free education. Overseas students are expected to pay a higher level of fees reflecting the full cost of their education.

Children of expatriates working outside the EU on a temporary basis may be treated as if they are in ordinary residence in the UK. However, children of expatriates who normally live outside the UK are likely to be considered as overseas students, and as such they do not qualify for financial assistance and must pay full university fees. In 1998/99 the annual tuition fees for UK and EU students are £1000 for classroom-based courses, £1600 for laboratory-based courses. The median fee for overseas students in 1998/99 is £6290 for classroom-based courses, £8480 for laboratory-based courses and £15,600 for clinical medical courses. The actual fee can vary by 30 per cent around this median. Accommodation charges and day to day expenses (food, local travel, books etc) which are not included in the fees, must also be met by overseas parents.

In order to clarify their status parents are advised to consult their local education authority and obtain a copy of its current regulations. Those students who may be entitled to a grant to help with living costs or with fees must apply to their LEA. Their award will be determined by taking the following into account: the fees which are charged by the university and the maximum maintenance grant for which the student is eligible this means the basic rate of grant plus any extra allowances which can be claimed in the light of the students parents income. In 1998/99 the *maximum* allowance available for studying at a publicly-funded institution is up to £1000 towards the cost of fees and the basic maintenance grant of £1225 for students living away from their parents home and studying in London; £810 for those living away from home and studying elsewhere in the UK; and £480 for students living at their parents home.

Since 1990 the government has been funding a loan scheme for students in higher education who are ordinarily resident in the UK. The loan is intended to help meet maintenance costs and is not means tested. The loan repayments start in April of the year after the student has ceased to attend his course, and are in monthly instalments. Outstanding loans bear interest at a rate linked to inflation. For 1998/99 the *maximum* loan for students living away from their parents home and studying in London is £4370 for the first year and £3790 for the final year, and for those elsewhere in the UK is £3545 for the first year and £3075 in the final year. For students living at their parents home, the maximum loan for the first year is £2805 and for the final year £2450. Note that all students must be attending an eligible course at the time of application. Under present regulations, most borrowers are required to repay their loans over a maximum of six years. The Student Loans Company publishes a leaflet giving full details of the scheme which may be obtained from the Student Loans Company Limited, 100 Bothwell Street, Glasgow G2 7JD, freephone: 0800 405010.

Further information on student finance is given in the DfEE publications, *Financial Support for Students* and *Mandatory Awards for those Living or Working Overseas*, available from the DfEE Publications Despatch Centre, PO Box 5050, Sudbury, Suffolk CO10 6ZQ, tel: 084560 22260, fax: 084560 33360. Advice is also available from the COBISEC Secretariat (address page 134).

Concluding remarks

Most schools will go to considerable trouble to make arrangements to see prospective parents, often at short notice. Where possible take your child with you when you visit a school and listen to his or her comments. Whatever your personal feelings about education, it is essential that those of your child are fully respected. Many children have sensible views about what is best for their own development and, where necessary, they should be persuaded rather than instructed.

Your child may be eager to make the transition from state to private school and adapt well to a new environment. However you should be aware that moving back to the state system can be difficult for ex-independent school pupils. These difficulties can also be encountered by children returning to a local school routine after the cultural diversity of an international educational environment.

The major problem for most children of expatriates is the lack of educational continuity, particularly when they are obliged to move from country to country, and school to school, every few years. If your child is to realise his or her potential you must try to provide educational stability. Much can be done to ease the process of transition by providing a new school with a detailed profile of your child. Reports, syllabus information, titles of books which he or she has been using and levels of attainment can enable a teacher to assist your child to settle happily into life in a new school with the minimum of disruption.

10

Adjusting to Living and Working Abroad

Living and working overseas can be extremely rewarding in personal, financial and career terms. It is also likely to herald a dramatic change of life style. All expatriates, no matter to which country they are posted, have to make some adjustment to life overseas, and all members of an expatriate s family will be affected by the move, whether or not they venture abroad. If, as a married person, you go abroad on unaccompanied status , you and your family will have to make a number of adjustments to living separately. There is much to be gained in going abroad as a married couple, but in so doing you may be asking your spouse to give up a career and possible future chances of employment, disrupting your children s education, and removing your family from their normal sources of comfort and support.

Much of the burden of adjustment falls on the expatriate wife, who is required to establish a home in a new country where, in spite of not speaking the language, she has to cope with shortages, difficulties of communication and, above all, different ways of doing things. If your wife and family fail to adjust to the tensions between home and work, it will make it harder for you to concentrate on the job you are there to do. Should you or your family fail to adapt, you may decide to terminate your contract early. Such unscheduled returns to the UK tend to cause considerable disturbance and hardship to all concerned. There is a high turnover rate among expatriates, so before you commit yourself and your family to working abroad it is important to discuss the likely consequences of the move with other members of your family.

In contemplating a move overseas you have probably tried to imagine what it will be like. Most people think about the physical differences: the heat, the humidity, the dirt etc, although they are rarely able to assess how these differences will affect their daily lives. How will working in 90 per cent humidity impair your effectiveness? Could you negotiate an important contract in an atmosphere more suited to the tropical house of your nearest botanical gardens? It is difficult to appreciate how much of the background to daily life is taken for granted; for example, drinking water from a tap, flicking a switch for light, pushing a button for instant entertainment. In underdeveloped countries many of these basics of everyday life either do not exist or function irregularly. While it is easy to imagine that things will be different, it is hard to envisage how this affects the quality of daily life and your sense of well-being.

But the differences that prove the greatest barrier to adjustment are the ones which cannot be seen and which are not normally even thought about. Despite regional differences in the UK most people have grown up with common experiences and expectations of how the world works. In any given situation, most people have a fairly clear idea of what is expected of them and what they expect of others. However, different nationalities do not necessarily share the same assumptions and expectations about life, or about how other people should behave. In Britain we share a common culture and, on the whole, common beliefs about what is right and proper. Other cultures, though, have quite different underlying values and beliefs, different expectations and concepts of normal behaviour .

Britain is nominally a Christian country, yet although much legislation and ordinary behaviour have their origins in Christian teaching, a relatively small proportion of the population would see Christianity as the driving force of British society. By contrast, in Saudi Arabia, Islam underlies everything. It regulates the legal and political system and the conduct of all aspects of everyday life and is so perceived by its own nationals. It can be difficult to understand how other people operate; it is easy to assume that the motivations of others are understood, while misunderstanding them utterly. In Britain the ground rules of human behaviour can be taken for granted, but overseas they must be questioned and come to terms with. For example, in Malaysia it is not uncommon for expatriates to feel that their local subordinates are disloyal when, instead of discussing some decision with which they disagree, they simply choose to ignore it. Yet to the Malaysian it would be unpardonable to cause a superior to lose face by questioning him in public; far more polite simply to ignore what is considered to be a poor suggestion.

Even unconscious behaviour is open to misinterpretation. For example, in the UK an individual who avoids eye contact would usually be categorised (unconsciously) as shifty or guilty. In Nigeria the same individual would be seen as respectful, because to avoid eye contact with an older person is a mark of respect. The classic example of how the smallest physical cues are subject to different interpretations is one of distance. The British tend to feel comfortable standing two to three feet apart when chatting; the Saudis prefer to stand closer together. A Saudi and a Briton talking to each other will each unconsciously try to establish the distance at which each feels comfortable. The Briton will feel threatened when the Saudi edges nearer and the Saudi will feel rebuffed as the Briton sidles backwards. Neither will appreciate the impact of his unconscious behaviour on the other. This kind of disorientation is experienced constantly by the fledgling expatriate, causing many expatriates to respond aggressively when no hostility was intended.

The expatriate experiences considerable anxiety when faced unknowingly with the loss of minor cues: the familiar signs and symbols which are taken for granted in the UK but are open to different interpretations in the host country. This constant disorientation is unnerving and can cause considerable stress. The syndrome is so common that it has been given a name culture shock. Doctors have long recognised that changes in normal life style can result in stress, and ultimately physical and mental illness. Change of home, change of friends, change of job, change of life style, loss of or separation from the marital partner may all be experienced by the expatriate, who may be deprived of his traditional means of support and solace. A new job is always stressful, but when the job is in a new (and seemingly hostile) environment, the tensions are even greater. Most expatriates eventually settle down, more or less successfully, but there is a predictable cycle to the adjustment and three main stereotyped responses to adaptation.

First, there is the chauvinistic expatriate, whose response to his predicament is to try to create a mini encapsulated UK or Little England . This expatriate s attempts to understand the local way of doing things, or local colleagues, are minimal. Faced with the difficulties of this new environment he retreats from what is perceived as a hostile host country and people. The blame for misunderstandings is never anything to do with him, but is always the fault of the stupid locals. This expatriate falls into a trap of denigrating everything local and idealising everything from home, ultimately provoking real hostility from local counterparts and making a reality of his view of himself alone against the world. Local expatriate clubs are full of this kind of expatriate, who often indulges his aggression over more drinks than are good for him.

The chauvinistic expatriate is experiencing culture shock. He is disorientated by his environment and feels constantly at sea. The symptoms of this state are incessant complaining, glorifica- tion of the UK, alcoholic over-indulgence, marital difficulties and general aggression. At this stage the expatriate will find it hard to work with local colleagues or clients and will be perma- nently miserable. It is at this stage also that expatriates tend to terminate their contracts, prior to completion, with major repercussions for· their families and their own careers. Fortunately for most expatriates, this is a passing stage and after their first home leave, when the realities of life in Britain are forced upon them, they manage to adapt successfully.

The second, much rarer, response is to go bush . This expa- triate eschews the company of his fellow expatriates, and tends to over-idealise all things local. He identifies totally with the host culture, which many of his local colleagues find both patro- nising and suspect.

The third and probably most appropriate response, but the most difficult to achieve, is that of the open-minded expatriate who, without abandoning his own values, is able to accept the new culture and attempt to understand it. This involves understanding how the host society s values are reflected in everyday behaviour. Decisions are made without the necessity for qualitative judgement. While differences are acknowledged, they are not categorised as better or worse.

If, prior to arriving abroad, you can come to terms with the idea that there are real cultural differences which need to be understood, you will find it much easier to adjust. These cultural differences affect work and home life. Often at work the differences are hidden because on the surface the work to be done is the same as at home, but local colleagues may have different ways of doing business and different attitudes to time and concepts of loyalty. Management styles may differ and motivation and discipline have quite different connotations. For example, many other nationalities find Western haste in business negotiations unpalatable; it is good manners and a useful way of assessing a business associate to chat seemingly inconsequentially before getting down to real negotiations. The Westerner considers it a waste of time, even insulting. In many parts of the world ethnic loyalty is a salient feature of everyday life, and a member of one tribe may be under an obligation to find jobs not only for his extended family, ie sons and daughters of aunts, uncles, cousins, and children of his father s other wives, but also for members of his own ethnic group. Outside the West, age is still considered to bestow authority and seniority, even at work. Social adjustment can also be difficult. Business is often conducted at social events; business entertaining at home may be the norm. Social life can be restricted, as in many areas expatriates make little attempt to get to know local people and mix almost entirely in expatriate circles. This can cause considerable pressure, as any minor upset at work or at home is common knowledge and long remembered.

The married expatriate living alone abroad often has the most difficulty in adjusting, both when he is working and when he is on leave. Single people often feel excluded from much social activity which revolves around the family. Single women suffer especially, as other expatriate women may resent or even fear them, and friendship with local colleagues can be misinterpreted. However, it is often the wives who bear the brunt of culture shock and have the greatest difficulty in adapting. At home most expatriate wives have had their own careers, or run their own homes. Abroad the opportunity of working is usually denied them. Neither do they have sole charge of their homes. While domestic help can be one of the boons of life abroad, dealing with domestic staff can be difficult, especially as many women find their staff taking control and fulfilling their own home-making role. Deprived of work, home role and often identified only by their husband or his job, many women experience a loss of confidence and self-identity, which makes dealing with the everyday difficulties of getting things done in a foreign country, in a foreign language, with none of the usual means of support, even more difficult. Many women go through a cycle of depression or boredom syndrome , made worse by the fact that they feel they ought to be enjoying themselves. Thinking the problem through in advance can do much to reduce its potency, especially if a determined attempt is made to try out new interests and activities.

So how can you, as a prospective expatriate, prepare yourself and your family to make the appropriate adjustments? First, you and your family should try to find out as much as possible about the country before you accept the assignment, and preferably before you go to the job interview. Once you have accepted a job offer, some employers will give you a briefing of some description. Relatively few employers seem to appreciate that the cost of staff turnover, in money, time, effort and damage to relationships with their clients, merits an outlay on briefing expatriates and their families before their departure.

You will need to know something about your employer, the nature and responsibilities of your job, the terms and conditions of your contract and whether the benefits offered match the prevailing conditions in the country. You will want to learn about the country, its history, geography, climate, politics, economics, form of government, people and religion etc. Much of this basic or factual information will be available in standard publications from the national embassies and tourist offices (although most countries naturally like to present a favourable picture of themselves). There are a number of specialised directories available in public reference libraries containing this information and some banks, such as the Hong Kong and Shanghai, produce factual booklets. The DTI produce a vast range of publications aimed at business abroad, many of which contain information of value to intending expatriates. A full list is provided in the Export Publications Catalogue, available FOC from DTI Export Publications, Admail 528, London SW1W 8YT, tel: 0171 510 0171, fax: 0171 510 0197, as well as details of other services. Your local Government Office or Business Link is another source of information linked to the DTI. Corona Worldwide (see page 111) produces its own *Notes for Newcomers* which contain background on each country with advice on setting up home.

The financial problems of expatriate life such as personal taxation, insurance etc, and other aspects of interest to expatriates are covered in several magazines catering specifically for their needs, available on subscription: *Home and Away* (monthly; £75 for 6 issues, £120 for 12 issues) is published by Expats International, 29 Lacon Road, East Dulwich, London SE22 9HE, tel: 0181 299 4986/7/8, fax: 0181 499 2484; *Nexus* (monthly) is published by Expat Network, International House, 500 Purley Way, Croydon CR0 4NZ, tel: 0181 760 5100, fax: 0181 760 0469, e-mail: expatnetwork@demon.co.uk, web site: http://www.expantnetwork.co.uk and *Resident Abroad*, published by FT Finance, and available via the Subscriptions Department, PO Box 387, Haywards Heath RH16 3GS; tel: 01444 445520, fax: 01444 445599 (Europe £59 plus VAT at local rates, rest of the world £69).

Expat Network offers a total support service for expatriates. Expat Network is a leading expatriate membership organisation enjoying a firmly established reputation within the overseas recruitment sector. The expatriate community and the overseas employment market need a level of understanding which can only be achieved over time. Most things are different, from the way in which contracts are negotiated, the job search itself, the problems involved with tax, personal finances, currency, locations, social security, pensions, etc. Expat Network can offer advice for each and every eventuality. A number of services are offered. The monthly magazine *Nexus* deals with expatriate issues, offers in-depth industry features, contractual news and has a 12-page job supplement. If you are available for work you can opt to go onto a register which is sent to a number of key recruiters who can then contact you direct. In addition the organisation also publish directories which list hundreds of contacts. *The Contract Directory* alone has 500 contacts   country-specific directories include: *The Former Soviet Union; The Far East; South East Asia.* The aim of these publications is to help you move smoothly on to a contract in your chosen location. When urgent vacancies materialise, companies will often contact the Expat Network before advertising to initiate a database search of the membership. Many people have been selected in this way. When you are working overseas Expat Network will give advice on location information, a gift service to keep you in touch with family and friends, a free tax consultation, etc.

However, the most effective way of gaining information is a briefing course. Some companies run their own; others use outside organisations. If your employer will not pay for you to attend a course, it would be worthwhile paying out of your own pocket. Ideally, husband and wife should both attend, and children can also benefit.

Corona Worldwide runs one-day Living Overseas briefings for men and women (price around £250) providing information and advice on living abroad and a one-to-one briefing, with a recent returner, on the country of your posting. Prices quoted are subject to revision. Emergency telephone and other briefings are also organised   fees for these can be obtained on request.

The Centre for International Briefing provides residential programmes and training for men and women taking up long-term appointments or short-term contracts abroad, and for home-based managers responsible for international personnel. Cultural and business briefings cover all major regions of the world, include all aspects of living and working, and allow a rapid transition to the destination country. Customised programmes provide training in international negotiation and communication skills, intercultural communication, international team-building and skill-transference in a foreign culture.

The Centre s programmes help individuals find a level of personal fulfilment which will increase effectiveness and protect the company s investment. Couples are encouraged to attend together. The intensive and demanding courses are residential and last from one to five days. Language tuition is also available, and the Centre s Language Plus programme combines intensive language and communication studies with business and cultural briefings. Details of programmes are available from the Customer Services Department, The Centre for International Briefing, Farnham Castle, Farnham GU9 0AG, tel: 01252 721194, fax: 01252 719277.

For expatriates going to Japan, China, Korea or other East Asian countries, individually prepared briefing and language sessions are available from East Asia Business Services at the University of Sheffield. Contact the Director, Dr John Bland, EABS, 317 Glossop Road, Sheffield S10 2HP; tel: 0114 222 8060, fax: 0114 272 8028, e-mail: EABS@Sheffield.ac.uk. These briefings are tailor-made and can be residential or in-company, according to the client s requirements. Family participation is encouraged. Sister organisations in destinations can provide further services. Briefings are modular and designed to provide new skills and practical knowledge. Sessions are conducted by business people with specific experience of the region.

The External Services Division of the School of Oriental and African Studies within the University of London provides a wide range of briefing and language services for business/government and private individuals. Open briefings on Japan and China are offered on a regular basis, including the two-day Japan Business Orientation Programme and the China Business Orientation Programme. Briefings may be integrated with language tuition if required and are offered on a tailor-made basis for most of the countries or regions of Asia and Africa. Details are available from the Co-ordinator, Ms Dzidra Stipnieks, SOAS External Services Division, University of London, Thornhaugh Street, Russell Square, London WC1H 0XG; tel: 0171 323 6396, fax: 0171 637 7355.

Going Places Expatriate Briefing, 84 Coombe Road, New Malden, Surrey KT3 4QS, tel: 0181 949 8811, provide tailored briefings to individuals or groups, in-house or in the home. Briefings last from three hours to a full day and cover preparation, living in-country, working in-country, coming home. Expertise is available on over 50 countries for both the working and accompanying partner. Guideline costs indicate £950 plus VAT per day per individual or couple; £100 a head thereafter. Going Places will provide its own facilities if more convenient.

These courses, and some employers, arrange for you to meet recently returned expatriates, and this is particularly useful if you can work out in advance, preferably in the form of a checklist, what you and your family really need to know. Such a checklist can also be helpful if you are offered, as occasionally happens for senior positions, the possibility of a look-see visit to the location in question.

Some expatriates have reported that the British Council are often helpful in terms of overcoming entry shock and giving advice and information about local amenities and activities.

A further aspect of learning about the host country is to master a few basic greetings in the local language. Even when it is not strictly necessary, familiarity with the sound of a language makes everything seem less strange and it is appreciated locally.

Once you arrive overseas you should take it easy, adjusting to climatic changes, as they will affect your physical and subsequently your mental state. Coping with so many new stimuli all at once is overpowering and you will need time to find your bearings. Tiredness and depression make it hard to react positively to your new situation. It is part of the adjustment cycle to feel frustrated and depressed, but if you can make the effort to understand the underlying cultural reasons for your frustration, you will be well on your way to adjusting successfully and enjoying your life abroad. After that you just have to cope with the culture shock of returning to the UK at the end of your tour.

11

An Employment Conditions Checklist

Salaries for jobs abroad nearly always sound like the proverbial offer you cannot refuse. Bear in mind, though, that you will incur a whole range of expenses which would not arise if you were employed here. It is vital to consider these expenses and to check whether your remuneration package covers them, either directly or in the form of fringe benefits.

If you are going to work for a reputable international company, it will probably know what the score should be. But if your employer is new to, or inexperienced in, the game of sending people to work abroad (especially if he is a native of the country to which you are going and therefore possibly not aware of expatriates standards in such matters as housing) here are some of the factors you should look at in assessing how good the offer really is.

To help you arrive at realistic, up-to-date answers to the following questions, it is worth trying to talk to someone who has recently worked in the country to which you are thinking of going, as well as reading the relevant sections in this book.

1. Is your employer going to meet the cost of travel out from the UK for your family as well as yourself?
2. Is he going to provide accommodation?
   (a) Of what standard?
   (b) How soon will it be available after you arrive?
   (c) Furnished or unfurnished? If furnished, what will be provided in the way of furniture?

3. If accommodation is not free, but there is a subsidy, how is this assessed?
    (a) As an absolute sum? In this case, is it realistic in the light of current prices? If not, is there any provision to adjust it?
    (b) As a proportion of what you will actually have to pay?
4. Who is going to pay for utilities (gas, water, electricity, telephone)?
5. If there is no subsidy and accommodation is not free, are you sure your salary, however grand it sounds, is adequate? Do not accept the job unless you are sure about this.
6. Will the employer subsidise or pay for your and your family s hotel bills for a reasonable period until you find somewhere to live? Is the figure realistic in the light of local hotel prices?
7. Will you be paid a disturbance allowance?
    (a) Is it adequate to cover the cost of shipping (and, possibly, duty at the other end) for as many household and personal effects as you need?
    (b) Will your eventual return to the UK as well as your departure be taken care of?
8. What arrangements will be made
    (a) To cover legal and other fees if you have to sell your UK home?
    (b) To cover the difference, if you have to let your UK home while you are away, between the rental income and such outgoings as insurance, mortgage interest and agent s management fees (see Chapter 7)? Will you be compensated for any legal expenses you incur, eg to get rid of an unsatisfactory tenant?
    (c) To cover the cost of storing household effects?
9. Will you be paid a clothing allowance, bearing in mind that you will need a whole new wardrobe if you are going to a hot country? Will it cover just your clothes, or those of your family as well?
10. Will your employer pay for or subsidise household items (eg air conditioning) that you will need in a hot climate and that are not included in an accommodation package?
11. Will your employer provide/subsidise the cost of domestic servants? If not, is your salary adequate to pay for them

yourself, if they are necessary and customary in the country and at the level at which you are being employed?

12. Is a car going to be provided with the job with or without driver?

13. Will the employer pay for or subsidise club membership and/or entrance fees?

14. Will you be paid an allowance for entertaining?

15. If your children attend UK boarding schools, what arrangements are there for them to join you in the holidays? Will the employer pay for their air fares and if so will this be for every holiday or only some of them? If the latter, can you arrange for them to be looked after at Christmas or Easter?

16. What arrangements are there for your own leaves? Does the employer provide return air fares to the UK or another country of your choice? Will these cover your family? And for how many holidays?

17. Will the employer pay for/subsidise all or any additional insurance premiums you may incur? In some countries (eg Saudi Arabia) it is advisable to insure your servants. Or costs of motor vehicle insurance may be inordinately high because of poor roads and low driving standards.

18. If social security payments are higher than in the UK (eg some EU countries) will your employer make up the difference?

19. Will he contribute to your medical expenses if free medical attention is not available or is inadequate?

20. If your salary is expressed in sterling would you be protected against loss of local buying power in case of devaluation? Equally, if your salary is in local currency, would it be adjusted for a rise in sterling against that currency?

21. Is your salary in any way index-linked to the cost of living? How often are the effects of inflation taken into account in assessing and adjusting your current level of remuneration?

22. If there are any restrictions on remittances, is your employer prepared to pay a proportion of your salary into a UK bank or that of some other country with a freely negotiable currency? This would not attract UK tax if you are away for more than 12 months.

23. Will your employer contribute towards language teaching for you and/or your wife?

24. Is the legal status of your appointment clear? If you are held to be your employer s sole or principal representative you may be personally liable in some countries for any obligations he incurs, eg the payment of corporate taxes or social security contributions.

25. Have all the terms of the job and the provisions of the remuneration package been confirmed in writing?

26. Are the contract and conditions of employment subject to English law and, if not, do you or your advisers clearly understand how they should be interpreted should a dispute arise?

27. If the job is with a foreign company, particularly a locally based one rather than a multinational, there are a number of points that need special attention:

    (a) Are the duties of the job clearly spelled out in writing in a contract of employment?

    (b) Are the normal working hours laid down? How long will your journey to work be?

    (c) Are all matters affecting pay, including when it is due and whether you will be paid for overtime, clear and in writing?

    (d) If there is a bonus, are the conditions under which it is due unambiguous?

    (e) Are there satisfactory arrangements for sick pay?

    (f) Would there be any restriction on your changing jobs if you got a better offer from another employer or decided to leave? (This one obviously has to be handled with particular tact!)

    (g) Do leave conditions clearly specify whether the leave is home or local? For the former, has the employer unambiguously declared his intention of paying your return air fare and that of your wife/family, if you are married?

    (h) Will legitimate expenses be paid in addition to salary?

    (i) Have you taken any steps to check the bona fides of the prospective employer, eg through a Chamber of Commerce (the local/British Chambers of Commerce to be found in many main centres are often more oblig-

       ing and better informed than commercial sections of
       British embassies), bank, trade association, or Dun &
       Bradstreet s Business Information Services?

28. Is there a legal obligation on the employer in a high-risk
country to continue to pay your salary if you are taken
hostage?

29. Will the employer offer you a special training course to cope
with the risks involved in living in a very high-risk country?

Part 2
Country Surveys

Some International Comparisons

Table 1 Comparison of net wages and resulting real worth for selected countries

Country	Middle manager @ £30K UK equivalent salary		Senior manager @ £40K UK equivalent salary		Senior manager @ £55K UK equivalent salary	
	Net pay %	Net wealth UK equivalent	Net pay %	Net wealth UK equivalent	Net pay %	Net wealth UK equivalent
UK	76.5	100	72	100	68.5	100
Australia	71	99	65	96	60.5	94
Austria	71.5	81.5	66.5	81.5	63	80.5
Belgium	60	74.5	53	70	47.5	65.5
Denmark	55	59.5	49	56.5	45	54.5
Finland	59.5	70.5	54	68	48.5	64
France	76.5	93	73	94	70	94
Germany	68.5	85.5	66.5	88	61.5	85.5
Hong Kong	89	100	85.5	103	85	107.5
Irish Republic	67	92	63	91.5	59.5	91
Italy	63.5	91.5	60	91.5	57	91
Japan	79	54	75.5	55	69.5	53.5
Netherlands	66	86.5	58	80.5	53	77
Norway	76	79.5	69.5	78	65.5	76.5
Singapore	76	96.5	77	103.5	77	109
South Africa	66.5	109	62.5	108.5	60	109.5
Spain	73.5	110.5	67.5	108.5	61	102
Sweden	66.5	79.5	62	78.5	58.5	78
Switzerland	80	79.5	75.5	79	69	76.5
USA	70.5	92	68	94.5	65.5	95.5

Net wealth is obtained by incorporating purchasing power of the net wages and comparing this with the UK standard. Hence, in Japan you would enjoy 2.5% more of your gross wage of £30K than in the UK, but sadly, cost of living in Japan means this would be the equivalent of nearly halving your UK net wage. These figures reveal just how expensive some countries are, although there are some surprising exceptions, eg the way Singapore becomes a better bet the more you earn. Apart from higher salaries, other contractual benefits for expatriate workers are essential to offset high costs of living. Source: courtesy of Employment Conditions Abroad (ECA).

Table 2 Classification of countries according to their relative hardship West European base

A (0-50 points)	B (55-85 points)	C (90-125 points)	D (130-165 points)	E (170-205 points)	F (210+ points)
Australia/Melbourne, Sydney	Bahamas/Nassau	Argentina/Buenos Aires	Bolivia/La Paz	Belarus/Minsk	Algeria/Algiers
Austria/Vienna	Bahrain/Manama	Botswana/Gaborone	Bulgaria/Sofia	Cameroon/Douala	Angola/Luanda
Barbados/Bridgetown	Chile/Santiago	Brazil/Rio, Sao Paulo*	Burkina Faso/Ouagadougou	China/Beijing, Shanghai	Bangladesh/Dhaka
Belgium/Brussels	Czech Republic/Prague	Brunei/Bandar SB	Colombia/Bogota	Djibouti	Cambodia/Phnom Penh*
Bermuda/Hamilton	Greece/Athens	Costa Rica/San Jose	C te d Ivoire/Abidjan	El Salvador/San Salvador	Congo/Brazzaville*
Canada/Montreal, Toronto	Hong Kong	Dominican Rep/Santo Domingo	Cuba/Havana	Ethiopia/Addis Ababa	Liberia/Monrovia*
Cyprus/Nicosia	Hungary/Budapest	Fiji/Suva	Ecuador/Guayaquil, Quito	Haiti/Port au Prince	Libya/Tripoli
Denmark/Copenhagen	Malaysia/Kuala Lumpur	Israel/Tel Aviv	Egypt/Cairo	Honduras/Tegucigalpa	Rwanda/Kigali
Finland/Helsinki	Namibia/Windhoek	Jamaica/Kingston	Estonia/Tallinn	India/Bombay (Mumbai), New Delhi	Sierra Leone/Freetown*
France/Paris	Netherlands Antilles/Willemstad	Japan/Tokyo	Gabon/Libreville	Iran/Tehran	Sudan/Khartoum
Germany/Berlin, Bonn	UAE/Abu Dhabi, Dubai	Jordan/Amman	Gambia/Banjul	Kazakstan/Almaty	Yemen/Sana a
Irish Republic/Dublin	Uruguay/Montevideo	Kuwait/Kuwait City	Ghana/Accra	Madagascar/Antananarivo	Zaire/Kinshasa*
Italy/Milan, Rome	USA/Los Angeles	Mauritius/ Port Louis	Guatemala/Guatemala City	Mali/Bamako*	
Luxembourg/Luxembourg City		Mexico/Mexico City	Guyana/Georgetown	Mozambique/Maputo	
Netherlands/Amsterdam		Morocco/Rabat	Indonesia/Jakarta	Myanmar/Rangoon	
New Zealand/Auckland, Wellington		Oman/Muscat	Kenya/Nairobi	Nepal/Katmandu	
Norway/Oslo		Panama/Panama City	Korea Republic/Seoul	Nicaragua/Managua	
Portugal/Lisbon		Puerto Rico/San Juan	Latvia/Riga	Nigeria/Lagos	
Singapore		Qatar/Doha	Lebanon/Beirut	Pakistan/Islamabad, Karachi	
Spain/Madrid		St Lucia/Castries	Lesotho/Maseru	PNG/Port Moresby	
Sweden/Stockholm		Seychelles/Victoria	Lithuania/Vilnius	Russia/Moscow	
Switzerland/Geneva, Zurich		Slovakia/Bratislava	Malawi/Blantyre, Lilongwe	Sri Lanka/Colombo	
United Kingdom/London		South Africa/Johannesburg	Paraguay/Asuncion	Tanzania/Dar es Salaam	
USA/New York		Swaziland/Mbabane	Peru/Lima	Uganda/Kampala	
		Thailand/Bangkok	Philippines/Manila	Ukraine/Kiev	
		Trinidad/Port of Spain	Poland/Warsaw	Vietnam/Hanoi, Ho Chi Minh City	
		Tunisia/Tunis	Romania/Bucharest		
		Vanuatu/Port Vila	Saudi Arabia/Jeddah, Riyadh		
		Zimbabwe/Harare	Senegal/Dakar		
			Surinam/Paramaribo		
			Syria/Damascus		
			Taiwan/Taipei		
			Turkey/Ankara, Istanbul		
			Venezuela/Caracas		
			Zambia/Lusaka		

* Significant deterioration ≥ 10 points in personal security/socio political tensions between September 1996 and September 1997.

Countries that score borderline or close to borderline on a UK base may move into next group (up/down) depending on the expatriate s nationality.

Please note that Zaire is now known as the Democratic Republic of Congo .

Table 3 World value of the pound (averaged in June 1998)*

	Local unit of currency	*Value of £ sterling*
Australia	Australian $	2.67
Austria	Schilling	19.70
Bahrain	Dinar	0.61
Belgium	Belgian franc	57.74
Brunei	Brunei $	2.45
Canada	Canadian $	2.34
China	Yuan	13.30
Denmark	Danish kroner	10.70
Egypt	Egyptian £	5.46
Finland	Markka	8.52
France	French franc	9.39
Germany	Deutschmark	2.80
Greece	Drachma	508.99
Hong Kong	Hong Kong $	13.02
Ireland	Punt	1.10
Italy	Lira	2773.14
Japan	Yen	212.84
Kenya	Kenya shilling	99.72
Kuwait	Kuwait dinar	0.50
Luxembourg	Lux franc	57.74
Malaysia	Ringgit	7.34
Mexico	Mexican peso	16.21
Netherlands	Guilder	3.15
New Zealand	NZ $	3.22
Nigeria	Naira	35.15
Norway	Norwegian krone	11.87
Oman	Rial Omani	0.62
Papua New Guinea	Kina	2.37
Portugal	Escudo	287.38
Qatar	Qatari riyal	5.85
Saudi Arabia	Saudi riyal	6.06
Singapore	Singapore $	2.80
South Africa	Rand (financial rate)	8.98
Spain	Peseta	238.39
Sweden	Swedish krona	12.36
Switzerland	Swiss franc	2.28
United Arab Emirates	UAE dirham	6.00
United States of America	US $	1.61
Zambia	Kwacha	2128.49
Zimbabwe	Zimbabwe $	26.00

* Exchange rates are determined largely by interest rates. Fluctuations in exchange rates both of sterling and of other currencies (if you are paid in a foreign currency) are crucial to your real earning power, so keep in touch with changes. Your bank manager or financial adviser will be able to offer assistance in this area.

Europe

Western Europe

The following section gives information about European Union
(EU) member states Austria, Belgium, Denmark, Finland,
France, Germany, Greece, Ireland, Italy, Luxembourg, the
Netherlands, Portugal, Spain and Sweden, plus Norway and
Switzerland. It does not cover the UK.

The European Union

The European Union is the world s largest single trading
group, and the largest market. It accounts for just over one-
fifth of the total global trade in goods. It is heavily dependent
on international trade more so than either the US or Japan.
Increasingly, this trade is extending from manufactured goods
to services: the fastest growing sectors are banking, insurance
and telecommunications.

The Single Market, in force since 1993, allows unrestricted
trade and free movement of capital and currency within the EU.
Union citizens are entitled to travel, reside, study and work
wherever they wish within the EU. Anyone is entitled to apply
for a job and sign a contract of employment in another member
state, without losing pension or health insurance entitlements
acquired elsewhere in the EU. Inevitably, however, things are
not quite that straightforward.

One of the main problems for the EU recently has been the
next step in the completion of the Single Market monetary
union. Although this debate is mostly political, few economists
can agree on what the real result will be for the economies of the

EU after the scheduled start of the system in 1999. What is evident is that, despite an EU average inflation rate for 1995 of 3 per cent, national finances are being affected in the uncertain run-up, eg the outflow of private investment from Germany. In general, it seems that the effect is one of stagnation, making it more difficult for governments to act to prepare themselves for the deadline. In some cases, like France, this process is having a bad effect on employment. Perversely, this situation is making life easier for some countries than it might otherwise be, for, while Western Europe is very well-off, it is also very expensive, for governments as well as workers. Overall, therefore, employment prospects in the EU are perhaps not as bright as they should be.

The most important change so far this decade has been   in terms of employment   the right of any fully-qualified professional from one EU or EEA state to be recognised as a member of the equivalent profession in another state without having to requalify (subject to a few safeguards). The rule applies to all professions to which access is in some way restricted by the state (or by Royal Charter in the UK) and which require at least three years university-level education. This is creating many more opportunities for a whole range of professionals to work, set up businesses and offer services in other parts of the Union. Further details are given in the Department of Trade and Industry booklet, *Europe   Open for Professions*, available from DTI Business in Europe Hotline (0117 944 4888).

Other points that are worth noting are:

Passports and permits. A British citizen can work in EU countries without a work permit; all he or she needs is a valid passport showing that the holder is a British citizen.

Job opportunities. For details of job prospects and conditions, see the following sections on various European countries. In general, skilled or highly skilled workers and those with professional qualifications or particular technical expertise will be able to find employment, but priority will usually be given to qualified nationals. The best opportunities are with multinationals or with British firms operating in other European countries (lists can usually be obtained from the British embassy in that country, although embassies *cannot* help people to find jobs). Details of job opportunities can be obtained from your local Jobcentre, which keeps in touch with the employment centres of EU countries about vacancies (see page 35). Before you accept a job, it is important to know exactly what to expect in the way of terms and conditions. A useful leaflet entitled Working Abroad , as well as others detailing specific countries, are available from Jobcentres or the Overseas Placing Unit of the Employment Service. The DTI Business in Europe Hotline can also provide a number of useful publications.

Unemployment benefit. If you have been unemployed in the UK for four weeks, you can continue to draw unemployment benefit from the UK for up to three months while job-hunting in the EU. You will need to sign on fortnightly at the local employment services office, and will receive the UK rate of benefit in the local currency. However, in view of the fact that this is nowhere near enough to live on while job-hunting, people who decide to prospect should make sure they have enough money to keep themselves during this period, or to get home at the end. Furthermore, many EU countries have made this right very difficult to exercise.

Driving licences
Newly qualified drivers are now issued with a pink EU driving licence. It is no longer necessary for drivers to exchange their old licence for a licence from their new country of residence within the EU.

Austria

Background
Austria lies in the middle of central Europe. It has an area of 32,500 square miles, orientated rather narrowly on an east west axis. Forty-seven per cent of the country is covered by forest. Most of the big towns and cities are in the east, where the bulk of the population of 8 million live; the average population density being a pleasant 246 per square mile. Austria is bordered by Switzerland, Germany, the Czech and Slovak Republics, Hungary, Slovenia and Italy.

The national language is German, although the rights of Slovene and Croat minorities in the south and east are protected. English is spoken widely and fluently. Typically, Austrians are extremely well-educated, culturally sophisticated and great lovers of outdoor pursuits. On the down side, Austrian society can be found by some to be rather reserved, if not staid.

The historic capital, Vienna (Wien) lies on the River Danube and has a population of 1.5 million. Other large towns are Graz, Linz, Klagenfurt, Salzburg and the Alpine sports capital, Innsbruck. The population is predominantly Roman-Catholic.

Austria is a presidential federal republic, with a two-house national assembly. The present head of state is Dr Thomas Klestil, who was elected in 1998. Parliament is characterised by long-running coalitions, currently between the Social Democrats and the People s Party (Conservatives). Since its re-establishment as an independent state in 1955, Austria has followed a policy of strict neutrality between East and West. The lifting of the Iron Curtain allowed Austria to look afresh at its position, and following a referendum, Austria joined the EU on 1 January 1995.

Exchange rate: Austrian schilling 19.94 = £1.

The economy

Although Austria is self-sufficient in agricultural production, the economy is based on industry (steel, chemicals, transport equipment) and tourism. In 1994, over 19 million tourists visited the country. More than 80 per cent of trade is with other European countries, predominantly Germany. Consequently, Austria s entry into the European Union has enhanced these trade links.

Austria has also developed strong links with the emerging nations of eastern Europe, particularly Hungary, where Austria is involved in a number of joint ventures, and also in Slovenia, Slovakia, and the Czech Republic. Many businesses undertaking work in eastern Europe base themselves in Austria.

Currently, inflation is 1.3 per cent with economic growth at around 1.5 per cent. Per capita GDP in Purchasing Power Units (PPU) is 17,140. PPUs are a common unit representing an identical volume of goods and services for each country.

Working conditions

In general wages are higher in Austria than in the UK; for managers, up to 150 per cent more. The standard of living is therefore higher, but not by much. Taxation and social security payments are somewhat higher too, as is the cost of living   at least 15 per cent more. In most other respects, working life in Austria is similar to that in the rest of western Europe. It is normal for managers and professionals to be granted up to 30 days paid vacation. A good knowledge of the German language is a basic requirement of any type of employment.

Living conditions

Food prices in Austria are considerably more expensive than in the UK. An identical basket of different food and beverage items costing £50 in London would set you back £70 in Vienna. Clothing is roughly comparable in price for both men and women, unless you try *haute couture*. In the latter case, an outfit comprising a ready-to-wear suit, a blazer, a shirt, a pair of shoes and socks could cost you up to twice what you would pay in the UK.

Accommodation prices also vary by comparison. Rents for a furnished four-room apartment in Vienna range from £1850 to £795 per month (about 15 per cent more expensive than London), whereas rents for an unfurnished three-room apartment are vastly cheaper: £795 £300 in Vienna, compared to £1050 £700 in London. Long-term residential costs are also much less in Austria. In general, household goods cost about the same, or only slightly more. General running costs and services average at about 10 per cent more than in the UK.

Cars of all makes can be bought easily and are about 15 per cent cheaper than in the UK. A VW Golf 1.8 would cost around £10,500. Vehicle taxation is even cheaper, costing about £100 per year for a 4-door standard saloon. Servicing, however, will cost you nearly twice as much per annum, so opt for newer or more reliable makes, and preferably those which are popular in Austria, eg any German types. With effect from 1 January 1997, Austria has introduced toll charges for the use of highways and motorways. These are available from Automobile

Touring Clubs in 13 European countries, and also from petrol stations, post offices and service areas.

A double room with en suite in a first class hotel in Vienna would cost about £190 for two, per night. The cost of eating out is comparable with London prices a two-course meal, excluding drinks, in a good restaurant will be at least £20 per head.

Given the extensive modern road and rail networks and the wide-spread use of hi-tech communication systems, the mountainous nature of the country no longer poses a problem. The state-owned railway system is extensive and efficient. Public transport is adequate and is cheaper than in the UK; taxis are expensive. Airline passengers are served by six commercial airports, principally at Vienna and Innsbruck. In addition there is considerable trade through the Danube ports by both local and foreign shipping.

There are four national radio and two national television channels, together with three national and 12 regional daily newspapers. Education is free and compulsory between the ages of 6 and 15. There are good facilities for secondary, technical and professional education. There are 12 state maintained universities and six colleges of art. Vienna is the cultural as well as the political capital, and boasts a wide range of entertainments, and the best social scene. There are also a large number of visitor attractions. With such easy access to a huge amount of upland countryside, most sporting and recreational opportunities revolve around the outdoors: hunting, fishing, hiking, skiing, mountaineering, etc.

Belgium

Background
Belgium has about 10 million inhabitants, who live in an area of 12,000 square miles one of the world s highest densities of population. Most of the country is flat, highly cultivated and built over. In the south, towards Luxembourg, are the rolling hills and forests of the Ardennes.

The country is divided into French-speaking Wallonia and Flemish/Dutch-speaking Flanders. German is also spoken in the Eastern Cantons. Constitutional reforms, introducing a high level of regional autonomy, have given the Flemish-, French- and German-speaking populations a degree of control over their own affairs. Belgium is now officially a federation of the states of Brussels, Wallonia and Flanders.

Brussels and Antwerp each have nearly a million inhabitants, and other important cities are Ghent, LiĿge, Louvain and Charleroi; these six cities account for one-fifth of the total population. The majority are Roman Catholic.

Belgium is a constitutional monarchy, with a two-chamber national Parliament. The regional governments have wide powers. The head of state is Albert II, King of the Belgians. Since the Second World War its governments have been coalitions.

Exchange rate: Belgian franc (financial rate) 62 = £1.

The economy

During the latter part of the 1980s Belgium attracted wealth and investment out of all proportion to its size. At the cross-roads of Europe, and host to the main EU institutions, Belgium has been well placed to attract investors. One of the most obvious signs of this has been extensive commercial and residential property development in Brussels.

Old industries have been restructured and small, hi-tech firms have been encouraged. The service sector now accounts for the majority of national income, with financial services making a major contribution. Nevertheless, Belgium is still very much a manufacturing country, and is one of the largest car exporters in the world.

Although fairly wealthy, Belgium s public debt is one of the highest in the developed world. However, inflation is under control at less than 3 per cent and Belgium has succeeded in reducing unemployment more rapidly than any other EU member state. Most of the leading economic indicators look good, and Belgium is well placed to exploit its central position as the capital of Europe. Per capita GDP in PPU (see Austria) is 17110.

Personal finance

The level of managerial and executive salaries is higher than in the UK. An upper-middle ranked executive could expect to earn at least £55,000 a year. Increasingly, a company car would be provided in addition to the basic salary.

Taxation

Income tax is levied at a progressive rate on all annual incomes. The rate is graduated from 25 to 55 per cent and is considerably higher than in the UK. Additional taxes are the municipal tax (8 per cent) and a crisis contribution surcharge of 3 per cent. Tax reliefs are given in the form of reductions for dependants and allowances for business expenses. However, there are very substantial tax concessions available to expatriates who are not permanently resident in Belgium.

Working conditions

EU nationals with valid passports are free to come and go, but they must register at the local town hall within eight days of arrival. A temporary residence permit, valid for three months, will be issued and can be extended for another three months if you have a job. After this initial period of six months, a one-year permit can be obtained. Children must also be registered.

If you are looking for work in Brussels, a knowledge of French is essential and of Dutch or German an advantage, depending on the area. You can advertise in the Belgian papers or seek out the local offices of Office National de l Emploi (Boulevard de l Empereur 7, 1000 Brussels). Belgium is so near that visits from the UK to hunt for a job are easily made. There may be opportunities with international organisations, such as the EC, and NATO which have headquarters in Brussels. But the best hope is probably with Belgian-based British firms in areas such as insurance, banking, management consultancy, public relations and construction. A weekly English-language journal, *The Bulletin*, is available at Avenue MoliŁre 329, 1050 Bruxelles (tel: 02 343 9909). There is also the British Chamber of Commerce at rue Joseph II 30, 1040 Bruxelles and the British Embassy at Rue D Chlon 85, 1040 Bruxelles.

Living conditions
The enlargement of the EU has inevitably increased the cost of living in Brussels, though in most respects it is cheaper than Paris or Bonn. Food is somewhat dearer than in Britain; here are some examples:

	BFr
Bread (1 kg)	73.19
Butter (250 gm)	57.79
Cheese (500 gm)	164.96
Chicken (1 kg)	144.95
Coffee	
ground (500 gm)	144.20
instant (250 gm)	383.32
Cooking oil (1 litre)	60.32
Eggs (12)	81.81
Milk (1 litre)	36.32

Mineral water (1 litre)	18.54
Potatoes (1 kg)	30.04
Rice (1 kg)	105.21
Steak (1 kg)	489.87
Sugar (1 kg)	42.07
Tea bags (250 gm)	193.98

Beer (the Belgians are great beer drinkers) is reasonably cheap at around BFr41 for a 50 cl bottle and a 75 cl bottle of wine can be bought for about BFr222 231. A bottle of Scotch costs upwards of BFr570, and a packet of 20 cigarettes about BFr120.

Cars of all makes can be bought easily and are a good deal cheaper than in the UK. A Ford Mondeo CLX would cost about BFr650,000. Petrol costs slightly less than in the UK, BFr40 per litre.

Though the influx of diplomats and businessmen has tended to push prices up in Brussels and Antwerp, there is no serious shortage of rented accommodation. Most people find houses or flats through agents or press advertisements and the Belgian Embassy can provide a list of estate agents. Rents have increased but are still reasonable in comparison with London. Leases are usually for three, six or nine years, and the deposit is related to this. There is relief of customs duty on removal goods provided they have been used and are for personal use.

Household goods are a little more expensive than in the UK. Electric current is AC, 220V, 50 cycles (in a few localities, 110V). Clothes are dearer than in the UK, so it is as well to shop at home.

Distances are so short that most travel is done by train or car. Rail services are efficient and there is a good network of roads and autoroutes, with ring roads round the large towns. Urban transport in Brussels is adequate, but buses and trams get very crowded.

The health services are part of the general social security system, which is a very comprehensive one. Everyone has to belong to a *mutualitØ/mutualiteit* (sickness insurance fund). You have to pay for a visit to a doctor and for prescriptions but about 75 per cent of the cost of medical treatment may be reimbursed by the *mutualitØ*. Many hospitals and clinics are run by different denominational groups. People who are currently insured under the UK social security scheme should obtain the necessary forms for reciprocal treatment from the DSS before leaving the UK. An English-speaking medical helpline operates on 02 648 8000.

Education, both primary and secondary, is free and compulsory for all Belgian children between 6 and 18. As well as the state schools there are many Catholic and independent schools in Brussels and elsewhere. There are a number of European and International Schools. The International School of Brussels takes in children from 3 to 18 in kindergarten, elementary and secondary schools and has over 1000 boys and girls, the majority being from the USA. There is a smaller International School at Antwerp. The British School of Brussels, which is co-educational and follows the UK National Curriculum, has over 1000 students aged 3 to 18. The majority of students transfer from British schools (or vice versa), but the school is genuinely international, with over 60 nationalities represented. There is also a school in Antwerp offering a British curriculum. The small English Primary School in Brussels caters for children from 3 to 12. The St John s English-speaking school at Waterloo, near Brussels, caters for children between 3 and 19 and takes in boarders.

There are French- and Dutch-speaking free universities at Leuven and Louvain-la-Neuve, state universities at Ghent and LiŁge and university centres at Antwerp, Mons and Diepenbeek. Education is free and standards are high.

The Belgians are a reserved and cautious people. The business community tends to be formal and punctilious.

There are plenty of cinemas, theatres and places of entertainment in Brussels, though there is no night life on the scale of, say, Paris. Coastal resorts like Blankenburg offer golf, sailing and tennis, as well as casinos and night clubs. Attractive towns like Bruges and Ghent are within easy reach of Brussels and the Ardennes is a good place for holidays.

Shopping and business hours are usually 8.00 or 9.00 am to midday and 2.00 pm to 5.00 or 6.00 pm. Most establishments take about one hour for lunch.

There is a sizeable British community in Brussels, including staff of the EC, NATO and many international organisations which employ English-speaking personnel. There are a number of British shops (eg Marks & Spencer and W H Smith) and some British pubs.

The closeness to the UK and a cosmopolitan atmosphere make Brussels an attractive city to most British people. Despite its central role in the administration of the EU, which has produced a great influx of administrators, diplomats, translators and their ancillary staff, prices have not rocketed, accommodation is still available and reasonably priced, and Brussels is still less expensive than, for example, Paris, Dusseldorf and Geneva.

Denmark

Background

Denmark consists of the Jutland peninsula and numerous islands linked by road, rail and ferry. The capital, Copenhagen, is situated on Zealand, the largest island, and contains about one-fifth of the total population of 5.2 million. Population density and climate are broadly similar to the UK. Other major cities are Aarhus, Aalborg and Odense. Greenland and the Faroe islands are semi-autonomous and do not belong to the EU, so work permits will be required.

The Danes have a well-earned reputation as a hardy, industrious, democratic and liberty-loving people. They pay high taxes, but welfare benefits are generous and public services efficient. Denmark was the first country to appoint an Ombudsman. It belongs to the EU and NATO, although there is as much controversy over Maastricht as there is in the UK.

Denmark is a constitutional monarchy. The single chamber Parliament (*Folketing*) of 179 seats is elected on the basis of proportional representation. The government is a social-democratic-led coalition.

Copenhagen was the 1996 European cultural capital , involving a year-long programme of more than 1800 events at a cost of £115 million.

Exchange rate: Danish kroner 10.79 = £1.

The economy

Denmark is traditionally an agricultural country and nearly three-quarters of its land is still used for farming and horticulture although employing only 6 per cent of the workforce. Though reduced in area since the end of the war, agriculture is highly efficient and food and dairy produce account for about one-fifth of total exports. The UK is a long-established market: Danish bacon and butter are found on many British breakfast tables. There has been a marked shift of resources towards manufacturing, the most important industries being food processing, metal and electrical engineering, transport equipment, textiles and clothing, paper, furniture, glass and brewing. Firms are small scale; about two out of three manufacturers employ fewer than 50 workers. Standards of design, styling and craftsmanship are high. However, by far the greatest proportion of the population works in the service sector. Despite recent spending increases and a trading deficit, inflation remains under 3 per cent, while unemployment has fallen throughout 1997. Per capita GDP in PPU (see Austria) is 16,710.

Personal finance

The level of management salaries is appreciably higher than in the UK but deductions for tax and social security are higher too. However, the base rate of tax is being lowered to align it more with other EU countries.

Income tax is payable both to central and local government. It is levied on a PAYE basis and imposed at a percentage rate. The combined rates may not exceed 63.5 per cent (1995). You should obtain a tax card (*skattekort*) from your local town hall. Local councils fix their own rate of tax which is assessed on the same taxable income as for central government tax. There is a dividend tax, a capital or wealth tax on assets and a small church tax. Income tax is subject to the usual range of deductions. Expatriate workers are allowed a special tax rate of 25 per cent provided they are not working in Denmark for more than three years and are paid by a foreign employer. VAT (MOMS) is 25 per cent.

Working conditions

It is not easy for foreigners to find work in Denmark, despite the free movement of labour provisions of the EU. Work permits are required for non-EU nationals, and are rarely granted. Most Danes speak English, but it is difficult to find employment unless you have a good knowledge of Danish. Rented housing is scarce and people are advised to try to arrange accommodation beforehand. Foreigners must apply for a residence permit to stay in Denmark for more than three months. Enquiries about residence permits should be made in advance to the Danish Embassy in London, or in Copenhagen to the Directorate of Immigration, 53 Ryesgade, DK-2100 Copenhagen 1 (tel: 31 393100). Holders of the residence permit must also get a personal code number from Folkeregisteret, Dahlerupsgade 6, 1640 Copenhagen.

The Danes have a good record of stable labour relations and co-operation between employers and unions. They have one of the lowest strike records in Europe.

The system of social security provides full cover against sickness, accident, retirement and other contingencies.

Living conditions

Denmark s per capita income and standard of living are among the highest in the EU, but living costs are also relatively high, noticeably in Copenhagen. The table below gives a selection of recent prices:

	DKr
Beer (50 cl)	8.58
Bread (1 kg)	19.64
Butter (250 gm)	10.18
Cheese (500 gm)	47.52
Chicken (1 kg)	35.12
Coffee	
ground (500 gm)	36.72
instant (250 gm)	79.40
Cooking oil (1 litre)	33.93
Eggs (12)	21.57
Milk (1 litre)	6.16

Mineral water (1 litre)	8.29
Potatoes (1 kg)	9.87
Rice (1 kg)	19.96
Steak (1 kg)	169.84
Sugar (1 kg)	10.59
Tea bags (250 gm)	66.37
Whisky (75 cl)	247.70
Wine (75 cl)	62.22
Cigarettes (20)	29.81
Petrol (1 litre)	5.82

Clothes are much dearer than in the UK and so are most consumer goods, so it is not advisable to buy locally.

Accommodation is relatively inexpensive but difficult to find. An unfurnished, three-bedroomed house in Copenhagen would cost around DKr14,875 a month. It is very hard to find apartments in central Copenhagen at all, but houses can be rented 15 to 20 kms outside the city. Unfurnished flats and houses are slightly cheaper. Service costs are among the highest in the world. As far as owner-occupied accommodation is concerned, contrary to previous years, Denmark is now experiencing a sharp growth in house prices. A permit from the Ministry of Justice is required to purchase a property if you have not been resident in Denmark for more than five years. Hotel costs are higher than in the UK but are not exorbitant. Eating out costs about the same. Cars are much more expensive to buy and run.

Copenhagen has an international airport (Kastrup) with frequent flights to European cities and to internal centres. Rail transport is efficient and reasonably priced   there are numerous concessions for families travelling together although public transport is expensive.

Driving is on the right, and the roads are good. As in other Nordic countries, there are strict regulations against drinking and driving.

The standard of medical treatment in Denmark is high. Health services have recently been remodelled on British NHS lines, with the emphasis on group practice and preventive medicine. Hospital treatment is free. Charges for doctors visits and prescriptions are refundable.

Education is compulsory from the ages of 7 to 17. English is taught in all schools. In Copenhagen there is an International School for 4 19 year olds with an international/US curriculum; Rygaards School at Hellerup offers a UK curriculum for the age range 5 16. The Education Act of 1975 reformed the existing system and placed greater emphasis on teacher/parent relationships. The Danes pay great attention to adult education and vocational training. There are three main universities and three university centres, and a number of higher technical and scientific institutions.

The Danes are extremely hospitable, and many speak excellent English, although Danish is essential for most jobs. Almost all belong to the established Evangelist-Lutheran church. Liquor laws allow drinking at most hours. Beer and schnapps (*akvavit*) are the most popular drinks, often taken with open sandwiches (*smorrebrod*).

Copenhagen has a reputation for being one of the most permissive cities in Europe. It is also one of the most beautiful and lively, with facilities for shopping and entertainment, and a large number of restaurants, theatres, cinemas and concert halls, as well as open-air activities. The Tivoli amusement park in Copenhagen is a must for visitors.

Finland

Background
Finland is situated at the head of the Baltic Sea, and sits between the rest of Scandinavia and Russia. Much of the land away from the Baltic coast enjoys a climate of cold winters and warm summers; the Arctic Circle cuts through the North of the country. Forests cover about 70 per cent of the land area of 130,500 square miles. The population of just over 5 million (population density of 38 per square mile) comprise 93.6 per cent Finnish speakers, 6 per cent Swedish, and 2500 Lapps. Both Finnish and Swedish are used for administration and education. The Finnish language is an area of intense linguistic

curiosity, as it appears to be disconnected from every other European language with the possible exception of Basque.

All the main towns lie in the very south of the country, near the sea. The capital, Helsinki, has a population of 0.5 million. Other centres are Tampere, Turku, Espoo, Vantaa and Oulu in the north. Altogether, these towns account for 25 per cent of the population, which is predominantly Evangelical Lutheran.

Finland is a presidential republic, with a single chamber parliament, the *Edeskunta*, composed of 200 elected members. The first direct elections for the presidency were held in 1994, won by Martti Ahtisaari. The present government is a social democratic-led coalition. Before the collapse of the Soviet Union in 1991, Finland was neutral, and had a large trade by barter with its neighbour. Finland joined the EU on 1 January 1995 after a national referendum. Finland is also a member of the European Monetary Union.

Exchange rate: Finnish markka 8.80 = £1.

The economy

Finland is a highly industrialised country. Forestry, which used to represent a large part of Finnish exports, now accounts for 31 per cent of the total. Metal engineering, particularly electronics such as mobile phones, and shipbuilding, now constitute 50 per cent. Finnish glass, ceramics and furniture enjoy high international reputations. Other important industries are chemicals, pharmaceuticals, foodstuffs and electronic equipment.

The economy has been adversely affected by the collapse of trade with Russia. In the early 1980s, trade with the former Soviet Union accounted for 20 per cent of exports; in 1997, this was down to 5 per cent. After the worldwide recession GDP has started to pick up rapidly at the rate of 4 6 per cent, after huge falls. In 1998, unemployment is 12.5 per cent. Inflation is under 2 per cent. Per capita GDP in US$ is 24,433 (1996).

The government has introduced austerity measures raising taxes, reducing health and social welfare spending and overseas development budgets in order to curb the high levels of public debt.

Working conditions

In general, wages are higher in Finland than in the UK. Tax and social security deductions, however, are much greater, as are other living expenses, so that the net result is likely to be a standard of living equal to, or perhaps less than, that in the UK. On average, the cost of living in Finland is about 20 per cent more than the UK. Working hours are roughly the same. Holiday entitlement is greater. Although English is widely understood, at the very least a working knowledge of Swedish would be useful.

Living conditions

Food prices in Finland are about the same level or a little cheaper. Clothing is a little more costly, but not by so much a basic medium quality man s working wardrobe might set you back £400.

Rented property is vastly cheaper up to half the price of similar London properties. A 4-room apartment in Helsinki could be yours for £720 £470 per month, while an unfurnished 3-room apartment would cost £490 £290. Long-term residential costs are not as cheap, though still considerably less than in the UK. Household goods are generally about 20 per cent more expensive, although electricity, water and gas are much cheaper than in the UK.

Hotels are plentiful and cheap, though there are few in the top-notch bracket: a double room in a first class Helsinki establishment would be around £120 one of the cheapest rates in Europe. Eating out costs about the same as at home. Finnish cuisine is similar to the hearty fare found elsewhere in Scandinavia. There are many restaurants, but most entertaining tends to be done at home. Specialities and traditions include crayfish, eaten during the summer season of July/August and almost treated as a festival, afternoon coffee, and Baari inexpensive eating places serving drinks and snacks. Care should be taken with Finnish vodka and berry liquers they are excellent but deadly. Also note that Finland shares the strict drink-driving laws found in neighbouring countries.

The road network is comprehensive and of good quality in the south of the country. Traffic drives on the right. Cars cost about the same as at home, but servicing is cheaper. It is better to adopt a flexible approach to transportation. The state railway system is comprehensive, efficient and popular. Public transport is cheap, as are taxis. Finland also has one of the densest and cheapest domestic airline networks in Europe. Finnair operates to 20 internal airports, the northernmost being about 130 miles north of the Arctic Circle! In addition, there is a comprehensive range of international and domestic ferry services operating on the Baltic and the numerous inland lakes.

Newspapers, books, plays and films appear in both Swedish and Finnish. There are a very large number of newspapers to choose from. State-provided education is co-educational, free and compulsory from 7 16 years. There are 21 universities or schools of similar level.

The Finns are a health-loving race a very popular form of vacation is the health resort holiday and are credited with the invention of the sauna. Be aware, however, that Finnish ideas of health revolve around the outdoors, whatever the temperature! Summertime is when Finns head upcountry: camping, hiking and hostelling are the pastimes of many, but to far more this is the season of the summer cottage, usually set in delightful secluded surroundings and with lots of facilities. Although there are plenty to rent, it is more traditional to build or buy your own and take an extended summer break with the family.

France

Background

With a population of 57.2 million and an area of 213,000 square miles, France is at the heart of Europe. Its neighbours are Belgium, Luxembourg, Germany, Italy, Switzerland and Spain; the Rhine, the Channel, the Atlantic, the Pyrenees, the Mediterranean and the Alps are its natural boundaries.

France s population, which declined in the inter-war years, has since grown rapidly as a result of a high post-war birth rate and immigration. However, this growth has now levelled off. Greater Paris has the largest concentration of population, with just over 11 million inhabitants, of whom more than 2 million live in Paris itself. Other important cities are Marseille, Lyon, Lille, Bordeaux, Nantes, Nice, Toulouse, Grenoble and Strasbourg. The climate in the north is temperate, while in the south it is Mediterranean.

The French are intensely patriotic and proud of the country, its language, culture and achievements. There are wide interregional variations and differences in attitude and character. The inhabitants of Brittany, Provence, Corsica, French Catalonia, Alsace and the Basque region are not at all like the Parisians; many have their own language and support federalism or even separatism. France is predominantly Roman Catholic.

France is a democratic republic with a written constitution under a presidency, and is an energetic member of the EU. Politically, France has recently swung to the right. The president is Jaques Chirac.

Exchange rate: Fr9.91 = £1.

The economy

A flagging economy and crippling strikes resulting from an attempt to cut government spending have caused dire problems. Unemployment is now over 12 per cent and growth is forecast at little over 1 per cent. Although France is one of the largest industrial powers in the world, it is the world s second largest agricultural exporter. Foreign companies now account for 27 per cent of manufacturing output and 30 per cent of exports. Per capita GDP is 17,610 PPU (see Austria).

France is well off for natural resources, with coal, natural gas, iron ore, potash, bauxite and fluorspar. However, despite an ambitious nuclear power programme, a steep rise in the price of oil could still wreak havoc.

Trade is primarily with EU countries, headed by Germany, with the UK as its third largest export market. Principal exports are food, wine and dairy produce, petroleum products, metals, steels, chemicals, cars, non-ferrous metals, and a wide range of consumer goods. Fashion and luxury items, and tourism, are also important sources of revenue.

Industry is fairly evenly dispersed, though Greater Paris has the largest and most heterogeneous concentration and some areas, such as Brittany and the south-west, are under-industrialised. Textiles, coal and steel have declined but new technologically advanced and science-based industries, such as chemicals, electronics and nuclear engineering, have been developed particularly in the Lyon Grenoble region.

Agriculture, largely dominated by small family farms, is still of major importance and influence, even though the numbers working on the land have steadily fallen and there has been a drift to the towns and cities.

Personal finance

The level of managerial salaries is around 30 to 40 per cent higher than in the UK. Employers contributions to social security are among the highest in Europe, but direct taxation is relatively low. Secretarial salaries are much the same as in the UK.

Taxation

The French system seems immensely complicated, so it is advisable to check with your employer or the income tax people exactly what your liabilities are. There is no PAYE system.

British subjects living in France are liable to the personal income tax (*imp t sur le revenu*) as are the French. There is a double taxation agreement between the UK and France.

Income tax is assessed on actual income, derived from all sources, eg salaries, dividends, profits, rents and also certain capital gains.

The global taxable income is charged at progressive rates from 0 per cent and rising to a maximum of 56.8 per cent. There are plans for a new tax to alleviate social security debts.

For people with dependants, there is a complicated points system of relief. There is also a range of allowances and exemptions. The French Embassy may be able to offer assistance or put you in touch with the income tax inspectorate in France. VAT varies from 2 to 22 per cent.

Working conditions

European Union citizens do not require work permits but after three months must apply for residence permits from the town hall or police, which can prove difficult to obtain without a job. This is valid for five years, or the length of your contract if this is less than 12 months. The 39-hour week is standard. French workers are entitled by law to five weeks annual leave. There are 11 public holidays. Many firms and offices are shut for much of August.

Most wages are fixed by collective bargaining at national level. Equal pay is theoretically obligatory the gap between men s and women s pay is narrower than in most EU countries. There is also a minimum legal wage. Given the current economic problems, these areas are under a great deal of pressure for change.

Many fringe benefits are provided and most employers have to contribute to housing and welfare. The practice of a 13-month bonus is widespread and most manual workers are now paid monthly, instead of fortnightly, and enjoy staff status. French workers attach as much importance to social security and fringe benefits as to money wages.

Living conditions

France compares with Britain on cost of living, with Paris dearer than London for food prices. In Paris inner city transport (metro and buses) is relatively cheap and so are taxis. Prices outside Paris are considerably lower, apart from in the main tourist areas, although a recent survey has shown that this is becoming less of a certainty. According to American Express, British overseas visitors rated France as being worst value for money in 1995.

The following are recent sample prices; for many items there is a fairly wide range:

	Fr
Beer (50 cl)	5.40
Bread (1 kg)	20.67
Butter (250 gm)	9.17

Cheese, Cheddar type (500 gm)	26.32
Chicken (1 kg)	32.01
Coffee	
ground (500 gm)	30.69
instant (250 gm)	55.54
Cooking oil (1 litre)	11.79
Eggs (12)	16.66
Milk (1 litre)	6.12
Mineral water (1 litre)	2.28
Potatoes (1 kg)	6.67
Rice (1 kg)	16.07
Steak (1 kg)	99.15
Sugar (1 kg)	7.47
Tea bags (250 gm)	41.47
Whisky (75 cl)	87.38
Wine (75 cl)	33.98
Cigarettes (20)	15.60
Petrol (1 litre)	5.95

There is usually no problem about hotel accommodation in Paris, except at peak tourist periods. A double room in a first-class hotel costs around Fr1215 a night, but there are plenty of smaller hotels where you get good value for money, and outside Paris prices are lower.

Household goods, such as refrigerators, electric cookers, vacuum cleaners and TV sets, are dearer than at home.

Houses and apartments can be found by personal contact, or through house agents and/or newspaper advertisements. Rents vary according to the district and have been increasing steadily. An unfurnished, four-bedroomed house would be around Fr12,900 a month. Alternatively, it is possible to buy a house or flat home ownership is becoming increasingly widespread in France. Electric voltage is usually 220V but this may vary.

Some families have a domestic servant living in, but it is more usual to employ a *femme de mØnage*, often foreign; domestic help is hard to get as so many women go out to work. If you or your spouse do your own cooking, you will probably prefer to shop at local markets and round-the-corner shops rather than at bigger shops and supermarkets. The smaller shops shut for a long midday break and stay open until late in the evening, but are often more expensive than supermarkets.

There is a reciprocal health agreement with the UK. Medical attention is expensive but 75 per cent of the fees for doctors and dentists working within the French sickness insurance scheme can be reimbursed. A proportion of the cost of prescriptions can be refunded (40 70 per cent), as well as outpatient hospital treatment (80 per cent) although this system is under review, and may face cuts. Private treatment is costly. There is a British hospital in Paris, the Hertford, and a more expensive American one.

Some expatriate parents send their children to local schools, which are of a high educational standard and where they can acquire a good knowledge of French. There is free compulsory education from 6 to 16 and below that age there are many crØches and nursery schools. Secondary education is in two cycles, from 11 to 15 and from 15 to 18. Those who complete the second cycle can take the BaccalaurØat examination before proceeding to university or institutes of technology. American and British schools in Paris cater for children of diplomats and businessmen. The British School of Paris is geared to the UK system; it takes pupils from 4 to 18 and offers boarding facilities. (See ECIS and COBISEC in Chapter 9.)

Main centres are linked by internal airways and there are airports at Lyon, Marseille, Nice, Bordeaux, Strasbourg and Toulouse, as well as two in Paris: Charles de Gaulle and Orly. The railway network is highly efficient, with a number of express and TGV (260km/hour) trains. Fares are cheaper than in the UK. Direct rail link with the UK is now possible via the Channel Tunnel. The roads are good and there is a network of motorways on which tolls are payable. These can be expensive on a long journey. Driving is on the right. Paris is congested and parking difficult, but the traffic flows. If you take your own car you are obliged to have it fitted with seat belts back and front; yellow headlamps are no longer compulsory for motor vehicles.

All makes of car can be bought new or second-hand. A small car is useful for city driving. A Peugeot 405 GR would cost about Fr106,500. Car repairs and servicing are much cheaper than London prices.

Most provincial regions have their own newspapers, but some Paris papers, such as *Le Figaro* and *Le Monde*, circulate nationally. There is a wide range of weeklies, the best known being *Paris Match* and *L'Express*. TV is state controlled with limited advertising, although cable and satellite facilities are expanding rapidly. There are one state, four commercial and a number of local private radio stations.

Paris and the main cities provide a variety of entertainment and opportunities for leisure activities. Outdoor sports are available shooting and fishing have always been popular and camping (in extremely well-equipped sites) is increasingly so. There is a centre for alpine and winter sports in the area east of Grenoble. Paris is rich in theatres, music, cinemas, museums and art galleries, as well as in night-life and restaurants. You can eat well at reasonable cost in the smaller family-run bistros off the beaten tourist track. Life is very different slower and more reserved in the provinces and outside the cosmopolitan centre of Paris it is even more important to have a fluent command of the language as an *entrOe* to local life.

The French spend about a quarter of their incomes on food and it is still an important part of national life, with each region producing its own specialities. Business is often transacted over a restaurant lunch but entertaining is increasingly done in the home. If you don t appreciate good food and wine, France is wasted on you! Fast food outlets are becoming more common.

A book entitled *Living as a British Expatriate in France* is available from the French Chamber of Commerce, 5th Floor, Knightsbridge House, 197 Knightsbridge, London SW7 1RB tel: 0171 304 4040), priced £10.00 (including post and packing).

Germany

Background
The German nation, reunified in October 1990, has a population of over 82 million, made up of 65.4 million from West Germany

and 15.7 million from the East. The country is 45 per cent Protestant and 40 per cent Roman Catholic. There is a Turkish minority of nearly 2 million; 9 per cent of the population are non-Germans. Its formal name is still the Federal Republic of Germany, but it is usually simply referred to as Germany.

The new Germany covers an area of 138,000 square miles. The capital, Berlin, with a population of 3.44 million, is by far the largest city, overshadowing Cologne (1 million), Frankfurt (647,000), Hamburg (1.66 million) and Munich (1.24 million). There are 16 Federal L nder (states), a two-house parliament and a president appointed by electoral college. Bonn remains the seat of government until 2000, when the switch to Berlin is scheduled for completion.

Over the next few years the dominant task facing Germany s government will be the continued integration of the two Germanies. In the 1998 election, Chancellor Kohl lost to the Social Democrat candidate, Gerhard Schr der.

Exchange rate: DM2.70 = £1.

The economy
Since reunification the German economy has shown strongly diverging trends: while the West was booming, the East was struggling to adapt to a market economy. Monetary union, which preceded the political union of the two Germanies, immediately created enormous pressures in the East ailing industries were exposed to the full blast of competition from advanced Western countries, whose goods flooded into the shops, while demand for indigenous products collapsed.

Unemployment has risen slightly to 10.1 per cent, but job cuts in both the public and private sectors have been swingeing. Problems are greatest in the old industrial areas of eastern Germany and the Ruhr. There has even been talk of accepting a reduction in standards of living, which, considering Germany s pride in its social achievements, is a major admission. There have been proposals to raise taxes, particularly VAT, and lower social security budgets, but no consensus has been reached. Consequently, there have been widespread strikes and bankruptcies have been running at an all-time high.

There are suspicions that Germany will not make the entry criteria for European monetary union, as public debt is running at 2.7 per cent, while reduced tax revenue is exacerbating the situation. One proposal has been to provide businesses with tax concessions to hire more workers. Nevertheless, unemployment is scheduled to remain as high as 10 per cent, while growth will hover around 2 per cent. Inflation is around 1.8 per cent; per capita GDP is US$ 20,497 (1995).

Germany s wealth, originally based on coal, steel and heavy engineering, is now founded on a broad spread of modern industries, including petrochemicals, artificial fibres, electric and electronic equipment, machinery, machine tools, scientific instruments and cars. New industrial development has been particularly noticeable in the south.

For many years the West German economy has relied on migrant labour particularly from Turkey, Greece, Yugoslavia and Italy and has also had a liberal policy towards refugees, both from the East and from the Third World (1.6 million in 1996). The presence of large numbers of foreigners has created tensions in German society, exacerbated by the influx of refugees from Eastern Europe. There is a serious housing shortage but it is too early to tell what policy the new Social Democrat government will follow.

In 1996, the government passed a new law ordering that all EU citizens working in Germany in manual jobs must be paid the German minimum wage, as well as social security benefits. Essentially, this means that the market for foreign labour (eg the 80,000 Britons in construction) has been removed at a stroke, as the whole point was that these workers were outside the German employment and taxation laws. However, with more than 5000 building companies bankrupted in the past year, it is doubtful if the rule will have the required effect. The most basic work is often undertaken by workers from eastern Europe for little more than £2 per hour. But prospects for technical and managerial personnel, and for teachers of English, should remain reasonable.

Personal finance
At managerial level, the Germans do considerably better than the British. Secretarial and skilled worker salaries are slightly higher than in the UK. The cost of living is lower in Germany than in the UK. The British Chamber of Commerce publishes annual surveys of salaries and fringe benefits.

Taxation
Income tax is levied on a graduated scale ranging from 25 per cent to a maximum of 53 per cent. A solidarity tax of 5.5 per cent is a recent development. A married couple can file a joint tax return, even if only one partner has an income. There are also compulsory payments for health care, social security and unemployment insurance, but benefit levels are much higher than in the UK, and business deductions are more generous: for instance, the cost of journeys to work can be deducted by employees.

Working conditions
British and other EEA nationals are free to enter and move about the country; if you intend to stay for more than three months you will need a residence permit, valid for five years, from the Foreign Nationals authority at the local town hall or area administration centre.

The standard working week is 36 40 hours for five days in many cases. There is a minimum of 25 30 days holiday, plus 10 13 public holidays.

Wages and salaries are determined by collective bargains which usually have the force of law. There are separate arrangements for senior executives (*leitende Angestellte*). Individual contracts are usually for an indefinite period and terminated by written notice, with compensation according to age and length of service.

There is a long-established and comprehensive system of social security, with benefits related to earnings. Employers may provide, by law or by custom, additional benefits, eg 13-month bonus and group/performance bonuses, and help towards housing, meals, transport and recreation.

The complex matter of identifying a job opportunity in Germany, including related aspects like qualifications, social security and taxation are dealt with in a useful factsheet, *Working in Germany*, published by the Employment Service Overseas Placing Unit, Level 4, Skills House, 3 7 Holy Green, Off the Moor, Sheffield S1 4AQ (tel: 0114 259 6051, fax: 0114 259 6040). The factsheet is available in all Jobcentres throughout the UK.

Living conditions

Germany is a high cost/standard of living country. Prices are higher than those in the UK.

The price of clothes is about the same as in the UK. Household and consumer goods are no dearer DM1205 for a refrigerator and DM341 for a vacuum cleaner. A colour TV set (22 in) would be DM1358.

House prices vary according to region and district, being highest in cities. The monthly rent for an unfurnished, three-bedroomed apartment in a good area in a major city such as Cologne, Frankfurt or Stuttgart would be upwards of DM3667. Electricity is 220V. Germans in cities live in flats rather than detached houses.

Medical treatment is of a high standard and most costs are met through insurance funds. Charges are made for dentistry, medicine, drugs and medical aids. Refunds are possible if you exchange your Form E111 for a *Krankenschein* certificate issued by the German health insurance companies through the Local Sickness Fund.

Education is compulsory from 6 to 18 (including three years at a vocational school on a part-time basis). A monthly fee is charged for nursery education between the ages of 3 and 6. The standard is high and thorough, and many expatriate parents send their children to local schools. Others want their children to continue education in the UK. There are International Schools at Dusseldorf, Frankfurt, Hamburg and Munich. The British Embassy runs a preparatory school in Bonn for children from 4 to 13. Fees vary, so it is necessary to check (see ECIS and COBISEC in Chapter 9). Schools for the children of British military personnel sometimes admit those of civilians.

There is a highly sophisticated network of air, rail and road transport, serving all parts of the country. All major cities are linked by motorways (*Autobahnen*). Every make of car can be obtained   German produced Volkswagen, Opel and Ford cars take the biggest share of the market. Prices are broadly similar, though taxation is less. Driving is on the right.

There is always plenty to do, winter or summer. Often even the smallest towns have their own opera and most towns have theatres, cinemas, concert halls, museums and art galleries. Hotels and restaurants range from the very expensive to the cheaper family *Gasthaus* types. German cooking is usually good, though sometimes on the heavy side.

There are abundant facilities for sport, rambling, riding, swimming and sailing, etc and some very beautiful country, especially along the Rhine and in the southern mountains.

There is a sizeable British community in most main cities, and the British Chamber of Commerce in Germany has seven regional groups of members; contact Mecklenburg House, 16 Buckingham Gate, London SW1E 6LB (tel: 0171 233 5656, fax: 0171 233 7835). The Chamber also provides a variety of useful publications: a magazine called *Trade Partners*, a *Members Bulletin*, information papers and reports on doing business in Germany. You don t have to know German for business dealings in western Germany, although in eastern Germany it is almost essential, but it would be difficult to live in Germany for any length of time without being able to speak the language.

The Bundesverwaltungsamt publishes a brochure *Merkblatt 119* (with two additional brochures), covering in detail aspects of living conditions, household costs, price index on consumer goods, housing costs, labour law, education, driving licences etc. The publication can be ordered from   ffentliche Auskunftsstelle F r Auslandt tige, Grosse Bleichen 23, 2 Stock, 20354 Hamburg (cover charge DM20.00).

Greece

Background

Greece covers an area of approximately 51,000 square miles, its islands accounting for nearly one-fifth of the total. It has common borders with Turkey, Bulgaria, Albania and former-Yugoslavia. Much of the country is mountainous, and there is little flat or cultivatable land, apart from some areas in the north. There are over 2000 islands, but only 154 are inhabited. The highest mountain is Mount Olympus. The climate is Mediterranean hot and dry in the summer, though it can be cold inland in winter.

The population is 10.5 million. About one-third live in the Greater Athens area, which includes the capital city, the port of Piraeus and a number of suburbs. It contains about 50 per cent of Greece s industry and is the country s principal commercial, financial and diplomatic centre. Efforts have, however, been made to decentralise the economy and the second city, Salonika (Thessaloniki) with its major port, has grown rapidly in population and industrial development. Other important towns are Patras, Larissa, Volos and Iraklion on the island of Crete.

Greece is a parliamentary democracy, currently led by a social democrat government. Pasok is the majority party and Costas Simitis is the Prime Minister. Parliament has a single chamber elected by proportional representation.

Greece has been a full member of the EU since 1981. There are tensions with the old rival, Turkey, and with the former-Yugoslavic Republic of Macedonia although these have lessened somewhat in recent years.

Exchange rate: Dr517.48 = £1.

The economy

The solid improvement of Greek macroeconomic fundamentals in the last few years continued in 1997, with real output expanding at an estimated rate of 3.5 per cent, inflation falling to 4.7 per cent in December 1997, general government deficit falling to 4.0 per cent of GDP and government Debt-to-GDP ratio for the first time declining to 108.7 per cent. The current account deficit, on the other hand, is estimated to reach 3.7 per cent of GDP. In the last few years, Greek economic policy has focused on gradually meeting the convergence criteria for joining the European Monetary Union. Policy makers aim at Greece joining the EMU by 2001 at the latest, one year before the common currency (Euro) is introduced in physical form. Real GDP growth has been significant in the last four years. In the last two years, Greek growth rates have been amongst the highest in the EU. Of more importance is the fact that the high rates of growth are accompanied by even higher investment growth rates which, on average, are more than twice as high as the corresponding EU rates over the 1994 1997 period. In addition to a restrictive incomes policy, the government announced its intent to speed up a number of structural reforms which enhance the supply side of the economy and hence improve both inflation and the economy s productive capacity. These include: measures that enhance the flexibility of labour markets, improvements in the social security system, restructuring public sector enterprises and speeding up most privatisations within 1998 and 1999.

The Greek economy was traditionally based on agriculture, with small-scale farming predominating, except in a few areas in the north. In common with all developing countries, there has been a steady shift towards industry, and although agriculture still employs nearly 19 per cent of the labour force, it accounts for 11.16 per cent of GDP. The principal products are tobacco, cotton, vegetables, wines, fruits and olive oil. An important part is played by the fisheries.

Greece is fortunate in having considerable reserves of minerals and ores, including bauxite, lignite, nickel and magnesite. These resources have yet to be fully exploited. Oil prospecting is intensifying.

In manufacturing, which accounts for 21.35 per cent of GDP, Greece s performance is hampered by the proliferation of small, traditional, low-tech firms, often run as family businesses. Food, drink and tobacco processing, textiles, chemicals, metal manufacture and engineering are the most important sectors. There are some steel mills and several shipyards. Shipping is of prime importance to the economy. There are major programmes under way in the areas of power, irrigation and land reclamation.

Greece has experienced severe balance of trade problems but to some extent these have been mitigated by healthy invisible exports, especially shipping, industrial products, tourism and migrants remittances. Over 10 million tourists visited Greece in 1994. Trade is mainly with EU countries.

The economy, however, remains in poor shape. The government s major concern has been to combat inflation, which is now down to 5 per cent. Wages and earnings, though well below the general EU level, have risen progressively but there is still a large public debt, and a vibrant black economy. The war in Yugoslavia has not helped matters.

Personal finance

The level of executive salaries is around 50 per cent lower than in the more prosperous northern EU countries but these are improving.

Taxation

Income tax is raised progressively on taxable income, allowances against which tend to be fairly generous. The top rate of tax is 45 per cent. On an average executive salary tax and social security payments would be around 30 per cent. Tax is deducted monthly, and the final balance is adjusted annually.

Working conditions

The EU provisions about free mobility of labour apply in Greece. You can freely take up employment, or enter the country to look for work, but you will need to register with the police (or the Alien s Department Office if you are in Athens) within eight days. You will need a residence permit for a stay of longer than three months. Greek bureaucracy is fairly intimidating, and can appear chaotic.

Job prospects for foreigners are slim at present, the best being with British firms with branches or subsidiaries in Greece or with multinational companies, especially in technological fields or in tourism. It is not very easy to find work and priority is given to Greek nationals. Military service is compulsory for men over 19.

Working hours are as in any hot country. In the summer (April to October) these are from 8.00 am to 2.00 pm and from 5.00 pm to 8.00 pm. Meals are eaten late and many people take a siesta in the afternoon.

There are 11 public holidays, including religious holidays. Annual leave is a minimum of four weeks after one year of service.

Living conditions

Wages and salaries may be lower than the average EU rates, but the cost of living is also lower, though Athens is more expensive than the rest of Greece.

Here are some recent prices:

	Dr
Beer (50 cl)	223.69
Bread (1 kg)	527.35
Butter (250 gm)	599.00
Cheese (500 gm)	966.00
Chicken (1 kg)	858.17
Coffee	
ground (500 gm)	1631.58
instant (250 gm)	2379.05
Cooking oil (1 litre)	617.64
Eggs (12)	482.76
Milk (1 litre)	287.82
Mineral water (1 litre)	121.74
Potatoes (1 kg)	129.55
Rice (1 kg)	768.74
Steak (1 kg)	2649.69
Sugar (1 kg)	274.56
Tea bags (250 gm)	1997.54
Whisky (75 cl)	3321.43
Wine (75 cl)	1546.54
Cigarettes (20)	538.52
Petrol (1 litre)	225.90

Wine is inexpensive and the local lager-type beer is recommended. The local aperitif is ouzo (like Pernod) and most

Greeks drink retsina, a slightly resinated light wine, white or rosØ, with their meals. Both are acquired tastes.

The food is reasonable and most British people, accustomed to similar food in Greek restaurants at home, will find it palatable, though some say that too much oil is used in cooking. Restaurants range from the expensive establishments in Athens and Salonika to modest tavernas in villages. The same applies to hotels. A double room in a luxury hotel costs around Dr25,000 a night, but all hotels are graded and must, by law, display room prices.

Shoppers will find that fresh fruit and vegetables are the best buy. Canned goods and imported foods tend to be expensive. There are supermarkets and large stores in the big towns, but many people prefer to shop in local markets and smaller shops.

You can get quite a wide range of local clothing and you can have things made up by a local tailor or dressmaker. It is probably best to bring out your own electrical equipment. Electrical supply is 220V, 50 cycles AC.

Despite a lot of building in the towns and cities, accommodation may be hard to find. A three-bedroomed apartment in a good area of Athens would cost from Dr227,000 a month to rent. Landlords usually ask for two months rent as a deposit and one month s in advance. Contracts are usually for two years. House prices are very high. It is possible to obtain domestic help but difficult to find anyone prepared to live in.

Transport is on the whole efficient and reliable and you can choose between air, rail, sea or bus. Most international air flights are based on Athens, and there are also regular services to and from Salonika. Domestic airlines serving some 30 towns and islands are operated from Athens by Olympic Airways. The railways are efficient and serve the main centres north and south of Athens. Long-distance coach and bus services provide a means of seeing the country and many shipping routes connect the mainland with the islands.

Taxis and cars can be hired, though car hire can be expensive. ELPA, the equivalent of our AA, runs a national road assistance service. Like all European cities, Athens has its traffic problems. The main roads in Greece are good, but conditions on local roads can be difficult, especially in the mountains. Cars are expensive. A Toyota Carina costs around Dr6,250,500.

Greece has a comprehensive social security system. The majority of employees are covered by the Social Insurance Institute, financed by employer and employee contributions. Benefits include pensions, medical expenses and long-term disability payments.

Doctor and hospital treatment within the Greek national health system is free, but you will have to pay 25 per cent of prescription charges. If you are in a remote area, you can reclaim a proportion of private medical expenses.

Public education is provided free of charge from nursery to university level, and is compulsory between ages 6 and 15. Because of language difficulties, expatriate parents tend to send their children to schools in the UK or, if they can get in, to an International School. The British Embassy school, St Catherine s, in Athens is a preparatory school for British children of 3 to 13 years. The American Community School caters for boys and girls from 4 to 18. The fees vary according to age. Campion School in Athens offers education in English and enters pupils for GCSE and A-level examinations.

Greece is very beautiful and the climate is excellent, but Athens suffers from a yellowish smog, which has been improved on greatly in the last five years. There is always scope for outdoor activity, with trips to the mountains or the islands, sightseeing or swimming from the many splendid sandy beaches. There are also conventional sports, such as golf, tennis and riding. It is not surprising, with all it has to offer and despite the relatively low salary levels, that many British people put Greece at the top of their choice for a country to live and work in.

Language may present a problem. Learn Modern Greek if you can, if you are staying for some time or living outside Athens in areas where English is not generally understood, or at any rate get to know the Greek alphabet and common phrases.

Republic of Ireland (Eire)

Background
The Republic of Ireland has a population of 3.5 million. It covers an area of 27,136 square miles. Its nearest neighbour is the United Kingdom, which incorporates Northern Ireland. The two official languages are Irish, the national language, and English. English is the usual language of business and, outside certain areas in the west, is the language in general public use. Dublin, the capital, is on the east coast and has a population of 0.5 million. Other important cities are Galway, Cork, Waterford and Limerick. The population is over 90 per cent Roman Catholic.

The Irish Republic is a parliamentary democracy with a written constitution. It has no military alliance. It has five predominant political parties and the political scene is dominated by conservative parties, the strongest being Fianna Fail. The present government is a coalition of Fianna Fail and the Progressive Democrats. The Prime Minister (*Taoiseach*) is Bertie Ahern.

The economy
Although industry has expanded greatly since Ireland s entry to the EEC in 1973, the economy is still built predominantly on agriculture. Over 13 per cent of the workforce are employed in this sector. Main crops are wheat, barley and potatoes, and the produce of arable farming provides major exports.

Membership of the EU has been advantageous to the Irish, who have benefited from heavy farming subsidies. The EU has also encouraged the development of manufacturing industries, such as food processing, electronics and textiles. The government is also keen to provide incentives to business in all spheres, eg the current tax breaks for movie making. Tourism is the most important part of the service sector and, in recent years, has provided substantial revenue.

A chronic power shortage has recently been transformed by the discovery of natural gas fields off the south coast, although there is still a need to import coal and oil. Although inflation is

very low, unemployment and the public debt remain uncomfortably high. Per capita GDP in PPU (see Austria) is 12,530.
Exchange rate: Irish punt 1.10 = £1.

Personal finance
The level of managerial salaries is approximately the same as in the UK. Upper/middle ranked executives earn up to IR£75,000 and general managers up to IR£120,000. Company cars are common.

Taxation
British subjects residing in Ireland are subject to the same personal income tax as the Irish. Rates of income tax are high, because of the small work force, and rates are progressive. A worker earning IR£10,000 per annum will pay an average of 25.5 per cent tax on real income; a single earner with a salary of IR£75,000 will pay on average of 47.3 per cent. Allowances and exemptions are available for those with dependants. Employers national insurance contributions are high, at 12.2 per cent on earnings up to IR£25,000. VAT ranges from 0 to 21 per cent.

Working conditions
British and EU citizens do not need work permits. The Irish work an average of 40.2 hours per week. Agencies and Jobcentres are more common ways to look for jobs than through the press. The Irish language is *not* a prerequisite for most jobs, although teaching and some civil service jobs are notable exceptions. The normal holiday allowance is four to six weeks per annum. The gap between men s and women s salaries is similar to the rest of Europe, but closing.

Living conditions
Ireland is comparable to the UK on cost of living, but Dublin is considerably more expensive than the rest of the country. Urban transport is slightly cheaper; taxis are more expensive. The following prices are recent samples:

	IR£
Beer (50 cl)	1.39
Bread (1 kg)	0.98
Butter (250 gm)	0.79
Cheese (500 gm)	2.93
Chicken (1 kg)	3.24
Coffee	
ground (500 gm)	4.11
instant (250 gm)	5.58
Cooking oil (1 litre)	1.21
Eggs (12)	1.65
Milk (1 litre)	0.61
Mineral water (1 litre)	0.45
Potatoes (1 kg)	0.59
Rice (1 kg)	1.77
Steak (1 kg)	9.87
Sugar (1 kg)	0.90
Tea bags (250 gm)	1.37
Whisky (75 cl)	13.68
Wine (75 cl)	6.19
Cigarettes (20)	2.65
Petrol (1 litre)	0.61

Accommodation is readily available in Dublin. A double room for one night in a five-star hotel will cost around IR£82; lowest budget accommodation costs around IR£5 per night. Houses and apartments can be found through the press or property agents. Rent is low, even in Dublin: a furnished three-bedroomed flat in the city costs from IR£450 600 per month, and is cheaper in the rest of the country. Public transport prices compare with those in the UK. Urban bus routes are extensive and are now much improved. Season tickets are good value. One overground urban railway line (DART) services Dublin and runs north south along the coast. There is an inexpensive, extensive and frequent coach service to all parts of the country. Trains are more expensive, but still cheaper than in the UK.

Ireland s roads have been vastly improved over the last decade with new motorways and road widening. There are international airports in Dublin, Cork, Shannon and Knock. The health service is private, except for those on social welfare, but exemptions and relief are available. A high percentage of the populace have health insurance.

At both primary and secondary levels most schools are run by church groups (Roman Catholic or other), although largely state funded. Admission is usually possible for members of other religions. Primary education is generally free, and also most secondary education, although many church-run schools (especially in Dublin) charge fees to supplement their state funding; from IR£1000 and IR£1500 for non-boarders. Limited government grants are available for tertiary education, and competition for university places is very high. Two schools with experience in schooling for expatriate children are Blackrock College, Dublin (12 18) and Newman College, Dublin (15 18).

There are four national newspapers; the *Irish Independent* and *The Irish Times* are the most popular. There are also evening and Sunday papers. Ireland has two national TV stations and national and local radio stations. The country has a strong literary and musical tradition and Dublin has, for a city of its size, a rich cultural scene. Dublin has many first-class restaurants. Ireland s pubs have long been argued to be the best in the world (possibly by Irishmen), and hundreds of excellent traditional pubs can be found all over the country. Traditional Irish music is played in many. The night club industry is currently growing throughout the country.

Outdoor sports are popular: national sports are Gaelic football and hurling. Soccer, rugby, water sports, angling, sailing, golf, horse racing and mountaineering are also popular with the Irish as well as with tourists. Ireland s countryside is largely unspoilt, unpolluted and beautiful, particularly in coastal areas.

Shopping hours are generally from 9 am to 5.30 pm, although many supermarkets stay open until 8.30 pm, Monday to Saturday. Lunch breaks in businesses are usually from 12.30 to 1.30 pm. Few shops close for lunch. Banks are open from 10 am to 4 pm, Monday to Friday, except Thursdays when they close at 5 pm. A number of British and international stores have branches in Ireland.

Ireland is similar to the UK in language, fashions, business trends, etc but differs in many topical views and stances, cultural, religious and social customs.

Italy

Background

Italy covers an area of 116,000 miles and has a population of some 57 million. Its regions vary widely in geography, development, tradition and culture.

It lies wholly within the Mediterranean region. In the north, the Alps constitute a barrier against the rest of Europe, and the Apennines form a backbone which runs down the whole length of the country from the plain of Lombardy and the Po valley to the toe in the Messina straits.

The north, centred on Milan, Turin and Genoa (the respective capitals of Lombardy, Piedmont and Liguria), is highly industrialised and contains about half the total population. The south, by contrast, is underdeveloped and poor. Rome, the capital, in the centre, is the headquarters of government and many business organisations. It has about 3 million inhabitants. Milan is the commercial and industrial centre. Other important cities are Naples, Turin, Genoa (the main port), Bologna, Florence, Venice, Taranto and Trieste. The expatriate population in Rome is mainly diplomatic, and NATO personnel predominate in Naples. Milan and northern cities are the main centre for business expatriates, who include many British.

There is little love lost between Rome and the provincial capitals, many of whose people still regard themselves primarily as Venetians, Neapolitans, Tuscans or Milanese. There are a number of non-Italian speaking minorities   German is used officially in the Trentino-Alto Adige region; there are Slavs in the Trieste area and a kind of dog-Latin is still spoken in the interior of Sardinia which, like Sicily and Val d Aosta, is autonomous. There is a powerful nationalist political movement, the Northern League, which advocates autonomy for the whole of northern Italy.

The climate is hot in summer and mild in winter. It can be extremely hot in the plains of Lombardy during the summer.

Italy is a parliamentary democracy and has been governed since the end of the war by successive coalitions. Following the resignation of the Berlusconi government, in January 1995 Lamberto Dini was appointed as Prime Minister with a government comprising non-political experts. Early in 1996 Sr Dini was forced to resign and, after much confusion, the latest election produced a victory for the centre/left Olive Coalition led by Professor Romano Prodi.

Exchange rate: Lire 2765.43 = £1.

The economy

The Italian economy has been growing strongly in recent years but has recently hit recession. However, unemployment is high at around 11.5 per cent. Inflation is around 1.9 per cent (1997). Repeated austerity programmes by the government, primarily involving cutting welfare and wages and instituting large scale privatisation plans have resulted in an increase in GNP of 2.7 per cent. The lira has suffered massive devaluation since withdrawal from the ERM. Per capita GDP in PPU (see Austria) is 16,840.

Italy has few mineral resources, apart from scattered deposits of sulphur, iron ore, zinc and lead, and is therefore dependent on overseas trade. There are, however, significant gas and oil fields which are being exploited, and Italy provides over a quarter of the world s mercury. Its main exports are machinery, cars, metal manufactures, iron and steel products, artificial fibres, knitwear and hosiery, and a wide range of luxury and semi-luxury items, including food and wine of which Italy is now a bigger exporter than France. Tourism, of course, is a major revenue producer and is one of the country s largest industries.

Industry is unevenly distributed. The northern triangle Milan, Turin and Genoa produces about one-fifth of the national output and incomes are well above the national average. There has been a steady migration of labour from the impoverished south, both to the more prosperous north and to other EU countries. Successive governments have aimed at developing the mezzogiorno but, despite government and EU aid, the south has remained relatively poor.

Most enterprises are small or medium-sized, but larger units predominate in engineering and chemicals.

Many American and multinational companies operate in Italy. Most of the major British companies have branches or subsidiaries, based mainly in Milan and Rome.

Personal finance and taxation

Managerial and executive salaries are on a par with most EU countries. Income tax rates in Italy begin at 10 per cent and rise to a maximum of 51 per cent. There are also local taxes, including a property tax of 4 6 per cent. Italy, however, is where tax avoidance devices flourish and you should certainly seek qualified advice on your position if you are going there on a salary at the usual expatriate level. VAT (IVA) is 19 per cent.

Working conditions

Citizens of EU countries can enter Italy freely to look for and take up a job; they do not need work permits, but you will need a residence permit. Register with the local police within seven days of arrival. It is also necessary to obtain a tax number which will be asked for when registering a car, buying a flat or getting a job.

Given the high level of unemployment and language difficulties, not many British people find jobs in Italy unless they are working for Italian-based UK companies. A frequent complaint among expatriates is the difficulty of dealing with the well-entrenched bureaucracy. A personal visit to find a job may pay off. Speaking Italian is important.

The 40-hour, five-day week has become the general standard (overtime is rare). Salaries are sometimes paid in 14 16 instalments. Most collective agreements provide for four weeks paid leave for wage and salary earners. There are also ten public holidays. There is a growing trend towards accumulating public holidays for summer vacations, so as to minimise disruption. Most towns also have a holiday on the feast day of their patron saint, and there are a number of half-day holidays. Employers have to face many additional charges, including a 13-month or Christmas bonus; assistance towards housing, transport and canteens; children s nurseries and kindergartens. Most of these concessions, which are negotiated, are common among the larger enterprises, and, in the case of smaller firms, often arranged through consortia. Some firms have savings plans. There are works committees in firms employing more than 40 workers. The trade union movement is divided on political and religious lines. It is likely that many of these benefits will be reduced as the government continues its economic reorganisation.

Living conditions
The cost of living is higher in the cities than elsewhere, but on the whole Italian prices are lower than in most northern European countries. Food is comparable or somewhat cheaper than in the UK. Here are some examples of prices:

	Lira
Beer (50 cl)	1,482
Bread (1 kg)	4,871
Butter (250 gm)	3,352
Cheese, Cheddar type (500 gm)	6,969
Chicken (1 kg)	6,923
Coffee	
ground (500 gm)	8,266
instant (250 gm)	16,237
Cooking oil (1 litre)	3,473
Eggs (12)	3,875
Milk (1 litre)	1,903
Mineral water (1 litre)	622
Potatoes (1 kg)	1,217
Rice (1 kg)	3,944
Steak (1 kg)	25,155
Sugar (1 kg)	1,886
Tea bags (250 gm)	15,137
Whisky (75 cl)	18,207
Wine (75 cl)	6,228
Cigarettes (20)	4,920
Petrol (1 litre)	1,838

Pasta, in all shapes and sizes, is the staple diet of many Italians and is cheap. Wine and spirits are less expensive than in the UK.

It is not cheap to live in Italy; it can be very expensive, particularly in Rome and tourist centres such as Venice. But, with careful budgeting, good value for money can be had, particularly in comparison with Switzerland and Scandinavia. The fall in the value of the lira in 1994 95 has worked to the advantage of foreigners.

The cost of eating out varies enormously. You can eat a good, robust meal at an extremely modest price in a family-run trattoria or pay huge prices at a slap-up restaurant. Cigarettes are cheaper than in the UK.

Clothing is good value. Women s outfits (dress, skirt, tights and shoes) can be bought in department stores for about the same price as in the UK. The same applies to men s clothing, which is cheaper than in other EU countries. But shopping in boutiques or high-fashion shops in Rome, Florence or other centres is extremely expensive.

The cost of most household goods is similar to that in the UK. Hire purchase facilities are available.

Houses are practically unobtainable in the main cities, since most people live in apartments. An unfurnished, two- or three-bedroomed flat in Rome or Milan costs around L46.5 million. Rental contracts are usually for four years. Domestic electric voltages are nearly always 220V, AC 50 cycles; lamp-bulb holders are of the screw type, wall plugs of the round, two-pin continental type. Some older properties may actually have electricity at two different voltages. It is important to check the wiring. Pay your service bills promptly or you will be cut off within days.

Rail fares are lower than in Britain, but some main-line trains require supplementary payments. The main cities are served by a network of toll motorways (*autostrada*), and other highways are in good condition. Many filling-stations are open day and night. All makes of car are available from dealers, though there is a strict limitation on the number of Japanese cars. Needless to say, if you are living in Italy, a Fiat is the best bet from the point of view of servicing and running costs (a Fiat Tempra costs around L27.5 million). Small cars are handy in the appalling traffic congestion of Rome and other cities. Driving is on the right. Taxis and self-drive cars are available in all centres. Long-distance buses and coaches offer admirable services and a chance to see the countryside in comfort.

Telephoning is relatively cheap and efficient, but mail is slow.

The national health service covers the whole of the employed working population, including registered foreigners. Private treatment is expensive but most foreigners prefer it. Italy has the highest doctor/patient ratio in Europe. A number of hospitals are run by the Church.

There are American and English schools in Rome and Milan. (See ECIS and COBISEC in Chapter 9.) These schools, inspected by HM Inspectors of Schools, include St George s English School, Rome; The New School, Rome; Sir James Henderson British School, Milan; and the International School, Milan. There are opportunities for UK teachers to find jobs in some of the schools, though, as in other countries, would-be EFL teachers should beware of rogue employers (one sign of which is apparent unconcern with an applicant s qualifications to teach). State schooling is free (although parents buy books and stationery) and most private schools are Roman Catholic day schools.

Quite apart from working in Italy, many British people settle there permanently because they like the country and its way of life. British residents include many retired people, artists, writers, etc.

It is impossible to be bored in Italy; there are numerous theatres, concert and opera attractions, cinemas, museums and artistic treasures. All Italian cities are within easy reach of beautiful parts of the country, eg Lake Como from Milan, Capri from Naples; expeditions for sailing, swimming, climbing, fishing and skiing in the north can be made at weekends or on holidays. The Italians are friendly, gregarious and exuberant, particularly in the south.

Luxembourg

Background

The Grand Duchy of Luxembourg covers only 999 square miles and has a population of 481,300. The capital, Luxembourg City, has a population of 80,000. Luxembourgers have their own dialect (*Letzeburgesch*) which is the national language, but French and German are the official languages. English is widely spoken and understood. The people have a strong sense of nationality and independence. They are proud of their traditions.

The Grand Duke is head of state. The Chamber with 60 deputies is elected every five years and the government is usually formed by a coalition. The current President of the European Commission is previous Prime Minister Jacques Santer.

Luxembourg has maintained its position as one of the richest countries in Europe. Its central location within the EU and a liberal fiscal climate have attracted a large service sector there, particularly in international banking and finance. To some extent this has compensated for the decline in manufacturing. Both inflation and unemployment are low 1.5 and 3 per cent respectively. Thirty-four per cent of the population are foreigners attracted by employment prospects. Belgian currency is also legal tender, and the Luxembourg Franc is linked to the Belgian Franc. Per capita GDP in PPU (see Austria) is 21,260.

Exchange rate: LFr57.74 = £1.

Personal finance and taxation

Gross pay is 50 to 100 per cent higher than in the UK at senior levels; many enjoy company fringe benefits (eg car, house).

The taxation system is separate from that of Belgium. Taxpayers are divided into three classes for income tax purposes. Single and divorced fall into class 1. Class 1a includes widowed people, those over the age of 63 and those from their household. Married people taxed jointly are in class 2. There is a subdivision of classes 1 and 2 for people who are entitled to a child allowance. The basic graduated scale of taxation ranges from nil on the first LFr300,000 of taxable income to 33 per cent on incomes over LFr1,800,000. Other taxes include those on capital yields and property. Reliefs are given for children, age and special expenses or extraordinary burdens.

Working conditions

Procedure for permits is as throughout the EU. A good knowledge of French and German would be valuable as both languages are widely used in business, although English is widely spoken. A knowledge of the Luxembourg dialect may be required for some jobs. All salaries and wages are tied to the cost of living index. The 40-hour week is standard.

Holidays are 25 days for all workers plus ten public holidays. Most workers receive an end-of-year bonus. Salaried staff sometimes receive extra bonuses.

Living conditions
Living conditions are much as in Belgium, though prices of basic foods tend to be lower and clothes are cheaper and lodging is more expensive. The overall cost of living is about the same as in the UK.

The following table lists some recent typical prices in Luxembourg:

	LFr
Beer (50 cl)	28
Bread (1 kg)	66
Butter (250 gm)	50
Cheese, Cheddar type (500 gm)	142
Chicken (1 kg)	204
Coffee	
ground (500 gm)	98
instant (250 gm)	383
Cooking oil (1 litre)	83
Eggs (12)	80
Milk (1 litre)	30
Mineral water (1 litre)	16
Potatoes (1 kg)	17
Rice (1 kg)	106
Steak (1 kg)	270
Sugar (1 kg)	40
Tea bags (250 gm)	244
Whisky (75 cl)	493
Wine (75 cl)	160
Cigarettes (20)	78

Purchasing power is high and Luxembourgers are among the best-off communities in Europe. The climate is temperate, but cold in the winter and in the higher altitudes of the Ardennes.

Food and drink are good, with moderately priced wines from the Moselle and local delicacies from the Ardennes such as ham and p tØ. Eating out is relatively expensive. Petrol works out at about LFr27 per litre. Annual rent for a small, two-bedroomed, unfurnished flat in Luxembourg City is around LFr740,000. House rents (unfurnished or part furnished, three to five bedrooms) in the city average LFr1,105,000. As one would expect, rents are lower in country areas. There are several letting agencies recommended by the Luxembourg National Tourist Office, which will supply their names and addresses on request.

Medical facilities are of a high standard but costly, although social security reimburses most bills. Some doctors have been trained in the UK: many speak English.

There are three schools in Luxembourg which cater for non-national children and are English-speaking. The Ecole EuropØenne is intended for children of EU and ECSC personnel, but is open to others.

New building has kept pace with the influx of business people and EU officials. Shopping and business hours are as in Belgium.

There is plenty of social life among the foreign diplomatic and business communities, but less organised entertainment than in Brussels. Country-lovers will appreciate the beauties of the Ardennes, Little Switzerland , and the Moselle valley for walking, cycling or motoring. The airport, which is only four miles from Luxembourg City, is served by regular British Airways and Luxair flights from Heathrow and Stansted.

The Netherlands

Background
The Netherlands is one of Britain s main gateways to Europe. Amsterdam is less than an hour by air from London and there are regular flights to many UK cities. The port of Rotterdam, the biggest and busiest in the world, is at the hub of the EU s trade.

The Netherlands is small but densely populated: 15.2 million people live in an area of 16,000 square miles. The country is flat and low lying a quarter of its territory is below sea-level, and the Dutch have had to wage an unremitting battle against flooding, through land reclamation and dykes drainage. Half the population lives in a narrow industrialised strip, known as Randstad , bounded by Amsterdam, Rotterdam, the Hague and Utrecht. Dutch is the main language, although Friesian is spoken in the north east.

Amsterdam, with just over 1 million inhabitants, is the capital of the Netherlands, although the political and diplomatic centre is The Hague. Rotterdam and district (1.2 million) has become the most important industrial centre. Other centres are Utrecht, Eindhoven, Haarlem and Groningen.

The Netherlands is a constitutional monarchy, with a two-chamber Parliament. Queen Beatrice became head of state in April 1980. There are a number of political parties, and the country has been governed by coalitions since the end of the war. The present government is a coalition of Labour, the People s Party of Freedom and Democracy (VVD) and Democrats 1966 (D 66).

Exchange rate: Guilder (DFl) 3.19 = £1.

The economy

The traditional image of the Netherlands as a land of bulbs, windmills and wooden shoes is perpetuated for the sake of tourists but, in fact, its modern industrial basis and rapid economic growth have placed the Netherlands in the forefront of European Union economies. Industry accounts for nearly one-third of both the national income and the working population.

It has no natural resources, apart from natural gas and salt in the east. The Netherlands is thus highly dependent on foreign trade and experiences recurrent balance of trade problems. The Netherlands is dependent on overseas suppliers for oil, but has stepped up its natural gas production to counteract this. Trading, banking and shipping businesses are of particular importance to the economy. Inflation is around 2 per cent.

Agriculture, though its percentage contribution to GNP has fallen relative to industry, is still important and very efficient. Production continues to rise, with cattle and dairy products, fruit, vegetables and flowers as its principal products.

The main industries include electrical and mechanical engineering, textiles and clothing, steel, shipbuilding, processed foods and chemicals, with diamonds and furs in the luxury range. Oil refining and the petrochemicals sector dominate the Rotterdam area. The electrical and electronics industries are highly sophisticated and produce computers, telecommunications equipment and precision instruments. Coal mining, after being progressively run down, has ceased completely.

That the Dutch are internationally minded is shown in their industrial structures. The multinationals include Philips, the electrical giant, Unilever, Shell and other major oil companies. Joint German/Dutch enterprises have been set up in some sectors. Foreign investment is welcomed, particularly in the development areas in the north-east and south. The UK heads the list of foreign investors, with the USA second. Many of the large British companies have Dutch subsidiaries.

Traditionally a free trade/free enterprise economy, the state role is limited to setting a favourable climate for growth and investment. Per capita GDP in PPU (see Austria) is 16,220.

Personal finance

Executive salaries are about 30 per cent higher than in the UK; secretarial salaries are roughly comparable.

Taxation

There is a range of tax-free personal allowances   amounts depend on such factors as age, marital status and number of dependent children. The maximum rate of tax is 60 per cent.

Social security payments which have to be made by individuals in the Netherlands are very high   but so are the benefits, should you need to call on them. There is, however, a very important concession made to qualifying expatriates as far as tax on income derived in the country is concerned. If you are working for a non-Dutch company your Dutch income is reduced in certain circumstances by 35 per cent for tax assessment purposes, though some fringe benefits are taxable as income.

Working conditions

Many British people put the Netherlands at the top of their list of preferred locations overseas. It is near home, most people speak English and the way of life is not unlike our own. If you want to find work in the Netherlands, the procedure is as in other EU countries no visa is required for EU nationals for stays of up to three months but you need a residence permit from the local police, whom you should contact within eight days of your arrival. After five consecutive years a permanent residence permit can be granted.

A legal minimum wage is fixed for all workers aged 23 to 65 and is reviewed at least once a year in the light of movements in average earnings and the cost of living index. Apart from this, wages are determined by collective agreements the practice of plant agreements has grown with the increase in the size of firms.

Collective agreements usually lay down procedures for dealing with disputes and provide for reference to arbitration boards in the event of failure to settle. The country has been relatively strike-free. Most contracts are written and provide for a two-month trial period. Dismissals and resignations come under government supervision; length of notice is governed by the terms of individual contracts and length of service for managers the notice period is usually three months. In most industries the 40-hour week has become standard.

Workers are entitled to three weeks paid holiday and most get more through collective bargaining. Five weeks is normal for managerial staff.

Living conditions
The overall cost of living in the Netherlands is similar to that in the UK.

	DFl
Beer (50 cl)	2.40
Bread (1 kg)	3.21
Butter (250 gm)	2.41
Cheese, Cheddar type (500 gm)	7.73
Chicken (1 kg)	8.54
Coffee	
ground (500 gm)	8.47
instant (250 gm)	18.95

Cooking oil (1 litre)	3.93
Eggs (12)	3.54
Milk (1 litre)	1.33
Mineral water (1 litre)	0.97
Potatoes (1 kg)	1.25
Rice (1 kg)	4.06
Steak (1 kg)	35.57
Sugar (1 kg)	2.10
Tea bags (250 gm)	5.43
Whisky (75 cl)	31.31
Wine (75 cl)	10.03
Cigarettes (20)	5.75
Petrol (1 litre)	2.03

Wine and whisky are a little cheaper than in the UK. Most consumer goods are fairly expensive, eg a refrigerator would cost DFl 1223 and a colour TV set DFl 1575. The price of clothes and personal services is, on the whole, higher than in the UK.

Apartments are hard to get in spite of a massive house-building programme. Semi-detached and terraced houses are the norm for those who do not live in blocks of flats, and cost from DFl 2300 per month (three bedrooms). Mortgage interest is tax-deductible and mortgages easily obtainable from banks, which offer lower interest rates than in the UK.

A new 1600cc Toyota Corolla would cost around DFl 33,472.

Eating out is expensive, but less so than in Belgium or Scandinavia. There are many moderately priced restaurants in Amsterdam. Domestic help is difficult to find in the big cities. Electricity is supplied at 220V, 50 cycles AC.

The cost of living is relatively low in comparison with other northern European countries. The social wage in the Netherlands is among the highest in the EU: unemployment benefit, for instance, is far more generous than in the UK.

The Dutch health service is based on a mixture of compulsory and voluntary schemes. The compulsory scheme covers about 70 per cent of the population. Private medical treatment is expensive. The Dutch are healthy, and have the longest life expectancy of any EU nationals. There is a reciprocal health agreement with the UK.

Education is free (though some schools may request a voluntary contribution) and compulsory from 5 to 16, with part-time schooling for a further year. There are state schools and state subsidised denominational schools. Primary schooling lasts seven to eight years, followed by different types of secondary education general, vocational or gymnasium (grammar-school type). There are universities, technical universities, technical colleges, International Schools and British Schools in many cities.

The British School in the Netherlands is in the vicinity of the Hague and provides for children between 3 and 18 years. The fees compare favourably with other International Schools in the Netherlands.

There is a British Primary School in Amsterdam and a number of other International and American Schools in the major cities details of these can be obtained from ECIS and COBISEC (see Chapter 9).

Internal and urban transport are very efficient. Frequent train services link the main centres and there are country-wide bus services. The roads are good and not over-congested. Nearly everybody in Holland cycles and there are special cycle paths on the main roads.

British people like living in the Netherlands, both because there are few language obstacles and because the way of life is attractive. The Dutch are very hospitable and welcoming to foreigners, particularly the British. Most speak English, but it would be as well to learn the language. The Hague is more formal than Amsterdam. There is plenty to do, particularly in Amsterdam, with theatres, art galleries, concert halls, cinemas and many good restaurants. There is scope for outdoor sports, including swimming and sailing, and the Dutch coast with its long stretches of sandy beaches provides a perfect holiday for people with children.

Norway

Background

Norway is the fifth largest country in Europe and the least densely populated just over 4 million people live in its 125,000 square miles. The country is long and narrow, and its 1700 mile-long coast is indented with fjords. Nearly three-quarters of the total territory is mountainous and uninhabitable, and about half lies within the Arctic circle. The vast majority of the population live in the southern half, which includes Oslo, the capital (477,515 inhabitants), Bergen (219,810), Stavanger (102,539) and Trondheim (142,015). In the far north, as in Sweden, there are communities of Lapps, known as Sami people, with their own language and culture.

Norway has longer summer daylight and longer winter darkness than any inhabited country in the world. The Gulf Stream keeps winter temperatures higher along the Atlantic coastline than in the more easterly parts.

Like the rest of Scandinavia, Norway is a constitutional monarchy, with a uni-chamber Parliament (*Storting*), elected every four years. The present government is a Labour minority.

Norway actively supports the United Nations (it provided its first Secretary General, Trygve Lie) and belongs to NATO. The government has believed for some time that Norway would be better off in the EU, but, in the most recent referendum in late 1994, the electorate once more rejected the plan.

Exchange rate: Krone 12.20 = £1.

The economy

The exploitation of oil deposits in the North Sea revolutionised Norway s economy and transformed its entire industrial and social structure. Thousands of workers left their traditional occupations in farms, fisheries and forests to find work in the rapidly developing oil sector, leading to severe pressure on housing and other social resources.

The government, anxious to avoid too much disruption and the development of a gold rush mentality, proceeded cautiously, limiting rates of production and exploitation, and taking care of the pollution and preservation aspects. It participates in operations, through its ownership of Statoil and heavy taxation of companies. Norway is now the biggest oil producer in western Europe, accounting for 40 per cent of its exports.

Oil apart, Norway is rich in mineral resources and has taken advantage of its cheap and abundant water power (which meets virtually all electricity requirements) to develop modern electro-metallurgical and electro-chemical industries.

The most important of these are aluminium (based on imported bauxite), ferro-alloys and nitrates. Other valuable minerals include iron ore (the basis of Norway s steel industry), copper, zinc, nickel, dolomite and titanium. Fishing and forestry, together with the production of timber, paper and pulp, are important, though relatively declining, sectors. Shipbuilding has steadily expanded, and has increasingly turned to the production of oil rigs and platforms. Consumer and service industries have developed, eg food and fish processing, clothing and textiles, but half the nation s food still has to be imported. Two-thirds of the population are engaged in service industries predominantly connected with oil, shipping and tourism.

The state plans and regulates economic development. The steel industry is dominated by the state-owned concern in the far north. In some cases, the state is the majority shareholder, but most manufacturing, eg shipbuilding, is in the hands of private enterprise. The government welcomes regulated foreign investment, offering special incentives for underdeveloped and underpopulated areas. Inflation is under 3 per cent.

Sweden is Norway s major trading partner, but trade with other EU countries particularly the UK, Germany and Denmark makes an important contribution. Tourism is a useful revenue earner and many visitors are attracted to Norway by the midnight sun and the open-air, away-from-it-all life.

Personal finance

In general, salaries are higher than in the UK, but so are deductions, and this is combined with a high cost of living.

Taxation

As in other Scandinavian countries, Norway s citizens have a heavy tax burden to bear for their welfare state and social services. Both state and local taxes are graduated according to income and numbers of dependents.

Rates of tax vary from 0 to 13.7 per cent, plus employees social security contributions, and a local tax of 28 per cent. Expatriates may be taxed at 15 per cent if the stay is for less than four years.

EEA-nationals

The EEA (European Economic Area) Agreement secures nationals of the EU and EFTA countries the freedom of movement and establishment throughout the area. Under the provisions of the Agreement you may stay in Norway for a period of three months to seek employment provided you are financially self-supporting. Should you succeed in finding work during this period, you must apply in person for a residence permit at the nearest police station, taking with you your national passport, two photographs and a Confirmation of Employment from your employer. You may, however, commence work before a formal residence permit has been granted.

If you take up short-term work only and your total stay in Norway does not exceed three months, a residence permit will not be required. Neither are you required to report to the police.

Should you not find employment in the course of the first three months, but wish to extend your stay in Norway, you must report to the local police before the expiry of the three-month period and must be able to prove that you have sufficient means of support. Should you not be in a position to support yourself financially, you may be asked to return to your country of origin.

Nationals of other countries

A general ban on immigration has been in force in Norway since 1975. An exemption is most unlikely to be granted unless you have special skills which local job applicants do not possess. If you have received an offer of employment in Norway due to the demand for your qualifications you must apply for a work and residence permit through the Embassy which will transmit your application to the Norwegian immigration authorities. The time required to process the application is normally at least three months.

Applicants may not enter Norway during the period in which the application for a work and residence permit is under consideration.

The normal working week is 37‰ hours and overtime is limited. All employees have four weeks annual leave, and there are up to ten public holidays. Both sides of industry contribute towards a jointly managed training fund.

Living conditions

Oslo is one of the most expensive capitals in Europe, and it can be difficult to obtain personal and domestic services. The cost of basic foods is somewhat higher than in the UK. Here are some typical prices:

	NKr
Beer (50 cl)	18.88
Bread (1 kg)	15.00
Butter (250 gm)	9.25
Cheese, Cheddar type (500 gm)	34.00
Chicken (1 kg)	63.83
Coffee	
ground (500 gm)	38.89
instant (250 gm)	89.43
Cooking oil (1 litre)	33.39
Eggs (12)	23.00
Milk (1 litre)	8.80
Mineral water (1 litre)	8.20
Potatoes (1 kg)	9.00
Rice (1 kg)	27.73
Steak (1 kg)	169.73
Sugar (1 kg)	12.41
Tea bags (250 gm)	84.12
Whisky (75 cl)	309.31
Wine (75 cl)	90.97
Cigarettes (20)	44.56
Petrol (1 litre)	8.60

Clothes are a little more expensive than in the UK (a man s suit costs around NKr3550). A Toyota Corolla would cost about NKr208,000.

Consumer durables and services are expensive. Rents are about the same as in Sweden, and slightly more than in Denmark.

Scattered settlements, and the country s topography, used to make transport and communications difficult. Regular shipping services serve the coastal towns throughout the year. There are regular sea/rail links within Norway and with Europe, and Norway co-operates with Sweden and Denmark in SAS, which operates regular air services internally and externally. Foreigners must be particularly aware of Norway s very strict drink and drive laws. Anyone caught driving with more than 0.5 per 1000 ml alcohol in their blood must reckon with an almost automatic prison sentence plus suspension of their licence for at least a year.

Social life in the main towns and cities is very like that of Sweden, though the Norwegians are less formal. Their command of English is impressive. Conditions in the remote areas, particularly in the north where it is dark most of the day in the winter, are severe, but housing compares well with the south. Warm clothes are needed in the winter.

Norway has unlimited facilities for outdoor sports, such as sailing, fishing, camping, riding and skiing (until April), and the country is wild and beautiful. Facilities for culture, such as theatre and music, are comparable with medium-sized UK cities, and you may find the long dark evenings wearisome. TV entertainment includes Sky as well as several Norwegian TV channels, with Swedish TV in the east.

Portugal

Background and the economy
Like its neighbour Spain, Portugal has become a popular holiday destination for tourists over the last 30 years. The most favoured spot has been the Algarve in the south, but the rest of the country is also attractive and has great areas of fertile land. The climate is mild throughout, though warmer and drier in the south.

Portugal has a population of around 10 million, many of whom are engaged in agriculture and fishing. Industry is low tech and labour intensive. The biggest single sector is services (including public administration) which accounts for nearly 50 per cent of the working population. This probably explains Portugal s relatively low rate of unemployment (7 per cent) and reflects a political situation in which various slightly right-of-centre governments have had to make economic sacrifices in the interests of political stability. Inflation is at 2.2 per cent.

Portugal has long-standing historical ties with Britain, going back to the fourteenth century when King John I of Portugal married Philippa of Lancaster. Portugal has also been a member of the EU since 1986 and this has been followed by a growth of economic activity in the country and a liberalisation of the labour laws. The government has been working towards European monetary union. Recently the budget deficit has been reduced and now stands at 2.5 per cent of GDP. Portugal receives large amounts of EU aid, one result of which is the attraction of new foreign investment and initiatives.

The capital, Lisbon, has a population of over 2 million. The second city is Oporto. Parliament is elected every four years by proportional representation. The elected President retains a measure of power. The present Socialist government is led by Antonio Guternes. Portugal has something of an unsettled political history. Per capita GDP in PPU (see Austria) is 9740.

Exchange rate: Escudos ($) 288.45 = £1.

Personal finance and tax
Portuguese nationals are poorly paid by international standards. Expatriates could expect to be paid about 25 per cent more than the equivalent rate for the job in the UK.

Income tax is self-assessed annually and varies from 15 to 40 per cent. There is a local tax, and VAT varies from 5 to 30 per cent.

Living costs and conditions
Rents vary considerably, but tend to be expensive for those on Portuguese salaries. In Lisbon, for example, the annual rent for

an unfurnished, three-bedroomed detached house could be from Esc 2.6 to 7.2 million per annum. It is possible to buy property, but buying a house is a complex process, riddled with legal pitfalls for foreigners and should not be undertaken without trustworthy local, professional help. More information is given in *Living Abroad: The Daily Telegraph Guide*, 11th edn, Kogan Page 1998.

Food costs are seasonal and, as in other expatriate locations, it is much cheaper to buy in street markets than in supermarkets. By the same token, one can eat well and cheaply in restaurants frequented by locals. In the shops meat and dairy foods are inexpensive compared with the UK, fruit and vegetables are cheap. Overall it is estimated that the cost of living in Lisbon is about 25 per cent less than in London. Sample prices are given below:

	Esc
Beer (50 cl)	88
Bread (1 kg)	210
Butter (250 gm)	270
Cheese, Cheddar type (500 gm)	720
Chicken (1 kg)	460
Coffee	
ground (500 gm)	830
instant (250 gm)	1560
Cooking oil (1 litre)	260
Eggs (12)	216
Milk (1 litre)	136
Mineral water (1 litre)	55
Potatoes (1 kg)	66
Rice (1 kg)	287
Steak (1 kg)	1800
Sugar (1 kg)	190
Tea bags (250 gm)	1200
Whisky (75 cl)	2130
Wine (75 cl)	500
Cigarettes (20)	360
Petrol (1 litre)	168

Hospital treatment and essential medicine are free, but you will have to pay half the cost of non-essential prescribed medicines. There is a small charge for treatment by a doctor.

There is a sizeable British community in Portugal, a couple of British schools and a British Hospital in Lisbon. Portuguese is essential in most areas.

Spain

Background
Of all European countries, Spain is perhaps one that British people think they are most familiar with, but this familiarity is generally limited to small and in many ways uncharacteristic strips of the Mediterranean coast. Spain is, in fact, a large and varied country the second largest in Europe. It has a population of about 40 million, the main centres, apart from Madrid (3.2 million), being Barcelona, Bilbao, Valencia, Seville, Murcia, Alicante and Malaga.

Spain is a democracy with the King, as head of state, playing a limited but effective political role. In a hotly-contested election, the conservative Popular Party end the 13-year reign of the socialists in 1996. This was considered the result of continued corruption scandals, the highest unemployment in Europe (21 per cent) and renewed Basque separatist terrorism.

Although inflation, at 2 per cent, is low, it is coupled with a high growth rate and high unemployment. The immediate economic prospect is not very good, though the country has the resources to emerge from its present difficulties. Spain has a large and successful agricultural sector and plentiful mineral resources. Tourism is a major industry. Important manufactures include cars, ships, steel and chemicals. Foreign investment is high. Per capita PPU (see Austria) is US$ 13,580.

Exchange rate: Pesetas 238.39 = £1.

Personal finance
The principal jobs available for expatriates in Spain relate to employment with a multinational firm. Here international

salary standards apply and prospective expatriates at executive levels should earn at least as much as in the UK, plus removal and other disturbance costs.

Taxation

Spain is no tax haven, and income tax rates go up as high as 56 per cent. Taxes are levied at two levels: national and local. National taxes include corporate income tax, personal income tax, VAT, wealth tax, inheritance and gift tax. Local taxes are: property taxes, municipal gains tax, and various licence fees. Taxes are payable yearly, on 31 December.

Liability for income tax depends on residence (irrespective of whether a person has a work permit or residence permit); an individual is regarded as a resident if he or she is physically present in Spain for at least 183 days in the year. Residents pay tax on their worldwide income. A typical expatriate employee with a dependent spouse would pay 30 40 per cent of gross salary in tax and social security contributions. VAT (IVA) ranges from 6 to 33 per cent.

Working conditions

Working conditions in Spain increasingly resemble those in other European countries, with city offices abandoning the siesta. The normal working week is 40 hours, and overtime (paid at least 175 per cent of normal rates) cannot be forced. Annual leave is 30 days, plus 12 days public holidays.

Living conditions

Most of Spain has a hot dry summer, intensely so inland, where winters can also get very cold. Northern Spain is cooler and wetter and many Spaniards actually prefer to spend their holidays on the Atlantic rather than the Mediterranean side. The water is usually safe to drink. State education, compulsory between ages 6 and 14, is free; private education (much of it run by the Catholic church) is not as expensive as in other countries.

Under the social security system, hospital and medical treatment is free, and 40 per cent of prescription charges are covered, but you will have to pay for dental work other than extractions. About 40 per cent of hospitals are private.

Prices in Spain are now much the same as in the UK. The following are examples of recent prices:

	Ptas
Beer (50 cl)	116.23
Bread (1 kg)	333.94
Butter (250 gm)	293.53
Cheese, Cheddar type (500 gm)	712.31
Chicken (1 kg)	434.95
Coffee	
ground (500 gm)	489.23
instant (250 gm)	1063.37
Cooking oil (1 litre)	201.85
Eggs (12)	236.54
Milk (1 litre)	114.66
Mineral water (1 litre)	39.53
Potatoes (1 kg)	78.52
Rice (1 kg)	254.28
Steak (1 kg)	1952.20
Sugar (1 kg)	148.64
Tea bags (250 gm)	1400.70
Whisky (75 cl)	1490.76
Wine (75 cl)	636.58
Cigarettes (20)	289.55
Petrol (1 litre)	116.71

Although English is much more widely spoken than it used to be, it would be very difficult to get by without a good knowledge of Spanish, and even then there are some pitfalls for the foreigner. It is advisable to appoint a personal agent (known as a *gestor*) to deal with legal matters and licence applications. Particular care has to be exercised in buying property, since Spanish property tenure is very complicated. The naive or unwary may find themselves buying a property hedged about with so many legal encumbrances as to be practically worthless. The annual rent on an unfurnished, four-bedroomed flat in Madrid would be Ptas 3.8 million.

Personal effects can be imported duty free by foreigners intending to establish permanent residence in Spain, and by foreign owners of holiday accommodation, if they guarantee to keep it in their possession for at least two years. A British national can also bring in a car, free of duty, provided the car has been registered in his name for at least six months.

There are estimated to be at least a quarter of a million British residents in Spain and these have created a market for private English-speaking schools which exist in most of the main cities Madrid, Barcelona and along the east and south coasts and in the Balearic and Canary Islands. Up-to-date information on fees can be obtained from Mr A Muæoz, Legal Adviser, National Association of British Schools in Spain, Avenida Ciudad de Barcelona 110, Esc. 3a, 5oD, 28007 Madrid.

Sweden

Background
Sweden, covering 174,000 square miles, is nearly twice as large as Britain, and is the fourth largest country in Europe. It has only 8.8 million inhabitants and the lowest population density in Europe: 83 per cent of Swedes live in urban communities, and Greater Stockholm has 1,534,000 inhabitants. The port cities of Malm and Gothenburg in the south have 237,400 and 437,300 inhabitants respectively. Main towns in the centre are Uppsala, V ster s and Norrk ping, and Ume and Lule in the north. Ninety-five per cent of the population are Lutheran Protestant.

It is a land of lakes and forests, flat along the coastal plain and particularly in the south, where 8.5 per cent of the population is concentrated. The north is mountainous and thinly populated.

Sweden is a parliamentary democracy; Prime Minister G ran Persson took over from Ingvar Carlsson early in 1996. The ruling Social Democratic Party replaced a non-socialist coalition in the 1994 elections. The king is head of state, but has no political power. Its one-chamber Parliament (*Riksdag*) is elected every four years. It is the archetype of neutralism and has not been involved in a war since 1814.

In a referendum in November 1994 the Swedish people voted to take up membership of the EU.

Exchange rate: Krona 12.36= £1.

The economy
Sweden is one of the world s most prosperous and politically stable countries, rich in natural resources and with a highly diversified manufacturing sector, particularly strong in engineering. Its economy is mainly private. The standard of management is probably the highest in Europe, and the emphasis is on technologically advanced and science-based industry. Sweden suffered from the recession. Unemployment in 1995 was up to 8.3 per cent (the highest recorded level since the war). Recovery is now under way. The new government has pledged to reduce public spending and the large budget deficit by 1998 through budget cuts and tax increases. Per capita PPU (see Austria) is 15,440.

The government encourages foreign investment and offers special incentives for its northern and western development areas. UK companies are second to those of the USA, both in number and in the total of employees. Immigrant workers represent about 5 per cent of the labour force, over 50 per cent coming from other Nordic countries which form a common labour market. Inflation is around 1 per cent.

Personal finance and taxation
Tax rates were reformed in 1990 and many employees no longer pay national income tax; marginal income tax has been reduced to a maximum of 50 per cent. Tax is paid to both national and local governments. The national income tax is 20 per cent for earned income over a set level. Local income tax is proportional, at a percentage of taxable income that is fixed each year; the average is about 31 per cent. Employers pay social insurance charges. VAT is 12 25 per cent on services and goods. Unemployment insurance tax was introduced in 1994 for all employed persons.

Working conditions

Sweden became a member of the EU on 1 January 1995, so residence and work permits are no longer required.

Although Sweden has been, and still is, short of skilled workers, it adopts a cautious attitude towards the employment of foreigners. As in Norway, there are openings for people who possess exceptional technical qualifications. Most British people work in a managerial or specialist capacity in a subsidiary or branch of a UK company.

The 40-hour, five-day week is standard, though hours may be slightly shorter for salaried staff. Opportunities for overtime are limited. Swedish workers are entitled to five weeks annual holiday with up to 12 public holidays. (There is no substitute day if the holiday falls on a Saturday or Sunday.) Periods of notice according to age and length of service are laid down by law in agreements. Employer employee relationships are highly egalitarian both in practice and in terms of legislation. Possibly for this reason, industrial disputes are rare.

Many employers provide subsidised canteens and contribute towards transport, holidays, health and leisure facilities. They are obliged in certain circumstances to provide language teaching, as well as housing, for immigrants. They bear a heavy proportion of contributions towards social security and pensions.

Living conditions

Sweden has one of the highest standards and costs of living in Europe. The following table lists recent prices:

	Kr
Beer (50 cl)	16.00
Bread (1 kg)	27.80
Butter (250 gm)	17.50
Cheese, Cheddar type (500 gm)	25.00
Chicken (1 kg)	43.21
Coffee	
ground (500 gm)	30.00
instant (250 gm)	79.84
Cooking oil (1 litre)	39.80
Eggs (12)	22.21
Milk (1 litre)	6.10

Mineral water (1 litre)	9.97
Potatoes (1 kg)	4.00
Rice (1 kg)	20.77
Steak (1 kg)	162.55
Sugar (1 kg)	10.93
Tea bags (250 gm)	44.21
Whisky (75 cl)	250.11
Wine (75 cl)	45.00
Cigarettes (20)	30.72
Petrol (1 litre)	7.95

Clothes are expensive   to buy an off-the-peg summer dress in the cheaper ranges would cost Kr975 and a man s off-the-peg suit about Kr3580. Prices of consumer durables are variable and it pays to shop around, but the cost of such items is certainly higher than in the UK (a washing machine costs about Kr6670).

The housing shortage, particularly in Stockholm, remains a problem for many people. Accommodation is often expensive, though less than in several other European countries. Housing exchanges in most towns help with finding accommodation. Two-thirds of all Swedes live in apartments, but there has been a popular movement against high-rise blocks in city suburbs.

The level of health care is high, and charges are generally modest (free to the under-16s). There is a fee of Kr120 for a visit to the doctor; house calls cost Kr170. Specialist consultation is up to Kr180. Emergency hospital admission is Kr180 250 but once you are admitted to hospital your treatment is free. Medication for hospital patients is free, but outpatients and those who are prescribed medicines by their GP must pay prescription charges. There are 11.9 hospital beds per 1000 people. The dental service is subsidised, and is free for children up to 18.

State education is free, and of a high standard. A third of pre-school children go to nursery schools run by the communities. Children of foreign residents have special courses in the Swedish language if they attend Swedish schools. There is an International School in Stockholm for children from 4 to 15. The syllabus is American up to junior high school level. The school caters for about 300 pupils.

Public transport is clean, efficient and universally available.

The Swedes drive on the right. The roads are mainly good and there are some motorways between the main cities in the south. UK and international driving licences are accepted; after two years you must obtain a Swedish licence. The main car manufacturers are Volvo and Saab. A Ford Escort would cost Kr127,700 approximately. If you import a car from the UK it must pass the very strict Swedish roadworthiness examination which includes tough exhaust emission tests. It can be very expensive to bring a car up to the required standard if it fails. Seat belts are compulsory and the laws on drinking and driving are very strict.

The Swedes are hospitable and enjoy parties. Most of all they enjoy their outdoor life. Many of the Stockholm business community have lakeside villas or cottages and there are ample facilities for sailing, fishing and swimming, or skiing in the winter. The Swedish winters are long, cold and dark and it is important to have plenty to occupy yourself with in the evenings.

Switzerland

Background
Switzerland is a small (16,000 square miles), land-locked country in central Europe. A land of mountains   the Alps and the lower-lying Jura range, which together comprise 70 per cent of the land area   and a central plateau with its lakes, it is very beautiful and has a large tourist trade, particularly in the winter when its skiing resorts are full. The population is about 7.1 million of whom 1.39 million are foreigners.

Switzerland has a strong democratic tradition and this is reflected in the jealously guarded liberties of each of the 26 cantons of the confederation. Caught between the traditional great powers of Germany, France, Italy and Austria, it has wisely steered a course of political neutrality in the last 150 years but the neutrality question is being reconsidered in the light of possible EEA/EU membership. As the standard bearer of internationalism, it has become the home of bodies such as the Red Cross and various UN agencies.

Exchange rate: Swiss francs 2.28 = £1.

The economy

Switzerland is prosperous commercially, and the main cities of Zurich, Basle, Geneva and Berne (the capital) are leading European banking and commercial centres. Agriculture is efficient and economic progress has been sufficient to attract large numbers of migrant workers, particularly from Italy. Apart from tourism and banking (crucial invisibles which help to offset the visible trade deficit), Switzerland s main manufactured exports are machines and metal products, chemicals and pharmaceuticals, electrical goods, precision instruments, textiles, clothing and watches. Its main markets are the EU and the USA. The country is politically stable, highly developed industrially and commercially, and strong enough to insulate itself from the worst effects of recession. The unemployment rate is 4.7 per cent. Inflation is currently around 2 per cent.

Language in Switzerland reflects its position in Europe: 64 per cent of the population speak German, 19 per cent speak French, 8 per cent speak Italian, 1 per cent speak Romansh and 8 per cent speak other languages as a first language. In practice, many people are bi- or tri-lingual, and most members of the business community are fluent in English, French and German.

Personal finance and taxation

Managerial salaries are among the world s highest.

Tax rates vary from canton to canton and from municipality to municipality. Taxes and social security contributions are around 30 per cent of income. Most expatriate employees will be subject to tax, though some categories of foreign teacher are exempt. Guidance on tax matters should be sought from the Federal Tax Administration, Eigerstrasse 65, CH 3003 Berne, Switzerland (tel: 031 322 7129), the local tax authorities or a Swiss tax consultant (*Steuerexperte*).

Working conditions

The Swiss government is at present reluctant to grant visas to foreign workers, and has imposed numerical limits on long- and short-term labour permits. In general, long-term permits are available only to people with special skills or qualifications who have been offered a position by a Swiss employer. Unsolicited applications are, therefore, not encouraged and have little or no chance of success.

Similarly, the government has reduced the number of seasonal permits covering periods of nine months or less and annual work permits. Employment opportunities have been correspondingly reduced, though there are still opportunities in the hotel and catering trades during peak tourist periods.

It is clear, therefore, that the best chance of long-term employment is with a British or American firm, or international agency with offices in Switzerland. Once you have obtained a position with a Swiss employer, or UK company based in Switzerland, your prospective employer must obtain the labour and residence permits you need. On entering the country you will need to produce a valid passport and an assurance of residence permit or a visa from the Swiss consulate and an employment contract.

Cost of living

If you succeed in finding long-term employment, remember that prices in Switzerland, particularly in the major cities, are high. Though prices have increased more rapidly in the UK than in Switzerland in the last few years, the latter is still more expensive.

The following table gives average prices of various items:

	SFr
Beer (50 cl)	1.30
Bread (1 kg)	4.00
Butter (250 gm)	3.05
Cheese, Cheddar type (500 gm)	10.54
Chicken (1 kg)	8.25
Coffee	
ground (500 gm)	7.30
instant (250 gm)	13.20

Cooking oil (1 litre)	4.30
Eggs (12)	6.60
Milk (1 litre)	1.70
Mineral water (1 litre)	0.80
Potatoes (1 kg)	1.60
Rice (1 kg)	2.30
Steak (1 kg)	42.90
Sugar (1 kg)	1.55
Cigarettes (20)	3.00
Petrol (1 litre)	1.26

Private boarding school education is expensive as is membership of private sports clubs. Facilities for winter sports are, of course, excellent.

Living conditions

Communications in Switzerland offer no difficulties except in the upland region where, in winter, snowfalls are hazardous. The railway and air networks are dense and highly efficient. So too is the road system, despite the difficult terrain. Car prices are comparable with prices in the UK. Banking is highly developed and it will be easy to find a bank which will carry out transactions with your UK bank. Swiss currency can be freely exported.

Accommodation is not easy to find, and rents in good parts of the main cities are high. Ideally, your employer should look for good accommodation for you. For a reasonable, four-roomed, unfurnished apartment in urban districts, you might expect to pay from SFr1500 upwards per month. (Furnished apartments are almost non-existent in Switzerland, so you will have to arrange to bring your furniture with you.) A double room with bath in a luxury hotel will cost SFr190 380 a night.

Switzerland is, in general, a healthy place to live; however the incidence of AIDS in the country is among the highest in Europe. Expatriates are strongly advised, in their own interest, to join a health insurance scheme from the very beginning. You should seek information from your employer on this point. The insurance should comprise not only medical and hospital treatment but also adequate sickness benefit, since employees have only a limited claim to payment of wages in the event of illness. Most people in Switzerland are insured against illness and accidents through various kinds of insurance scheme. The most popular ones, the so-called *Krankenkassen*, try to exert control over physicians fees. For private patients and patients covered by other types of insurance, physicians usually charge more, according to income. Specialists, as a rule, charge significantly more than general practitioners.

Social insurance agreements between Switzerland and various other countries make it easier to join specific health insurance schemes and in certain circumstances shorten the waiting period. Under some agreements, moreover, the Swiss employer is required to make sure that an employee coming from the country concerned is insured for medical care (doctor and hospital) and, if he is not, to take out adequate insurance for him; he can deduct the contributions for this from the employee s wages. In cases of doubt enquiries should be addressed to the appropriate consulate.

The Swiss have a reputation for insularity and coolness, but this is misjudged. Expatriates will, for the most part, find them good colleagues and warm friends. Living standards are high and opportunities for recreation and entertainment are plentiful (though playing membership of, say, a golf club near one of the main cities would be very expensive). Your business and social life is greatly eased and improved if you can speak one or more of the indigenous languages, and few employers now send people to Switzerland who do not have some proficiency in French and/or German.

Eastern Europe

Some trends are now beginning to emerge in the expatriate job market in Eastern Europe: Poland, Hungary, the Czech and Slovak Republics, former East Germany, Rumania, Bulgaria, and the former Soviet Union   Russia and the Commonwealth of Independent States (CIS).

A considerable number of American and West European companies have set up offices or bought or invested substantially in enterprises in these countries, but they are moving cautiously in an undercurrent of instability in the economies of several of them. Mostly they are putting expatriates in the top jobs and hiring locally below that level. They are also sending out middle-ranking expatriates as project managers to kick-start or investigate the potential for new enterprises or to fill specific skill gaps and train locals to take over from them. The area most often cited here is in financial management, a discipline unknown under Communism.

This also highlights a cultural problem that Western managers encounter when they go to work in Eastern Europe. People who have had this experience report that their local subordinates and colleagues are largely unfamiliar with concepts like profitability, decision-making, acting on their own initiative or taking responsibility. Though often technically very competent the standard of education and training in spheres like engineering is very high throughout Eastern Europe the extent of management in Eastern Europe under Communism was to fulfil the plan , or target in Western terms, no matter what. That accounts, for instance, for the appalling environmental pollution to be found throughout the area. In fact environmental clean-up is one of the areas of opportunity for firms and individual specialists from the West.

The economies of the East, and hence the job opportunities that they offer, vary widely. The Czech and Slovak Republics are generally reported to have made the most progress. By 1995 over 90 per cent of Czech state enterprises had been privatised. Output and GDP have grown since 1993 and unemployment is low at 4 per cent. However, in Slovakia the privatisation programme was suspended in 1994 after the election of a new coalition government with a lukewarm attitude to economic reform. Hungary, which was the first of these countries to break with Communism, has been a disappointment, and the economic transition has been difficult there, although privatisation and new small businesses have been successful. The government introduced an austerity budget in March 1995 to reduce inflation. East Germany has also had difficulties, with post-unification output falling by 60 per cent, and high unemployment. Economic improvement started in 1994 with both inflation and unemployment falling dramatically. Russia s economy remains turbulent despite a period of stabilisation in 1994/5 when inflation was temporarily under control. It is too early to tell if the economy will be able to restabilise and if it does, how long this will take.

The differences illustrate the impact of cultural factors on economics. Hungary, for instance, has a strong entrepreneurial tradition but not a strong corporate one. Small enterprises are doing better than larger joint ventures between Hungarian and Western firms. The unexpected success of the Polish economy has been put down to the readiness of Polish ØmigrØs to return and train their fellow countrymen in Western ways.

The relative failure of East Germany to change may be due to the lack of flexibility in the German management culture, as well as what are now seen to have been mistakes at the time of reunification: notably, giving parity to the East German Mark and the DM. This has made it virtually impossible for the rust-belt industries of the East to compete with the West. The resulting high unemployment in East Germany, coupled with a wave of immigration of people from poorer economies hoping to use the East as a staging post to West Germany, have resulted in social unrest.

Throughout Eastern Europe, crime is now a new factor to be faced by expatriates. It is a product of rising unemployment, coupled with inflation, both of which are generally understated in the official figures. Average inflation throughout Eastern Europe is reckoned to be around 20 per cent. Prices in countries which were comparatively cheap two or three years ago, notably Hungary, Poland and Czechoslovakia, are now comparable with those in Western Europe. Rents are high too, but these are mostly paid by the employer, as are local taxes.

On the positive side, except in Russia almost everything is obtainable, though quality remains a problem. This is also true of services. Expatriates report long waits and poor workmanship from tradesmen like plumbers, electricians and telecommunications workers. In fact, the poor standard of the communications network is widely cited as a problem in both personal and business terms.

There are also occasional shortages of everyday goods. A manager in Budapest tells of not being able to hang pictures in his new office because hammers were not available in the shops that week. The reason for such shortages, he says, is that shops cannot afford to hold back-up stocks. In Hungary the situation is exacerbated by the fact that the Forint is not negotiable so that imports have to be paid for in hard currency. This is also the situation in several other former Eastern bloc countries.

The Budapest manager has in fact elected to base himself in Vienna and to travel back there at weekends. He says that many expatriates in Eastern Europe would do the same if they could. With the exception of Prague, most of the cities are drab and there is little to do, especially for wives, whose employment prospects are very limited unless they can find jobs in another company with Western connections. Even that is difficult unless they have a good command of the local language.

You can get by in the principal cities of most Eastern European countries with English and German, but only up to a point. Ultimately, learning the local language is inescapable and essential for anyone working there. That is why many of the jobs on offer go to former refugees, or their children. European emigrants have a good record of keeping up their native language.

At top levels, what companies are looking for are good general managers who are financially aware, have good marketing skills and can provide some evidence of a track record in the field of international management. Functionally, the job opportunity most widely cited is, as stated above, in financial management. There is also a demand for marketing people. In East Germany, one recruiter reports that there is currently a shortage of managers and professionals in the building industry   somewhat surprisingly in light of the fact that this is one of the sectors that has been hardest hit by the recession elsewhere. Overall, one of the most important generic attributes that recruiters look for is the ability to train local managers in Western practices and attitudes.

The Middle East

The risks faced by expatriates in this region were brought home forcefully by the events leading up to the Gulf War. The long-term effect of these events is uncertain but expatriates will need to be more rather than less sensitive to local cultures.

The Arab Countries: Some Notes on Etiquette

One of the things that worries expatriates about living and working in the Arab world is the idea of having to conform to a society whose customs and etiquette are very different from our own. All sorts of stories circulate about niceties of social behaviour, failure to observe which will mortally offend the Arabs, but most Arabs you are likely to meet will have travelled or studied in the West and be quite used to Western ways. Of course, if, while talking to an Arab, you lounge in your chair in an arrogant or disrespectful fashion, it will not go down well. Nor will it be appreciated if you smoke, eat or drink in the presence of Moslems during the holy month of Ramadan, the time when their religion enjoins abstinence from such activities. But what one is really talking about then is simple good manners, and simple good manners will take you a long way in contacts with members of your host country.

This is not to say that there are not some points of etiquette that you should bear in mind on such occasions as you come into social contact with local people. If you are invited to dinner in an Arab country you will be expected to arrive on time (although Arab guests to your home will be much more casual about punctuality). You should be very careful about admiring any object in the house in which you are a guest because your host may press you to take it as a present, but he will, in due course, expect a present of at least similar value from you. When food comes, you will have more heaped on your plate than you can eat. It is not considered bad manners to leave most of it, rather the reverse, because to leave nothing on your plate suggests you think the host has not been sufficiently generous. If food is being eaten with the fingers (or indeed when you are offering anything to an Arab), use your right hand only; the left is considered impure, since it is associated with what one might politely call the exercise of intimate bodily functions.

If there are long periods of silence over dinner, do not consider yourself a social failure. Arabs do not regard constant talk as a social necessity. Nor should you be taken aback if they ask you rather personal questions this goes for talk between women in particular. They are not restrained as we are about the things concerning other people that we are dying to know but are always too polite to ask while hoping they will come back to us in the form of gossip. Nor should you feel the evening has gone badly if your Arab guests leave immediately after dinner. This is customary, and they expect you to do likewise. Incidentally, few Arabs, except the more westernised and sophisticated, will bring their wives in response to an invitation, and neither will they expect the guest to do likewise.

There are other points of social etiquette as well, and if you are being asked into an Arab home or vice versa, you should certainly seek advice from someone who knows the local scene. It is worth acquainting yourself before your departure with the dos and don ts of everyday behaviour. For instance, all Arab countries, even the more liberal ones, frown on what the Americans politely call public displays of affection between the sexes. Women wearing revealing clothes are apt to attract attention which varies, according to the country, from what would be described in the UK as rude stares to being told by the police to go home and put on something more suitable. It is unwise to argue with the police in an Arab country since the processes of justice are, to say the least, different from those in the West. This does not mean, even in Saudi Arabia, that they will cut off some valued part of your anatomy if you are found guilty of a crime; but they will unceremoniously put you on the next plane out of the country if they do not like your behaviour. The public flogging incidents which received so much publicity are extremely rare (as far as Westerners are concerned). This sort of punishment would only be put into practice in the face of the most open and provocative breaches of the law. However, in countries where Koranic law is strictly observed, particularly in Saudi Arabia, there is no right to representation in court and lengthy periods of arrest before trial can occur. On the positive side Islamic law lays great emphasis on the fulfilment of contractual obligations by both parties.

Drinking is severely punished in the various countries where alcohol is forbidden and it is criminal and foolish to try to smuggle it in. This does not mean to say that smuggling of alcohol does not go on. There are a few places where whisky is available, at prices of up to £80 a bottle. But it is best to leave smuggling to others; and if you are offered smuggled booze be very discreet about drinking it no raucous parties and avoid being seen under the influence in public.

The maxim about good manners getting you a long way also applies to business etiquette. There will be some things about business contacts that you will find frustrating or annoying but you will just have to accept them with good grace. For instance, Arabs are lax about keeping appointments; and when you do get to the person you may have waited hours or even days to see, all sorts of individuals will probably pop into his office while you are there and interrupt your conversation for minutes on end. Arab customs are also different concerning the acceptance of gifts. This is a tricky one for businessmen, but a lot of what we could castigate as bribery is the normal custom in an Arab country. This is not to say that you should go about trying to bribe people to get favours this is generally considered to be a bad idea because, as a Westerner, you would not know who to bribe and how to go about it for a start but if you are offered a present in a business context you should not refuse it, unless it patently *is* a bribe. To a Moslem, the return of a gift implies that it is unworthy of the recipient and can be a tremendous slap in the face for the giver. It is difficult to tread the narrow path between integrity and self-righteousness, but then few things about leaving home to go and work in another country are easy though they are nearly always interesting.

One final question that tends to be asked now is whether and to what extent the backlash against Western ways and influence which marked the Iranian Revolution has spread to other Moslem countries. Certainly, extremists seized on the furore caused by Salman Rushdie s book, *The Satanic Verses*, to advance the cause of fundamentalism, which means there is unlikely to be any loosening up of observances regarding alcohol consumption, dress, religious holidays and so on. But while the possibility of upheaval can never be entirely discounted in countries going through a period of such radical changes as at present, informed opinion regards them as unlikely.

Egypt

Background

Egypt is about four times the size of Great Britain, but about 95 per cent of the country is virtually uninhabitable desert, a fact which gives cause for alarm about its rapidly growing population, estimated at 65 million and increasing annually at about 3 per cent. An estimated 13 million people live in Greater Cairo and another 3.4 million in Alexandria. The rest are concentrated largely in the Nile valley and delta.

Politically, Egypt is a democratic socialist country headed by President Muhammed Hosni Mubarak.

During the past few years, support for Moslem fundamentalism has grown in Egypt, particularly among the poorer sections of the community, who see the establishment of a wholly Islamic state as a remedy for the country s economic and social problems. Early in 1995 there was a new surge of unrest against the moderate regime.

Exchange rate: Egyptian pounds 5.46 = £1.

The economy
The need for development aid is focused on the problem of housing and feeding Egypt s large, impoverished and increasingly urban population. The potential for instability has been brought to the fore on a number of occasions in the shape of serious rioting. Worrying factors are a fall in oil revenues and a sharp reduction in the inflow of money from Egyptians working in other Arab countries. Economic growth has improved under an IMF reform programme, with inflation falling to 7.3 per cent in 1994. Theoretically, with its large population, Egypt could become the manufacturing centre of the Middle East. It is here, in construction and in oil and hydro-electric power, that most of the development is going on and where European expatriates are mostly employed.

Personal finance and taxation
Unified tax rates are 20 and 32 per cent, plus 2 per cent development duty. Foreigners living in Egypt are liable to income tax, but allowances are generous and tax on an average expatriate salary would be around 30 to 35 per cent. Salaries for expatriates are generally lower than in the UK. Arrangements should be made to have some paid outside the country, since although in theory up to 75 per cent of one s Egyptian income can be remitted out of the country, in practice this is reported to be very difficult. A further advantage in having part of one s salary paid outside the country is that it is not then liable to Egyptian tax. It is, in fact, common for expatriate salaries to be paid in hard currency outside Egypt, with only as much as is required for living expenses being brought into the country.

A work permit is needed, which must be arranged by the local employer. It is advisable to take a plentiful supply of passport photos and duplicates of essential documents as bureaucracy in Egypt is an industry in its own right and there are many occasions on which form filling, supported by documents, is called for. Reserves of patience are also advantageous, for the Egyptians, though extremely nice people to deal with, are not noted for speed or efficiency.

Living conditions

The two main cities are Cairo and Alexandria. Both have long, hot summers, where the temperature averages 32 C and can be higher, and short winters. These run from November to March and though mild by European standards they do require warmer clothing and a certain amount of indoor heating on colder days. In upper Egypt temperatures are much higher, though it is a dry heat. Alexandria, on the other hand, is inclined to be humid because of its position by the sea.

Egypt need not be an expensive country to live in, provided one does not rely on imported food. Local fruit and vegetables are cheap and good, though it is essential to wash them if eaten fresh   preferably in boiled or filtered water, since tap water is not recommended. Overall, food is much cheaper than in the UK, though prices at the big hotels are geared to international standards.

Here are some examples of recent prices:

	£E
Beer, bottled (50 cl)	4.08
Bread (1 kg)	5.92
Butter (250 gm)	3.69
Cheese, Cheddar type (500 gm)	10.23
Chicken (1 kg)	8.19
Coffee	
ground (500 gm)	32.41
instant (250 gm)	46.15
Cooking oil (1 litre)	5.22
Eggs (12)	3.10
Milk (1 litre)	2.70
Mineral water (1 litre)	0.84
Potatoes (1 kg)	2.07
Rice (1 kg)	5.34
Steak (1 kg)	20.94
Sugar (1 kg)	1.92
Tea bags (250 gm)	14.63
Whisky (75 cl)	91.62
Wine (75 cl)	64.19
Cigarettes (20)	5.34
Petrol (1 litre)	1.06

Current annual rents in Cairo for a furnished three-bedroomed flat range from £E25,000 to 39,000; rents are lower in Alexandria. Many expatriates, however, are employed on remote sites (usually on single-status contracts), with purpose-built accommodation provided. In finding accommodation (if it is not provided by the employer) it helps greatly to work through an agent, whose guidance on local practice and general know-how should be well worth the 30 per cent of one month s rent he takes in commission. Two important and sometimes over-looked requirements to brief him on are the orientation of the windows they should not face the sun during the hottest hours of the day and the availability of a telephone, which otherwise can take months or even years to install.

Air conditioning, though generations of expatriates lived without it, is considered essential for modern standards of com-fort. Like other household effects air-conditioning equipment can be bought locally, but it is generally advisable to bring it with you. Electricity is provided at 220V, 50 Hz AC, but power cuts and unevenness in supply can play havoc with equipment. Plugs are usually the two-pin, round variety. A device called a voltage stabiliser is therefore an essential adjunct to any electri-cal goods you bring with you. There is little difference between the price of electrical goods in Egypt and the UK, so they are probably best bought locally.

Efficient household equipment is all the more necessary because good servants are increasingly difficult to find, though wages of £E250 a week (for 30 hours) for a live-out cook (£E300 live-in) and £E150 for a live-out maid are very reason-able. They generally work from 7.30 am to 3.00 pm and expect overtime for longer hours plus a modest yearly bonus. Dry cleaning is available only at the major hotels.

Locally assembled cars can now be bought and a Peugeot 405 will cost about £E80,000. Because of import restrictions, second-hand cars can be as expensive as new ones. The state of the roads is poor but improving, so cars need to be serviced every 1500 kilometres or so.

The local situation regarding schools is quite good but they are expensive. Medical attention is also good in theory Egyptian doctors are much sought after throughout the Middle

East but the standards of hygiene in hospitals can leave something to be desired. Private hospitals are much better in this respect. Egypt insists on HIV tests for anyone staying longer than a month. As far as recreation is concerned, Egypt has plenty to offer. Social life is much more relaxed and varied than in other Middle Eastern countries. There are no constraints on the consumption of alcohol and the practice of Islam, though universal, is not exercised with any degree of fanaticism.

French and English are widely spoken.

The Gulf States

Economies
Oil is the salient factor in the economies of all the Gulf States, although the level of reserves varies. Most of these countries are making efforts to diversify into other activities and to invest oil revenues in the creation of infrastructure. Bahrain is developing large-scale industrial enterprises, including aluminium smelting and shipbuilding; it has a longer-established trading tradition and is an important offshore banking centre. It is emerging as a regional centre for technology and light industry. Oman, whose oil reserves are modest by Middle Eastern standards, is developing copper mining and smelting, cement production and fisheries; it also has a programme to expand health, education, communications and public services such as electricity and water. Qatar produces fertilisers and cement, and is also making rigorous efforts to develop its agricultural industry.

Bahrain

Bahrain is composed of a group of 33 islands in the Arabian Gulf with a total land area of some 230 square miles. The capital city and chief business centre of the country is Manama, which lies at the north-east end of the main island, with Isa Town, a largely residential area, situated seven miles south of the capital. Oil was first commercially exploited in Bahrain in

1932 and now provides 75 per cent of export earnings. Owing to the gradual decline in crude oil production during the past few years and the fact that present reserves are forecast to last only until the late 1990s, the government is actively encouraging foreign investment in diversified industrial development with some success. Recent estimates put the population at about 550,000, increasing at a rate of 3.5 per cent a year, one-third of whom are expatriates.

There is at present much concern over the terrorist activities of the Shia Muslim Opposition who want the Sunni rulers to restore parliament, dissolved in 1975. Martial law has been threatened. The unrest is escalating, with recent bombs targeting luxury hotels. Westerners have been warned by their embassies to be careful.

Bahrain is governed by an hereditary Amir who is advised by a Cabinet of Ministers. Arabic is the official language but English is widely spoken, particularly in commercial circles. Although the usual Moslem observances are kept, Bahrain is generally thought of as one of the more progressive, relaxed and hospitable Arab states to which expatriates should have little difficulty in adjusting. There is no income tax.

Examples of prices may give some indication of the cost of living:

	BD
Beer (50 cl)	0.81
Bread (1 kg)	0.93
Butter (250 gm)	0.39
Cheese, Cheddar type (500 gm)	1.44
Chicken (1 kg)	1.26
Coffee	
ground (500 gm)	3.44
instant (250 gm)	3.45
Cooking oil (1 litre)	0.76
Eggs (12)	0.62
Milk (1 litre)	0.51
Mineral water (1 litre)	0.24
Potatoes (1 kg)	0.90
Rice (1 kg)	0.80

Steak (1 kg)	4.17
Sugar (1 kg)	0.37
Tea bags (250 gm)	2.20
Whisky (75 cl)	11.10
Wine (75 cl)	4.99
Cigarettes (20)	0.39
Petrol (1 litre)	0.10

Rents are variable: a three-bedroomed unfurnished apartment in Manama is about BD350 per month.

The basic unit of currency is the Bahrain dinar (BD), divided into 1000 fils.

Exchange rate: BDinars 0.61 = £1.

Kuwait

Kuwait lies at the head of the Arabian Gulf and is bordered to the north and west by Iraq and to the south by Saudi Arabia. Its land area comprises some 6900 square miles. The population is estimated at around 1 million, nearly half of whom are foreigners (the government intends to keep this proportion down to 40 per cent). The capital and commercial centre of the country is Kuwait City which is situated on Kuwait Bay. The rebuilding of Kuwait, liberated from Iraqi occupation in 1991, is generating renewed opportunities, and Kuwait is also rebuilding its armed forces, and replacing industrial managers. These expenses are a drain on the economy. However, up-to-date information remains difficult to come by. Certainly, it is not likely to attract any but the toughest, single-status, pioneering-minded expatriates though for them the rewards may well be considerable.

Salaries in Kuwait are still high, and there is a high standard of living, including free education and health care. English is the second language.

The unit of currency is the Kuwaiti dinar, divided into 1000 fils or 10 dirham.

Exchange rate: Kuwaiti dinars 0.50 = £1.

Oman

The Sultanate of Oman runs in a 1000-mile long narrow strip around the south-eastern corner of the Arab peninsula. Its most northern point is separated from the rest of the country by the United Arab Emirates. The total area is about the same as that of the UK, but 97 per cent of the country is desert or mountains. Population is 2 million of whom 623,000 live in the area of the capital Muscat and its neighbouring port, Mutrah, which is also the commercial centre.

Oman is an independent state, ruled by Sultan Qaboos Bin-Said. Politically and economically, it is favourably disposed towards the UK, which is reflected in the relatively large British community. It is fairly stable politically. Inflation is 1.4 per cent.

The government is steadily reducing the high percentage of expatriates in the labour force.

Anyone going to Oman, even on a non-business visit, must previously obtain a No Objection Certificate issued by the Sultanate immigration authorities and obtainable in the country by the employer or a local sponsor. The NOC is necessary in order to obtain a visa even for family visitors. This proviso does not apply, though, to visitors born in the UK, who can obtain visas in London for visits of less than 14 days duration.

The official language is Arabic, but English is widely understood in business circles.

The unit of currency is the Omani rial, divided into 1000 baiza.

Exchange rate: Omani rials 0.62 = £1.

Qatar

Qatar, which is one of the smaller OPEC countries, consists of a narrow peninsula of some 4000 square miles which juts northwards 100 miles into the Arabian Gulf with Saudi Arabia, Bahrain and Abu Dhabi as neighbours. Situated on the east coast of Qatar is the capital city and chief commercial centre, Doha, a fast-developing, modern metropolis from which 1080 km of excellent roads radiate to the rest of the peninsula. Other important urban centres are Umm Said, also on the east coast, which is the centre for industrial development and on the west coast, Dukham, which is a major oil-producing centre.

The population of Qatar is estimated at around 50,000 of which about 52 per cent live in Doha. Qatari nationals constitute about one-third of the total with large communities of Indians, Pakistanis, Northern Arabs, Iranians and Gulf Arabs. The British community is thought to number about 6000.

Qatar is governed by an hereditary ruler, His Highness The Amir Sheikh Hamad bin Khalifa Al Thani, who assumed power in June 1995 after overthrowing his father. A coup attempt in February 1996 was foiled, but the deposed Emir has vowed to return to power.

Provided the usual Moslem etiquette is observed (for example, both men and women should dress modestly in public), most Western expatriates will find their private lives are not markedly affected although expatriates have been warned to stay away from troubled areas. Expatriates can obtain a liquor permit from the British Embassy in Doha.

The unit of currency is the Qatar riyal, divided into 100 dirhams.

Exchange rate: Qatari riyals 5.85 = £1.

United Arab Emirates
Abu Dhabi

Abu Dhabi is the largest and richest of the seven Emirates which make up the UAE. Its ruler is also President of the UAE. It has a population of about 889,000 of whom only 22 per cent are Abu Dhabians, the rest being Arabs from other countries, Indians, Pakistanis and Europeans, of whom there is a sizeable community.

The main population centre is Abu Dhabi town, which is on an island ten miles long and which until relatively recently was little more than a fishing port. There are some handsome buildings, a choice of Western-style supermarkets, several sports clubs, and a surprising amount of greenery planted along boulevards and in parks.

A three-lane ring road including an airport link and downtown tunnel is under construction. Most of the rest of the Emirate, which is about the size of Scotland, is desert. The oasis town of Al-Ain, 100 miles inland, is a fast-growing population centre, however, and is the site of the UAE s university. Oil in large quantities has been found both on and offshore, the centre of the offshore oil industry being Das Island, about 80 miles out in the Gulf.

Dubai and Sharjah

Dubai and Sharjah are the two neighbouring Emirates to the north of Abu Dhabi. The population of Dubai is around 560,000 (three-quarters of whom are foreigners) and of Sharjah about 380,000. Most of them live in towns of those names, though Dubai actually consists of twin towns: Dubai and Deira. Sharjah town is only some nine miles from Dubai. In both of these Emirates oil has been discovered only in the last few years, though Dubai was an established commercial centre as an entrep t for Middle East trade for a century before. Constant building and road-making are indications of continuing prosperity. Dubai is promoting retailing with a view to sustaining the economy after the oil runs out in 2005.

Dubai is generally considered a more pleasant and sophisticated place to live in than Abu Dhabi. The area is becoming a tourist region; trees have been planted, resulting in greater rainfall.

The other emirates are Ajman, Umm Al Quwain, Ras Al Khaimah and Fujairah. Expatriates account for 90 per cent of the UAE workforce.

Living costs
The cost of living in the UAE is hard to judge; however, the following list of prices may be some guide:

DUBAI COLLEGE كلية دبي
Moving to Dubai?

(Established in Dubai (1978) by decree of H.H. The Ruler)

Dubai College is a British-style secondary day school of 650 pupils conveniently situated between Dubai and Jebel Ali in a purpose built complex with very good educational and recreational facilities, and an academic record well above the U.K. average.

Small classes of children in the age range 11-18, taught by graduates of British universities, follow a curriculum leading primarily to London University (Home Centre) G.C.E. 'A' Levels, K.S.4/G.C.S.E.

P.O. Box 837, Dubai, U.A.E.
Telephone (9714) 481212
Fax: (9714) 480175

	Dh
Beer (50 cl)	6.05
Bread (500 gm)	8.71
Butter (250 gm)	3.64
Cheese (500 gm)	13.66
Chicken (1 kg)	14.63
Coffee	
ground (500 gm)	28.94
instant (250 gm)	33.91
Cooking oil (1 litre)	9.17
Eggs (12)	7.86
Milk (1 litre)	5.01
Mineral water (1 litre)	1.59
Potatoes (1 kg)	3.93
Rice (1 kg)	7.80
Steak (1 kg)	37.00
Sugar (1 kg)	3.45
Tea bags (250 gm)	19.95

Whisky (75 cl)	77.53
Wine (75 cl)	48.19
Cigarettes (20)	3.87
Petrol (1 litre)	1.02

The currency unit of the UAE is the dirham (Dh), divided into 100 fils.

Exchange rate: UAE dirham 6.00 = £1.

The economy

The UAE is one of the richest nations in the world. Investment in productivity and infrastructure are increasing throughout the UAE. Oil is the main commodity. Dubai is an important banking centre, and its harbour is one of the largest in the Middle East. Abu Dhabi has invested in building up its infrastructure roads, schools, housing, hospitals, hotels and developing the harbour. Water is in short supply, so the development of desalination plants is another area of investment.

Personal finance and taxation

Expatriates should be earning considerably more than the equivalent UK salary, with generous fringe benefits: certainly free or heavily subsidised accommodation; provision for medical treatment; payment of school fees or help with them; six weeks home leave a year, with air fares paid in the case of married men and spells of two to three weeks leave every four months for bachelors; and probably provision of a car and, in the case of a managerial job, at least one servant. There is no personal income tax and there are no restrictions on the amount of currency which may be taken into or out of any of the Gulf States (but check UK tax regulations if employed by a UK domiciled company).

Working conditions

Work and residence permits, and a medical certificate, are required in every emirate. Dubai will only issue permits if skills are not available locally.

Throughout the Gulf, you would be well advised to take a supply of passport photos with you, to help speed up the process of obtaining official documents. You should also check for last-minute changes to visa requirements, which are apt to be brought in with minimal notice. At present, passports bearing evidence of a visit or a proposed visit to Israel will still cause some problems though this restriction may be lifted; you are advised to consult your nearest Regional Passport Office.

Friday is the weekly holiday. Saturday and Sunday are normal working days.

Living conditions
The region is characterised by hot and humid summers, with temperatures over 100 F, the worst months being July, August and September. Air conditioning and lightweight clothing are essential. It may be possible to find local tailors who will make copies of Western clothes at a reasonable price. Designer clothes are expensive compared with the UK.

With most expatriate postings, free or subsidised accommodation is usually offered along with the job, and it is usually of a high standard, fully furnished and air conditioned. Property cannot be bought, and must be rented. A three-bedroomed unfurnished house in Abu Dhabi costs from Dh14,000 per month. A municipal tax of 5 per cent in Dubai (or 2 per cent in Sharjah) is levied on rental. Servants are generally immigrants. A houseboy will cost Dh800 1400 per month, a good cook Dh1100 2000.

A car is essential, and most are large: four-wheel drives are popular. New models can usually be bought at prices slightly lower than in the UK, although not all British makes are available. A Toyota Corolla costs Dh53,450. Check with the local police about driving licence regulations; you will be able to obtain a UAE licence on payment of a fee, presentation of a valid British licence and passing an eye test.

Electricity is supplied at 220 volts, 50 cycles AC in Abu Dhabi and 240 volts, 50 cycles AC elsewhere, but can be unreliable.

On the thorny matter of alcohol, exercise discretion. Non-Moslems are usually able to buy alcohol for private consumption, but in the UAE it is necessary to obtain a liquor permit from the police.

There is usually a lively social scene in the form of parties and dinners. Leisure naturally centres on the outdoor life   bathing and fishing at the beach, picnicking and camping in the desert during the cooler part of the year. Facilities for organised sports such as golf or tennis are available through clubs or hotels, but they tend to be expensive.

Most expatriates in the UAE belong to private medical schemes, funded by their employers. However, state-run facilities are generally of a high standard. A health card (costing Dh250 per year) is required for non-emergency treatment at government hospitals.

There are a number of British and International schools with three months summer holiday, although many parents prefer to send their children to boarding school in the UK.

The official language throughout the region is Arabic, but English is spoken widely in business and official circles.

Saudi Arabia

Background

Saudi Arabia occupies over 70 per cent (approximately 920,000 square miles) of the Arabian peninsula and shares borders with many Arab countries; a large part of it is desert. A national census taken in 1992 showed a total population of 16.9 million, about a quarter of whom are nomadic or semi-nomadic. Two-thirds of the remainder are urban dwellers, mostly living in the larger cities: the capital, Riyadh, and Jeddah, the chief port and commercial centre, the sacred cities of Mecca and Medina, and Al Khobar and Dhahran, in the centre of the oil industry. That industry is situated in the eastern province along the Gulf. Saudi Arabia is the world s third largest oil producer and leading exporter of oil; new oilfields are still being discovered. Investment in manufacturing and light engineering is growing.

The country is ruled by its conservative royal family, headed by King Fahd. His brother, HRH Crown Prince Abdullah, took over power from November 1995 to February 1996 after King Fahd suffered a mild stroke. The rulers sympathies are strongly with the West, particularly with the USA.

Suadi Arabia is traditionally ultra-conservative and adheres to strict codes of conduct in moral and religious matters.

The unit of currency is the Saudi riyal (SR), which is subdivided into 100 halalas.

Exchange rate: Saudi riyals 6.06 = £1.

The economy

The backbone of the economy is, of course, oil. The country is rich in other minerals and much is being done to exploit them. Gold, silver and copper are now being produced. The income from oil has been largely devoted to improving the country s infrastructure, developments such as petrol refining, gas liquefaction plant and other petroleum-based activities, and the expansion of a wide range of manufacturing industries. There has also been a good deal of investment in agriculture to increase self-sufficiency. Another major form of investment has been in various measures of water conservation and deployment and there are now 33 desalination plants.

Apart from water, Saudi Arabia s scarcest resource is trained manpower and the country is heavily dependent on foreign skills (there are about 4.1 million foreigners residing in Saudi Arabia). For this reason a great deal of money is being put into education at all levels. In the longer term, this may reduce Saudi reliance on foreign labour, and already Saudi graduates have, to some extent, taken over middle-level posts in banking and administration which were previously held by Indians and Pakistanis. But at the extremes of the labour market highly skilled technicians and professionals, and labourers it seems unlikely that reliance on foreign workers can be reduced for some time to come. Inflation is 1.8 per cent.

Personal finance and taxation

Salary differentials between Saudi Arabia and the UK are not as high as they were, but you could still expect to increase your UK gross salary by up to 25 per cent, on average. Salaries are highest in the more arduous, inland posts. These high salaries are accompanied by generous fringe benefits, which include furnished accommodation, ample home leave with air fares paid, a car, medical attention, and free or subsidised education for children in the case of more senior jobs. The level of remuneration reflects the rather arduous social and climatic conditions in the country, which women in particular find hard to take.

There is no personal income tax in Saudi Arabia, and no restriction on the amount of currency that may be taken into or out of the country.

Working conditions

Work permits must be applied for by your Saudi agent, employer or contact in the country. When this is forthcoming you must supply its details to the Saudi Embassy which will issue a visa. This is apt to be a lengthy procedure and plenty of time must be allowed for the documentation to come through. It is a good idea to have smallpox and cholera vaccinations, and polio, TB and anti-tetanus are also advisable.

A particular point to bear in mind is that, if you arrive in the Haji (pilgrimage to Mecca) time, special precautions against cholera have to be taken and certified. Check details before leaving as conditions are sometimes changed without notice. The Saudi Arabian Embassy in London requires all expatriate residents in the Kingdom to undergo an AIDS test before they are issued with visas.

The working week runs from Saturday to Thursday. Work often starts early in the morning, at 7.00 or 8.00 am, with a long break in the afternoon, but working hours are variable, depending on region and prayer times.

Telephone services, internationally and between towns, have improved, as has the post. Deliveries are made to box numbers at the main post offices, except in the case of hotels and government offices.

Foreigners should carry their ID, driver s licence and residence permit at all times. It should also be borne in mind that exit visas are required to leave the country and these sometimes entail bureaucratic delays before you get them. You also need a letter of release if you are changing employers within Saudi Arabia. The conditions under which you can terminate your employment should therefore be clearly set out in your contract.

Many jobs, particularly at more junior levels, are single status. Where accompanying wives are allowed, you are advised to bring several copies of your marriage certificate.

Living conditions

For most of the year the places where expatriates are likely to find themselves in Saudi Arabia are extremely hot and summer temperatures of 42 50 C are usual. Almost all buildings are air-conditioned. Around Jeddah and the eastern province oilfields, humidity is high and even during the winter season (December to March), it is never really cool. The interior is dry and, though equally hot in summer, can get very cold in winter. Thus warm clothing is necessary in winter in places like Riyadh. There is little rainfall anywhere, although irregular heavy showers do occur in the winter months. Prevailing winds come from the north and sometimes produce uncomfortable dust-storms.

Clothing is available locally, but the range is limited and expensive (a man s suit costs about SR2300), so it is best to take it with you. Take plenty of lightweight articles and a few medium-weight things for winter wear. You must be careful about clothing etiquette. Men should not wear shorts in public and there are very severe restrictions on what is considered proper for women in public. Thus, no revealing dresses (dØcolletØ or see-through), no hems above the knee, sleeves at least to the elbow, trousers only if worn with a top that goes below the thighs and, on the beach, one-piece bathing costumes only.

It is best and not too expensive to buy electrical equipment locally. Electricity is supplied at 110V or 220V, 60 cycles AC and many places have facilities for both. Refrigerators (costing around SR2300) and air conditioners (or air coolers) are essential.

It is forbidden to take photographs of airports, military installations, or other sensitive buildings such as government offices or institutions and foreign embassies. Photography is better tolerated in rural areas than in the city, but care should be taken not to photograph individuals (without their consent) and particularly not veiled women.

Nearly all jobs advertised for Saudi Arabia offer free accommodation, usually furnished. A three-bedroomed house would cost SR80,000 24,000 per year to rent. A good hotel will cost about SR300 a night.

Executive jobs tend to include domestic help as a fringe benefit, though you will first have to find your servant. Saudi women are not allowed to work and the personnel available are Arabs from other countries, Filipinos, Indians, Pakistanis and North Africans. Ethiopians and Sudanese are considered the best bet, but you should try to get someone recommended to you by another expatriate. A driver is paid SR1200 2000 a month. Although members of the business community speak English, servants seldom do so and a basic knowledge of Arabic is therefore useful, as well as being a courtesy much appreciated by your Arab contacts. It is advisable to insure servants against injury as employers can be held liable for damages, and it is a good idea to get them to take a medical before you employ them.

All kinds of food are available in the large city supermarkets, including baby products. Here are some prices:

	SR
Bread (1 kg)	6.38
Butter (250 gm)	5.05
Cheese, Cheddar type (500 gm)	16.94
Chicken (1 kg)	10.61
Coffee	
ground (500 gm)	27.23
instant (250 gm)	32.42
Cooking oil (1 litre)	7.49
Eggs (12)	15.63
Milk (1 litre)	4.35
Mineral water (1 litre)	2.26
Potatoes (1 kg)	3.54
Rice (1 kg)	6.19
Steak (1 kg)	29.95
Sugar (1 kg)	3.31
Tea bags (250 gm)	18.03
Cigarettes (20)	3.94
Petrol (1 litre)	0.58

It is usual to carry cash, although cheques are accepted more often than previously. Women are not allowed to drive which means that they must either walk or take a taxi, unless they are lucky enough to have a chauffeur. In fact, although cars are essential and petrol is comparatively cheap, owning one is not without its hazards. Driving standards are poor but improving; there is no legal insurance requirement, but the compensation that has to be paid for an accident involving loss of life is high. Maximum comprehensive cover and third-party liability are most strongly advised, although expensive. However, the consequences of being involved in a traffic accident are always serious and the Saudi police tend to deal more strictly with offenders than is common in the West.

A wide range of models is available but British cars are not really a good buy. Japanese ones are the most popular. A Toyota Corolla costs around SR45,000. A car usually goes with the job, in any case with executive or supervisory posts. You will need a Saudi licence which may be obtained, with a three-month delay, on production of a UK one. Eyesight and blood tests are also required.

Facilities for recreation in Saudi Arabia are extremely limited, and boredom, particularly for wives, is a major problem. There are no tourist-associated facilities and, with the exception of restaurants, there are very few facilities for public entertainment, not even cinemas. A few of the big corporations expatriate townships have their own private recreational arrangements, but these are also very limited. There are, however, some good places for outdoor recreation, especially swimming and other kinds of water-based pursuits. Saudi television has an English-language channel. It is generally possible, also, to pick up English TV channels from Bahrain and other countries in the Gulf as well as Sky News, if there is a satellite dish. Video rentals are popular.

The health situation is good, though intestinal upsets are not uncommon. Some places are supplied with potable water, but in other areas it should be bought in bottled form. Expatriate jobs generally include free medical attention, and hospitals in the main centres are extremely good. Private treatment, of course, is very expensive   even an ambulance journey to hospital costs around SR600. Oculist services are improving but if you need glasses you should bring spare pairs with you. Sunglasses are also a good idea, because of the strong glare.

There are several International and American schools for children up to the age of 15. There are British private primary schools in Jeddah, Riyadh and Al Khobar. Below this level there are playschools run by expatriate wives. On the whole, taking children of school age to Saudi is not a good idea and in any case places are very hard to get.

It must be remembered that the import of alcohol is forbidden and visitors should not try to take alcohol with them, even in small quantities. The penalties are severe. The import of pork, pigmeat products, salacious literature, narcotics, firearms, games of chance and non-Islamic religious symbols/books is also forbidden. No formal religious practices other than Islam are allowed and discretion should be exercised when *informal* religious practices are engaged in.

Africa

Kenya

Background

Kenya is one of the most important and advanced countries on the African continent. It lies within the tropics, almost exactly astride the equator, and has long coastline borders on the Indian Ocean. It covers 225,000 square miles and has over 30 million inhabitants with a rapidly rising birth rate and a very young population. Nairobi, the capital and chief political and commercial centre, has around 1 million inhabitants and is a modern, prosperous and sophisticated city. It is followed in size by the port of Mombasa, an island set into the coast with some 800,000 inhabitants.

Kenya has borders with Sudan and Ethiopia to the north, Somalia to the east, Uganda to the west and Tanzania to the south. Over half the land is arid, but the central areas and west are fertile and cultivable, with plateau and upland country rising to high mountains   Mount Kenya is about 17,000 feet high, and Nairobi is 5432 feet above sea level. Its climate is pleasant and invigorating, whereas it is hot and humid on the coast. The main rainy season is from April to June.

The population includes Europeans, Asians and Arabs. There are some 35 tribal groups. The national language is Swahili and a working knowledge of this language is advisable, although English is used everywhere. There are Anglican and Catholic churches in most towns and other Christian denominations, as well as Moslem faiths.

Kenya, first colonised by the British in the 1880s, achieved independence in 1963, and is a republic within the

Commonwealth. Daniel Arap Moi succeeded Jomo Kenyatta as President on the latter s death in August 1978, and was re-elected in 1983, 1988, and 1997. Moi is President of the ruling party, KANU.

Exchange rate: Kenya shilling 99.72 = £1. (Though not an official unit of currency it is common practice to refer to a Kenya pound symbol £K to denote 20 Kenya shillings (KSh). There are 100 cents to the shilling.)

The economy

Kenya is best known for its tea and coffee, which form the backbone of the economy. Other crops include wheat, sugar, sisal, cotton, fruits and vegetables. Tourism is the most important source of foreign exchange, having overtaken coffee in 1988 as the main foreign exchange earner.

Eighty per cent of the population derive their livelihood from agriculture, which accounts for 52 per cent of exports.

There are few mineral resources, but the government is encouraging exploration. The manufacturing sector is being expanded it includes food processing, canning, chemicals, drink, tobacco, car assembly, paper and printing, metal products, textiles, clothing, footwear and cement. An oil pipeline links the Mombasa refinery with Nairobi.

The government welcomes foreign investment, but it is anxious to see that as much commerce as possible is handled by indigenous Kenyans. As part of the on-going economic reforms, the government has divested itself of many enterprises, some of which have been sold to foreign investors, who consider the Kenyan atmosphere a favourable one.

Economic development is based on national planning, with emphasis on agriculture and manufacturing and on encouraging export and labour-intensive industries.

Britain and Germany are the principal trading partners and the UK a major provider of external aid, particularly in sending experts, teachers and technical advisers.

There are serious balance of payments imbalances and annual inflation is in single digits. In 1995 it was 1.6 per cent. Unemployment and under-employment have remained serious problems, particularly among the young. These are exacerbated by Kenya s rapid population growth.

Coffee, which is of high quality, is Kenya s major crop, but has suffered from unstable prices and rising costs. Tea has also suffered from the same problems, and only a permanent recovery of tea and coffee prices would significantly reduce the strain on the economy. The government has decided to modernise coffee production, mainly carried on in small farms on the slopes of the mountains, and improve harvesting and distribution methods.

Despite deriving much power from hydro-electricity, Kenya has suffered because of rises in the price of oil. This has been accentuated by fluctuations in coffee prices and the effects of drought which also created poor economic conditions in Kenya s neighbouring export markets in East Africa.

Personal finance and taxation

Most employers provide housing and make allowances for children s education, cars, etc.

Income tax is charged on total income (including benefits in kind) and ranges from 10 per cent to 40 per cent. Personal allowances are given for single and married people, but there are no allowances for children.

Working conditions

A valid passport is needed, but most Commonwealth citizens do not need a visa, except Australian, New Zealand, Sri Lankan, Indian and Nigerian citizens and British passport holders subject to control under the Immigration Act of 1971. Many other nationalities qualify for a visa-free three-month stay. Entry permits vary according to the type of employment. Applicants must show that they have adequate financial resources and that their activities will benefit the country. It is advisable to check immigration regulations with the authorities, as these are liable to change.

A work permit must be obtained by the employer from the Principal Immigration Officer (PO Box 30191, Nairobi) before the employee leaves Britain. The PIO s permission is needed for dependants to work. Work permits for wives, unless they are professionally qualified, are hard to obtain.

Working hours are as throughout tropical Africa, ie 8.00 am to 5.00 or 5.30 pm. There are eleven public holidays, both religious and official.

Living conditions

The inflation rate has dropped to single digits and import restrictions have been repealed. Generally speaking, basics are cheaper, luxuries more expensive than in the UK. You can save money, and vary your diet, by shopping in local markets for meat which is usually of good quality, fish, dairy produce, vegetables and fruit.

Examples of prices are as follows:

	KSh
Beer (1 litre)	46.37
Bread (1 kg)	45.98
Butter (250 gm)	77.83
Cheese (500 gm)	281.22
Chicken (1 kg)	243.88
Coffee	
ground (250 gm)	281.37
instant (100 gm)	412.71
Cooking oil (1 litre)	115.16
Eggs (12)	73.99
Milk (1 litre)	29.96
Mineral water (1 litre)	52.61
Potatoes (1 kg)	25.45
Rice (1 kg)	54.52
Steak (1 kg)	302.26
Sugar (1 kg)	49.21
Tea bags (250 gm)	128.41
Whisky (75 cl)	1670.39
Wine (75 cl)	771.29
Cigarettes (20)	115.48
Petrol (1 litre)	33.96

There are occasional shortages of certain canned goods. The quality of meat is said to be good but often spoilt by bad butchering. Most people drink beer, which is of high quality. The local tipple, Kenya cane, is a cross between vodka and rum. Local wine is produced in the Naivasha region.

Prices of standard household goods are very much as in the UK, but those of imported consumer durables are considerably higher. A refrigerator, for instance, would cost nearly three times as much as in the UK.

Imported European and American clothes are expensive, but locally made clothes are sufficient for casual wear. Tailoring and dressmaking are usually of good standard, but it is advisable to bring as much as you need from home   lightweight clothes plus woollies for high altitudes. Most businessmen wear short-sleeved shirts and trousers, and many also wear a tie. Some hotels and restaurants require more formal dress.

There is no shortage of housing in Kenya, not even in Nairobi, where increasing numbers of international organisa-tions are establishing headquarters. Most employers supply accommodation, whether part or fully furnished, but it may be necessary for a newcomer to stay for several weeks in a hotel before a house or flat becomes vacant. It is probably advisable for the husband to travel out alone and send for his family later. Security is a problem. Burglary and more violent crimes are not uncommon and it is advisable to keep children playing at home rather than, for example, in the street or in public places.

There are excellent hotels in Nairobi and in the main tourist areas, guest houses and game park lodges. Prices at Nairobi hotels are around US$148 a night for a single room in a four-star hotel, with meals extra. Advance booking is essential during the high season (December to April). Details of hotel and guest accommodation can be had from the Ministry of Tourism, Utalii House, off Uhuru Highway, PO Box 30027, Nairobi, or from the Kenya Tourist Office, 25 Brook s Mews, London W1Y 1LF.

Electricity is supplied at 240V, 50 cycles AC in most centres and the supply is reliable. Lamps are mainly bayonet fitting; plugs are two-pin round and three-pin flat types. Adaptors are useful when travelling. Water is drinkable in the towns, and bot-tled water is widely available.

Most household and electrical goods can be bought in the main stores, and the range of locally produced articles is steadily rising. But it is probably cheaper to bring as much as possible check that electrical equipment from the UK is suitable for Kenya.

Most expatriates employ one or more domestic servants, who often live in, and wages are low (averaging about KSh1400 a month).

Housebreaking, car thefts, pickpocketing and pilfering are on the increase, so it is essential to take precautions. Mugging is also becoming increasingly common, particularly in Nairobi and Mombasa. Many expatriates employ guards.

Shopping hours in the main stores are from 8.00 am to 5.00 or 6.00 pm but many have late shopping some nights of the week and some open on Sunday. There are numerous banks, and they are open from 9.00 am to 3.00 pm Monday to Friday and 9.00 to 1 pm on certain Saturdays. Personal services such as dry-cleaning and hairdressing are fully available in Nairobi and Mombasa. Well-known brands of toilet articles and cosmetics can be bought, but at twice the UK price.

International and national air services operate from Nairobi and Moi (Mombasa) International Airports. The main railway line runs from Mombasa to Nairobi and beyond and services include sleeping compartments. Local rail and bus travel are usually avoided. State-controlled taxis and international car hire companies are found at both airports. A private car is essential for people staying any length of time and should be tough enough to withstand difficult conditions. New and second-hand cars can be bought locally, but are about twice as dear as in the UK. A new Toyota Corolla costs around KSh1,900,000. Servicing facilities are adequate in Nairobi, but if you are taking your own car it is advisable to contact the manufacturer beforehand about spare parts, etc. Roads are of fairly high standard. Driving is on the left. There is an AA of Kenya with headquarters in Nairobi. A valid British or international licence, which should be endorsed at a police station on arrival, is accepted for up to 90 days, thereafter exchanged for a Kenyan one no test is imposed. The AA and RAC have reciprocal arrangements with the Kenyan AA. Distances are given in kilometres, and petrol sold in litres.

Outside the cities, roads are poor. It may be necessary to have a Landrover-type vehicle there. Many expatriates have two cars, though cars are very expensive. If you have to buy your own it is best to go for a cheaper model; otherwise they are difficult to re-sell when you leave the country.

Airmail from Europe takes about four days, surface mail six to ten weeks. There are full facilities for telephoning, telex and fax.

Kenya is, in general, a healthy place in which to live, apart from the risk of AIDS which is now considered to be prevalent in many parts of Africa and is affecting both the male and female population. It is preferable to seek medical treatment only after consultation with the British High Commission. There are the usual tropical hazards, particularly along the coast. Anti-malarial drugs should be taken. Medical standards are high, particularly for private facilities in Nairobi. The National Hospital in Nairobi is managed, administered and staffed at senior levels by British staff. Doctors fees are expensive, however, and medicines, so bring out what you need. Hospital fees can be reduced through the National Insurance fund but, where insurance is not provided in their contract, many expatriates subscribe to a locally available scheme.

There is a network of district hospitals, clinics and dispensaries, and also mission hospitals. Very remote areas are served by a flying doctor service, which requires a small annual subscription.

Most expatriate parents send their children to private primary schools, but many of these have long waiting lists. There is generally no problem about placing children in nursery schools and kindergartens. The Nairobi International School takes in children for both primary and secondary schooling, though fees are high. It follows the US curriculum but most private schools are geared to that of Britain. There are schools in Mombasa and most other centres; some schools take boarders. There are a number of convent schools. Nairobi University, the Strathmore College of Arts and the Kenya Polytechnic admit students of all nationalities.

The main English language newspapers are the *Standard*, *Daily Nation* and *Kenya Times*; there are several weeklies and monthlies and most UK papers can be bought in Nairobi and Mombasa. There is one national radio station in Nairobi with provincial sub-stations in Mombasa, Kisumu and Mount Kenya. There are three TV broadcasting stations and one cable station. Recently, more companies have been licensed to operate TV and radio stations.

About 25,000 British people live in Kenya, mainly in Nairobi and Mombasa. There are also communities of Asians,

Americans and other Europeans. Life is more cosmopolitan and sophisticated, as well as more relaxed, than in many African countries. A number of clubs provide social and recreational facilities (many employers pay your subscriptions) and there are opportunities for sports, including motor and horse racing, and for museum visiting. Most towns have cinemas, libraries and swimming pools and Nairobi has a great variety of restaurants, of all nationalities and at all prices. It has a repertory theatre and a music conservatory. There are many local amateur dramatic and musical activities. In general, Western influences are inherent in the arts.

Most people spend their weekends and leave periods exploring the country, going on safari to the nature and wildlife reserves, camping, bird watching, riding, fishing, photographing or swimming and surfing at the coast. The wildlife, country and the coast are unbelievably beautiful.

British people in general feel at home in Kenya, where the climate is very agreeable and life is not so different from the UK as in some West and East African countries. The Kenyans are hospitable and mix easily with Europeans. There seem to be fewer frustrations in day-to-day life than in many developing countries. Kenya has been one of the most politically stable countries in Africa, maintaining good relations with all nations and, despite its current problems, has made considerable economic progress.

Nigeria

Background

Nigeria, covering an area of 356,000 square miles, has an estimated population of 116 million and is the largest and most influential state in black Africa. Despite the economic problems of the past few years, it still employs a considerable expatriate managerial and technical force from both European and Asian sources.

The country falls into two geographical parts: the southern tropical rain forest area that includes the coastal area, and the more arid northern plains that stretch to the fringe of the Sahara desert. Temperature in the south is generally about 84 F with a humidity almost as high. The rainy season begins in April/May and continues until September/October with a short break during August. Temperatures in the north are sometimes above 90 F and rain is restricted to the midsummer months. The *harmattan*, a dust wind from the Sahara, can be a nuisance to air traffic and is prevalent from November to February. The ethnic groups of the north, the Fulani and the Hausa, are mainly Moslem, while the people of the south are mainly Christian.

The commercial capital, Lagos, is in the south of the country, as are the other major ports of Port Harcourt, Warri and Calabar. With the movement to the new federal capital Territory Abuja of all the government ministries and parastatals, the population of the new capital has swollen to more than 3 million.

The British administered the country from 1914 to 1956 and granted self-government in 1956 and independence four years later. English is the *lingua franca*. The goodwill between Nigeria and Britain has been strained recently after an international outcry over executions and in November 1995 Nigeria was suspended from the Commonwealth for two years pending democratic elections. The political situation remains unstable after the death of General Sani Abacha and it is too early to see what policies his successor, General Abdulsalem Abubakar, will follow. There are estimated to be over 8000 British expatriates living there. Half of the total foreign investment in Nigeria is of British origin. American influence has grown in recent years.

The unit of currency is the Naira (N), which is divided into 100 Kobo.

Exchange rate: Naira 35.15 = £1.

The economy

Nigeria is a major oil producer, but during the 1980s much of its oil wealth was squandered and a huge external debt built up. To cope with the crisis, austerity measures   endorsed by the IMF   have been implemented since 1986. Further economic reforms were introduced in 1995, but Nigeria s economic prospects remain disquieting. Corruption is endemic, reforms difficult to implement, the infrastructure is deteriorating and unemployment rising.

Successive governments have been aiming to diversify the economy away from oil, to encourage the development of agriculture and industry, and to overhaul the infrastructure   particularly transport, power supplies and water. Increased spending on social services is also planned, to ease the adjustment of an urban population which has experienced falling living standards over the past few years.

Personal finance and taxation
Income tax is progressive, at rates varying from 10 to 35 per cent. To attract investment, the Federal Government, in the 1997 budget, removed all ceilings to amounts that could be remitted into or outside the country. An investor now has the right to wholly own a company or in conjunction with any person. There is no limit to the amount he could repatriate or bring into the country.

Working conditions
All visitors except nationals of certain neighbouring countries require a visa (easily obtainable for nationals of Commonwealth countries). A visitor s permit will last for a maximum of three months. Expatriates working in Nigeria require a resident s permit and this is obtained by the employer within the quota allowed to the company.

Nigeria acknowledges both Christian and Moslem holidays as well as May Day and Independence Day (1 October).

Living conditions
Motor maintenance and spares are costly. Comprehensive insurance may be about N2000. In Lagos road conditions have improved considerably, although there can be long delays at peak periods. Parking is a perennial problem and, to the uninitiated, driving (on the right) in Nigeria can be hazardous. Meals out are expensive. A meal at one of the few good restaurants will start at £30. Lebanese and Chinese restaurants provide the best food. A list of sample prices will give you some idea of day-to-day costs:

	N
Beer, bottled (50 cl)	34.26
Bread (1 kg)	136.79
Butter (250 gm)	129.67
Cheese, Cheddar type (500 gm)	389.73
Chicken (1 kg)	226.79
Coffee	
ground (500 gm)	864.91
instant (250 gm)	1139.75
Cooking oil (1 litre)	322.28
Eggs (12)	96.02
Mineral water (1 litre)	28.91
Potatoes (1 kg)	33.64
Rice (1 kg)	133.59
Steak (1 kg)	281.50
Sugar (1 kg)	96.06
Tea bags (250 gm)	408.00
Whisky (75 cl)	857.74
Wine (75 cl)	817.39
Cigarettes (20)	59.45
Petrol (1 litre)	11.00

Most manufactured goods are imported and are therefore expensive. There is, however, a vigorous black market in smuggled goods which may cost less than their UK equivalents.

Housing is expensive and difficult to find. Typical rents for an unfurnished, three bedroomed flat will be N550,000 to 850,000 a year in a good part of Lagos, though much cheaper elsewhere. Many companies, particularly construction companies, build and provide their own housing in company compounds for both single and married employees. While this has the added advantage of security, it does limit social contact with the indigenous population. The main voltage in Nigeria is 220 volts, however, most hotels/flats have outlets for 110 volts electric showers. You need a standby generator because of the supply situation. Household goods are also very expensive locally and your contract should include a substantial air baggage allowance. Surface mail takes months.

Most expatriates employ a cook/steward, a driver, a nanny and a night-watchman. A cook s wages would be N470 for 47 hours per week, plus accommodation in the south, but much less in the north.

Because of the conditions of working in Nigeria, leave tends to be generous, particularly with companies who operate in other overseas markets. Three tours of three months a year with one month s leave after each tour is not uncommon, although a tour of six months is more normal.

Anti-malarial pills should be taken regularly starting two weeks before each tour and continuing for four weeks after. It is also advisable to obtain immunisation against yellow fever, tuberculosis, typhoid, tetanus, polio, cholera, hepatitis A and B. There were epidemics of spinal meningitis, gastroenteritis, cholera and measles in the north of the country in early 1996. AIDS is also a problem in this area. Water should always be boiled and fruit and salads carefully cleaned. Swimming pools can be a health hazard and advice should be sought from residents. Exposure to the sun can be a danger, particularly in the north. If there is a need to be hospitalised it is best to return home if possible. AIDS is now considered to be prevalent in many parts of Africa, and is affecting both the male and female population. The virus can be contracted through sexual contact or through medical treatment involving the use of hypodermic or blood transfusion equipment which may be infected. It is advisable to seek such treatment only after consultation with the British High Commission. State hospitals have difficulty in maintaining international standards of hygiene while private hospitals tend to be expensive and commercially orientated.

Credit cards are not generally used in Nigeria and are accepted in only one or two hotels in Lagos. Credit is not usually given. There are good hotels in the major cities of Lagos, Abuja, Kano, Port Harcourt and Enugu. Hotels require a deposit covering all likely expenditure in advance and in cash, and payment by non-residents has to be made in hard currency or in foreign currency at the local rate of exchange. A single room in a 5 star hotel in Lagos will cost around US$100 to US$290 a night. Most hotels are air-conditioned but the equipment may not be functioning. There is often a shortage of water and electric power. Hotel food is poor but improving.

All retail purchases are made in cash. A cheque from one state to another can now be cleared within ten working days. Only certified cheques, or bank drafts, are accepted as currency. Cheques tend to be used only to draw cash from one s own local branch. Banking hours are 8.00 am to 3.00 pm on Mondays and 8.00 am to 1.00 pm Tuesdays to Fridays. Some banks now offer Saturday banking from 10.00 am to 3 pm.

Trunk roads linking the various state capitals have improved considerably in recent years. A motorway runs from Lagos to Ibadan, and from Lagos to Benin. However, within Lagos itself traffic conditions are horrendous. For instance, you have to allow about four hours to get to the airport. Poor road maintenance can cause some hazards, and road accidents in Nigeria are very frequent. It is not safe to drive after dusk because of the risk of accidents and highway robbery; be cautious about unsolicited assistance with transport or other facilities. Travel by rail is slow and not recommended.

Most state capitals now have airports, the most recent addition being Makurdi, Benue State. Regular services are frequent, but delays can occur because of poor weather conditions. Bribery, known as dash , may be necessary to clear customs and immigration. In the north, a private airline links the state capitals, in competition with Nigeria Airways, and has a good reputation.

Nigeria Airways and British Airways provide daily flights from the UK to Nigeria and many international airlines operate daily schedules to Nigeria. Most continental airlines have a weekly or bi-weekly service. There are three international airports: Ikeja, 17 miles from Lagos; Kano, in the north; and Port Harcourt, 22 miles from the town of Port Harcourt. Nnamdi Azikiwe International Airport in the new federal capital territory was commissioned in 1997. Where airports are some distance from the town only taxis operate. Care should be taken to ensure that the taxi is properly marked and that a reasonable fare has been agreed upon before the journey begins. Ideally, visitors should always be met at the airports.

The telephone system is notoriously inefficient. While it is now possible, within Nigeria, to call most of the major cities direct in theory, in practice it requires a lot of patience, owing to the overcrowded telephone system. International direct dialling services are being introduced and calls can be made direct to the UK from certain phones, including those at the offices of NITEL (Nigerian Telecommunications).

International post takes a minimum of six days (airmail) and four to six weeks by surface mail. Documents are better despatched by courier, particularly as mail can get mislaid. Internal post takes about seven to ten days.

Telex is fairly reliable, though this depends on an efficient and keen operator at the Nigerian end and also on a source of electric power, which on occasions can be unobtainable.

There are some fax machines in Nigeria, but it is not a common means of communication as it relies on an already congested telephone system.

The newcomer to Nigeria should understand that, while with care he will probably have a trouble-free tour, there *is* a crime problem in Nigeria. This takes a variety of forms: car thefts, usually only of new Peugeot cars, housebreaking, mugging and highway robbery. While appropriate precautions will vary from time to time, it is generally not considered safe to travel out of town at night.

Most state capitals still have the old British clubs alongside Nigerian ones and these provide opportunities for swimming, tennis, golf, squash, etc and for meeting both Nigerians and other expatriates. Membership of one club provides affiliated membership to the others. There are swimming pools in all the major hotels. Cinemas are to be found in most of the clubs and also in some of the larger hotels.

Most expatriates send their children to UK boarding schools at an early age and certainly for secondary education. There are private International Schools in Nigeria, often staffed by Europeans, which cater well for the ages of 5 to 9 and provide a congenial atmosphere. There are International Schools in Lagos, Ibadan, Kano and Kaduna. Fees tend to be somewhat higher than in equivalent schools in the UK.

South Africa

Background

South Africa is divided into nine provinces covering 471,000 square miles. Its 1996 Census gave a population figure of 37.9 million. Most of the white population of around 5 million live in the four main industrial centres: an area within a radius of 100 miles around Johannesburg; Durban; Port Elizabeth; and the Western Cape. Although South Africa is principally thought of in terms of mining and the country has large reserves of virtually every mineral with the significant exception of oil it does in fact engage in a broad range of industrial activities. The newcomer will see, in this respect, few differences between South African cities and those of any other industrialised nation.

The differences lie under the surface though not very far and are a product of racial tension and the political system which was evolved to control it. The white population is 13 per cent of the total racial mix of Europeans, Africans, Indians and people of mixed blood. Racial segregation has been dismantled, although the psychological effects will linger for many years to come.

The April 1994 election introduced a five-year coalition government with an African National Congress majority and Nelson Mandela as President, and a new interim constitution. The final constitution was passed in December 1996 and took effect on 4 February 1997. The National Assembly and Provincial Legislatures are elected by proportional representation, as was the Senate, which has now been replaced by the National Council of Provinces comprising ten delegates from each province. The federal-style government allows substantial devolution of power to the provinces.

There is now hope that, despite continuing violence in the townships, peaceful change is possible in South Africa. However, at present there are unstable regions in the country and it is dangerous to stray off the beaten track away from safe areas.

Exchange rate: Rand 8.98 = £1.

The economy
Inflation is around 7.7 per cent, and GDP is steadily rising. South Africa was hit not only by sanctions but also by the falling price of gold, its principal export. Since the lifting of sanctions at the end of 1993, inward investment into South Africa has been able to give a boost to industry, and provide funds for housing, jobs and education. Gold and commodity prices have stabilised   a positive development for trade.

Personal finance and taxation
South Africa has lately been declining in the world salary league table. Taxes are now relatively high, and there are few concessions in the way of rebates. New income taxation rates were introduced effective from 1 March 1997. So, for example, anyone (married or single) earning a salary of R80,000, would have to pay a flat rate of R20,850 plus 44 per cent of the amount over R70,000. The minimum rate of income tax levied is 19 per cent.

Fringe benefits are not a significant part of remuneration, although managerial jobs generally earn a car and holidays tend to be generous, six weeks a year being frequently quoted. Free or subsidised medical aid schemes are frequently offered to more senior people. If these are not available such costs, and they are considerable, should be borne in mind in assessing the true value of the remuneration package.

There is a wide variety of indirect sales duties, the most significant of which is on cars. The remission of duty on personal effects is marginal and it is not worth bringing a car into South Africa. A new Toyota Corolla costs around R60,000. You can drive on a UK licence for the first six months of your stay, but after that you have to apply for a South African one, which is normally granted to anyone with a recognised overseas licence.

If you are an approved immigrant you may, however, import one motor vehicle per family under full rebate of customs duty (but subject to VAT), provided that the motor vehicle has been owned and used by you and registered in your name, in your country of residence, for at least 12 months before your departure and before the date on which it was shipped to South Africa.

There are no restrictions on the amount of foreign currency you can bring in, but strict exchange control regulations are in force on taking money out of South Africa. For this reason, it is advisable to transfer no more of your assets than you need to South Africa unless you are absolutely sure you want to stay there. You have to declare the existence of overseas assets to the bank when you get to South Africa, but they will normally allow you to keep them abroad, subject to your making certain undertakings. For instance, you must not make them over to a South African resident, as this would be an obvious way of circumventing the regulations.

Working conditions

At executive and professional level, working conditions (ie hours and leave) are very similar to those in the UK. There has been little industrial unrest in South Africa, though it has increased recently. Wages are fixed by industrial councils and vary according to occupation and region. Welfare benefits are minimal compared with the UK, although health care is now free, and numerous private schemes for medical care, pensions, disability, etc do exist on a contributory basis and about 85 per cent of the white population belong to a scheme of some kind.

There is an active immigration scheme and most UK professional qualifications are recognised in South Africa. The scheme is selective, the criteria being primarily the state of the economy at the time and the extent to which the applicant s qualifications and experience fit in with its needs. However, immigrants are not allowed to change occupation without approval for three years after their arrival in South Africa. This is related to the availability of work. Prospective immigrants should write to the Chief Migration Officer, South African High Commission, Trafalgar Square, London WC2N 5DP for further information. If you are thinking of working in South Africa for a more limited period, application for a work permit may be made to the same address.

Living conditions

South Africa s climate is excellent, though by no means uniform. There is quite a difference at all times of the year between semi-tropical Natal, the Mediterranean climate of the Western Cape and the dry, cold winters and hot, thunderstormy summers of Johannesburg. These varied conditions make it possible for all foodstuffs to be grown locally, though they are no longer particularly cheap. All in all, and allowing for variations such as the fact that there is no National Health Service in South Africa, the cost of living is a good deal less than in the UK bearing in mind the international value of the Rand. A refrigerator would cost around R2400, a washing machine R2700, and a colour TV set R2700. Other prices are as follows:

	R
Beer (50 cl)	2.90
Bread (1 kg)	3.10
Butter (250 gm)	4.43
Cheese, Cheddar type (500 gm)	14.67
Chicken (1 kg)	11.48
Coffee	
ground (500 gm)	22.68
instant (250 gm)	28.26
Cooking oil (1 litre)	5.55
Eggs (12)	5.14
Milk (1 litre)	2.56
Mineral water (1 litre)	4.48
Potatoes (1 kg)	2.79
Rice (1 kg)	4.39
Steak (1 kg)	40.58
Sugar (1 kg)	3.36
Tea bags (250 gm)	9.44
Whisky (75 cl)	43.07
Wine (75 cl)	21.82
Cigarettes (20)	4.17
Petrol (1 litre)	2.02

As in any move to a new area, it is unwise to plunge into buying a new house without first disentangling the subtleties of congenial and uncongenial neighbourhoods. Rented accommodation is, however, in fairly short supply. An unfurnished three- to four-bedroomed house in Johannesburg will cost from R42,000 to R78,000 a year. House prices are lower than for similar properties in the UK but it is essential to check that good security arrangements have been installed. As in this country, it is highly advisable to consult a solicitor before signing either a lease or a deed of sale.

Many people in South Africa employ servants, who normally receive free meals and accommodation in addition to their wages, which are around R500 a month, or R6 an hour for part-time workers. A new Act sets out maximum hours and overtime for domestic workers.

Education in state schools is free, but schools are allowed to charge a small fee to cover miscellaneous expenses. There are, of course, plenty of private fee-paying schools as well. Children who will not have reached the age of six before 1 July of the year of admission will not be allowed to attend school, even if they have done so previously. The school year begins after the Christmas holiday. It should be noted that the syllabus and atmosphere of South African schools is markedly more traditional and restrictive than is the case in most other countries. University education is not free.

Zambia

Background

Zambia is over three times the size of the UK and its population at the latest estimate is about 8.6 million and growing rapidly. It includes about 20,000 expatriates, mainly Europeans.

The country is landlocked, bordering on Tanzania and Zaire to the north, Malawi and Mozambique to the east, Zimbabwe, Botswana and Namibia to the south and Angola to the west. Most of the land is plateau, with an elevation of 3500 to 4500 feet, intersected by rivers, of which the Zambezi is the most important. There are high peaks in the Muchinga mountains to the north-east.

Zambia is the most urbanised country in black Africa and more than a million people live in the Copperbelt. The capital, Lusaka, is a rapidly expanding city with around 1 million inhabitants. In the Copperbelt, Kitwe is the main city (348,500) with Ndola (376,500) on its outskirts. Livingstone (84,116) is the main centre in the south.

English is the official language. The principal African languages are Nyanja, Bemba, Tongu, Lozi, Lunda, Luvale and Kaonde. Christians make up 80 per cent of the population, but there are Moslem and Hindu minorities, and some Africans follow traditional beliefs.

Because of its altitude, the climate is temperate, with extremes of heat and cold in summer and winter. The rainy season is December to March.

Zambia became independent in October 1964, after the breakdown of the Central African Federation. The United National Independence Party (UNIP) waged a successful campaign against the CAF and its domination by white Southern Rhodesia. The UNIP governed the country from 1964 until 31 October 1991 when the first multi-party elections for 23 years took place. The elections were contested mainly by the two major parties the UNIP and the MMD (Movement for Multiparty Democracy) with the MMD gaining a strong majority. The MMD formed the first government with President F J T Chiluba as head of state, and is transforming the economy into a free-market system. The UNIP staged a coup in 1993 and allegations of corruption led to the resignation of MPs and ministers in 1993/94. Zambia is a member of the Commonwealth, the UN and the Organisation of African Unity (OAU).

The administration is divided into nine administrative provinces: Lusaka, Central, Copperbelt, Eastern, Luapula, Northern, North Western, Southern and Western.

Exchange rate: Kwacha 2128.49 = £1 (after declining rapidly in value between 1989 and 1993, the Kwacha has since remained stable). Foreign exchange shops exist in which currency can be exchanged at the prevailing market rate.

The economy

The economy is based on copper, which accounts for about 95 per cent of foreign exchange earnings, and is highly sensitive to fluctuations in world copper prices. As a result of falling world copper prices and increased oil prices Zambia has faced serious economic difficulties and a huge balance of payments deficit. The Zambian economy was adversely affected by drought during 1992 causing a decline in agricultural output and cuts in electricity generation.

About 50 per cent of the people are engaged in agriculture, the main crops being tobacco, sugar and maize. Farming is on a subsistence basis. Like other developing countries, Zambia has adopted national plans to develop and improve its farming, encourage diversification and reduce its dependence on imports. The scale of manufacture is still small, but a wide range of industries has been, or is being, established, such as food and tobacco processing, grain milling, production of steel sheets, cotton, furniture, clothing, plastics, cement, beer, soap and detergents, fertilisers and copper products, and vehicle assembly.

The MMD government is committed to abolishing monopolies, has commenced the privatising of parastatal companies and has introduced investment incentive schemes. Foreign companies can repatriate 100 per cent of after-tax profits.

South Africa has a trade mission in the Zambian capital. The aim is trade with all and sundry and international competition in investment Germany, China and Italy have all contributed towards major projects. Britain, however, has contributed most aid, mainly in technical assistance and experts. There is still a shortage of technical and qualified manpower. Many white mining technicians have left the country to work in the Middle East or South Africa. Government policy aims to entice back qualified Zambians who have left for other countries offering better wages and conditions.

Outside the Copperbelt and the main towns there is little paid employment and considerable poverty.

Personal finance and taxation

Expatriate employees of overseas companies usually receive benefits such as a car, a house, travel and education allowances which vary from company to company.

Expatriate inducement allowances are subject to taxation and the government intend to abolish inducement allowances altogether except for those professions such as medicine where there is a shortage of qualified Zambians.

Personal income tax ranges from 15 per cent to 35 per cent.

Working conditions

Visas are not required by holders of valid UK passports. Expatriates need a work permit, obtainable by the prospective employer from the Chief Immigration Officer (PO Box 31984, Lusaka). Dependants are not allowed to work without his permission. There are limited opportunities for women to work as doctors, nurses and teachers, but the authorities can be reluctant to issue work permits to expatriate wives. Voluntary work, however, is possible.

Working hours are as in other parts of tropical Africa, ie 8.00 am to 4.00 or 5.00 pm. There are 12 official public holidays. Leave arrangements for expatriates are negotiated individually.

Expatriates are usually expected to train Zambians working under them to acquire higher skills. This may not be explicitly stated, but it is assumed that sooner or later a job will be Zambianised .

Living conditions

Inflation, security fears and scarce transport make Zambia an expensive and difficult country in which to live. With the easing of import restrictions, the supply of goods has improved, and almost all items are available locally. Here are some examples of prices:

	Kwacha
Beer (50 cl)	623
Bread (1 kg)	891
Butter (250 gm)	1427
Cheese, Cheddar type (500 gm)	2869
Chicken (1 kg)	3252
Coffee	
ground (500 gm)	8813
instant (250 gm)	1263
Cooking oil (1 litre)	2261
Eggs (12)	1525
Milk (1 litre)	492
Mineral water (1 litre)	792

Potatoes (1 kg)	813
Rice (1 kg)	2639
Steak (1 kg)	3991
Sugar (1 kg)	833
Tea bags (250 gm)	2216
Whisky (75 cl)	12,811
Wine (75 cl)	6238
Cigarettes (20)	1365
Petrol (1 litre)	422

Inflation is high (roughly 200 per cent) and prices rise constantly. Meat is readily available and is of good quality as are local fruit and vegetables which are in plentiful and varied supply. Household necessities tend to be expensive, particularly of the imported variety. There is a limited choice in household furnishings, particularly electrical, and prices tend to be about double those of the UK. Most expatriates bring their own equipment with them. Locally produced clothing is of poor quality and imported items expensive; however, local tailors are skilful at making and copying clothes. A man s suit would cost around K120,000.

Informal dress   shorts for men, cotton dresses for women is preferred. Men usually wear suits or safari suits to the office. The golf clubs demand long trousers or shorts with long socks for men and both women and men must wear tops with collars. Temperatures drop rapidly at night and warm clothes are also needed in the cool season.

It is almost impossible to find accommodation for oneself. Housing *must* be provided with the job. The shortage of accommodation is so great that many newcomers often have to spend a long time in a hotel.

Electricity is supplied at 230V, 50 cycles AC and is available in towns; many people in country areas use bottled gas or paraffin.

Most expatriates have domestic help. Wages are upwards of K6500 per week for a live-in maid but are rising rapidly in line with inflation. Check the going rates with the local labour office. Servants also expect to be provided with housing, free utilities and uniforms, together with a bag of maize meal (the local staple) and/or ration money monthly.

Many families employ a day- or night-watchman and many also use the services of a security company such as Securicor. Housebreaking, burglary and petty theft have increased alarmingly. Thefts include cars and car fixtures, refrigerators and electrical equipment. Mugging and pickpocketing are also prevalent.

Hotels tend to get heavily booked, particularly in Lusaka. Prices in four-star hotels are around US$150 per night for a single room plus service and sales tax (10 per cent and 20 per cent respectively), which must be paid in hard currency for non-residents of Zambia. Hotel prices are lower outside Lusaka. Accommodation can sometimes be found in government rest-houses.

There are internal air services serving five major centres. Zambia Airways operate flights to the UK and leading African countries. There is a single-track railway system from Livingstone to the Copperbelt, and the Tazara railway, covering nearly 1600 miles, serves 147 stations between central Zambia and Dar es Salaam in Tanzania. Cross-country rail or bus travel is not recommended.

Most main roads are tarred, though secondary roads have potholed gravel or earth surfaces. Express buses link Lusaka with Livingstone and the Copperbelt, but urban transport is not much used by Europeans. Taxis and self-drive cars can be hired in Lusaka and other towns. Most car-hire firms do not permit self-drive.

The Zambians are exuberant drivers and have one of the world s highest accident rates. New arrivals in the country would be well advised to hire a car with a driver. Indeed, some companies employ drivers for their staff and these drivers services may be available, for an additional payment, out of office hours.

If you wish to drive yourself, you could consider bringing your own car. New immigrants are allowed under existing regulations to import one car per family duty free provided that the vehicle has been in their possession, or they have proof that they ordered it before their departure to Zambia, and provided that it arrives within six months of their own arrival in Zambia. Otherwise duty and sales tax will be payable roughly 84 per cent of the CIF value. The 1996 budget introduced a further excise duty on saloon cars of 25 per cent on those with 1500 cc or less engine capacity and 20 per cent on those over 1500 cc. (Advice on exporting a car can be obtained from the RAC.)

Foreign exchange payment for imported cars, many of which come from South Africa, must be proved to come from a source outside Zambia. Imported new cars can therefore be purchased partly in foreign exchange (covering the cost of the unit plus freight charges) and partly in kwacha (covering local elements of duty, sales tax, clearing charges, profit, etc). The cost of a Toyota Corolla is about K20,000,000. In order to drive in Zambia, you will have to take the Zambian driving test; this takes a long time to arrange and there is a high failure rate. An international permit is valid for one year. Be careful about security car thefts are frequent.

Health standards have declined in recent years with cholera becoming endemic, particularly during the rainy season, and an increase in strains of choloroquine resistant and cerebral malaria. AIDS is prevalent with an estimated 25 per cent of the adult population being HIV infected. However, Zambia is generally a healthy place, in part because of its elevation. Hospital and medical treatment carry only nominal fees, but there is a severe shortage of doctors, nurses, medical equipment and drugs. Dentists are few and far between. Most expatriate employers subscribe to private medical practices. The mining companies have their own hospitals and provide medical services for their personnel and families.

Education

Zambia has given high priority to its educational programme, and has had a long way to catch up. When it became independent, there were only 100 university graduates in the country and illiteracy was widespread. Now it has a number of teacher training colleges; the aim is universal education and an expansion of secondary education.

Zambian state schools are geared towards Zambian needs and classes are often overcrowded and facilities poor to non-existent. For expatriates in Lusaka there are four private schools, all of which have long waiting lists. There are also privately run Italian, French and Scandinavian schools and a limited choice of nursery schools for which there are long waiting lists. Elsewhere throughout Zambia there are a few other private schools and in the Copperbelt there are also trust schools and two private schools: Simba and Lechwe in Ndola and Kitwe respectively. Most expatriates send their children to be educated in the UK, Zimbabwe or South Africa from the age of 10, although some use home-teaching methods.

Social life is what you make it, as there is little organised entertainment. This is usually done at home, with lunch, dinner or cocktail parties barbecues (braai) are very popular. Dress is informal. Clothes should be lightweight and loose fitting, although woollens are required for the evenings and early mornings in winter. Sandals or canvas shoes are best.

There are plenty of clubs and sports facilities and most employers help with entrance fees. There is excellent fishing in Kariba lake and other waters and hunting is allowed outside game reserves. Camping and trekking are popular. Many expatriates take their weekend leave in neighbouring Malawi or Zimbabwe.

Most towns have cinemas and there are local amateur dramatic and music groups, some assisted by the Zambia Arts Trust. Broadcasting on TV and radio stations is in English. There are two daily newspapers the *Times of Zambia* and the *Zambia Daily Mail* and four weeklies the *Weekly Post*, the *Standard*, the *Financial Mail* and the *National Mirror*.

Expatriates often complain about the frustrations of daily life and about bureaucracy. Specific grievances concern housing, shortages, burglaries and servants.

For people who live near the Malawi or Zimbabwe border there are opportunities for trips to its well-stocked shops to make up deficiencies. (But beware the restrictions on dress in Malawi. Women may not wear trousers or shorts, and skirts must come below the knee. Men s hair must be short.) Most expatriates advise people to bring with them all necessary electrical goods, sports equipment, cooking utensils, gardening tools, shoes and clothing.

It is said to take about six months to get used to living in Zambia, but, once the adjustment has been made, most people find it an interesting and stimulating country. The Zambians are friendly and tolerant and there are no problems of race relations.

Zimbabwe

Background

Zimbabwe, formerly Rhodesia, has an area of 151,000 square miles. The country is landlocked, bordering on Botswana to the south-west, Mozambique, north and east, South Africa, south, and Zambia, north.

Most of the country lies 1000 feet or more above sea level and 80 per cent is above 2000 feet. The highest land is in the mountainous district near the Mozambique border, where mountains reach nearly 8000 feet. Because of its elevation the climate is healthy and pleasant, with daily maximum tempera-tures of 80 to 90 F for most of the year. The rainy season is from November to March; it is warm and dry from August to October and cool and dry from May to August. There is no need for air conditioning.

The population is 11.5 million and is increasing at a rate of 3 per cent per annum. Seventy-five per cent of the population live in the rural areas though urbanisation is now proceeding rapidly.

Harare, the capital, has a population of 1,184,169 and Bulawayo, the second largest city, 620,936. Both cities have mixed racial populations. Other towns include Mutare (Umtali), on the Mozambique frontier, Gweru (Gwelo), in the centre, and Hwange (Wankie) near the Zambian border.

Zimbabwe s first black government came into office in 1980, following elections supervised by the British. President Robert Mugabe s party again won a sweeping victory in 1995, gaining 118 out of 120 seats. Mugabe has encouraged Europeans to stay in the country, though many have emigrated to South Africa. Some are actually returning, as conditions stabilise in Zimbabwe but become more unsettled in South Africa. In theory, the con-stitution still provides for a multi-party system, but the main opposition party, Zapu, led by Joshua Nkomo, merged with the ruling Zanu PF in 1987 effectively creating a one-party state. Nkomo and other Zapu members were appointed to posts in the Zanu-controlled government, a government which is committed to the creation of a socialist society by gradualist means.

There are three official languages: Chishona, Sindebele and English.

Exchange rate: Zimbabwe $26.00 = £1.

The economy

The rate of inflation is declining at 22 per cent and is linked with the steady fall in value of the Zimbabwe dollar. Liberalisation of exchange control has made black market currency dealing superfluous. Bureaux de change are now found in most cities, with the majority found in Harare.

The mainstays of the economy are minerals and agriculture, dominated by tobacco, the major export crop, but the country also produces wheat, cotton, oilseeds, maize, cane sugar and beef and is self-sufficient in food. About 1.4 million Zimbabweans are occupied in agriculture, mainly at a subsistence level, and there are 4500 white farmers, many of whom employ efficient methods. Just over 2 per cent of the total population are employed in manufacturing and nearly 1 per cent in mining and quarrying (coal, copper, chrome, asbestos, nickel and gold). Tourism is increasingly important, as is horticulture.

With its plentiful resources and the President's policy of stability and unity and intention of promoting gradual, rather than revolutionary, change, Zimbabwe is re-emerging as a leading political and industrial force in southern Africa. There is still high unemployment (despite an acute shortage of skilled labour) and progress on the economic front has been disappointing, affected in 1995 by a severe drought.

Personal finance and taxation

Wages and salaries are highest in the mining sector and are above the African average; however, they are heavily taxed and are not high in expatriate terms.

A PAYE system of taxation is in operation, at rates rising from 20 per cent to a maximum of 40 per cent; a UK expatriate is likely to be paying tax near the top end of the scale. The remittance of funds is restricted to one-third of gross income, but tax on the remitted portion will have to be paid out of the local allowance. This is best illustrated by an example. A person earning Z$180,000, paying tax at 50 per cent, can remit the foreign currency equivalent of Z$60,000. He would pay Z$90,000 tax, leaving a local living allowance of Z$30,000. Remittance is subject to assessment by the authorities (who are anxious not to lose foreign currency and are particularly worried that white emigrants will remit their capital). It is possible to have the remittance paid into a UK or US offshore bank, while having a local living allowance.

Bearing in mind that you will be paid in local currency, the high inflation rate and falling dollar suggest that you would be well advised to negotiate six-monthly salary reviews.

Working conditions

UK nationals do not need a visa, but to work one needs a temporary employment permit and temporary residence permit. From acceptance of a job offer it could take your employer four months to obtain these. You need to be able to demonstrate good qualifications and the employer s application is likely to be refused if the authorities believe the job could be done by a Zimbabwean. Expatriate spouses are not permitted to work unless they are able to obtain their own work permit; this should be possible where there are shortages.

The term expatriate is not popular with the Zimbabwean authorities and it is preferable to use the expression employee under contract . Contract employees are recruited from outside Zimbabwe to fill vacancies in areas where there is a manpower shortage. They are normally recruited for a maximum of two years, with the option to extend their contracts for a further year. The consent of the Ministry of Public Service, Labour and Social Welfare is required for recruitment of contract staff. Conditions are covered by collective bargaining through industrial councils. There is provision for redundancy and severance pay.

Living conditions

Zimbabwe has a high standard of living by African standards, though it is not so high for the majority black population. Food and clothing are reasonably priced. The shops are usually well stocked, though there are frequent shortages of a number of items at any one time. This does not cause too much of a problem if you make provision. Anything imported is expensive. It is advisable to bring luxury and electrical goods with you. With servants being the norm, it is common practice not to have washing machines or vacuum cleaners. Check what furniture and household goods are provided by the employer; it is probably a good idea to bring anything you want which is not provided. Men s clothes and casual clothes for both sexes are easy to come by, but women and girls may find that smart clothes are not to European taste and will want to bring them. Children s toys are few and poor in quality.

The majority of villas (in Harare) have their own swimming pools and some have tennis courts. There is more competition for housing than in the past and this is reflected to some extent in rising prices. The power supply is reliable (voltage 220 230 AC). Tap water is potable. Harare is a sprawling city in which parks and gardens abound. Most suburban families employ a servant for the house and another for the garden. A maid, living in, would be paid about Z$400 per month.

There are good hotels in Harare and Bulawayo, at prices from about Z$900 single and Z$2700 double. There are restaurants both in the hotels and outside, including a number of very high standard establishments.

You need receipts of purchase on items you bring in that are less than six months old because duty is charged. Personal effects can be imported duty free but be prepared for a long wait to clear customs. The authorities will want serial numbers of luxury and electrical items to check that, when you leave, you take out what you brought in. Come armed with a list of numbers. If any goods are impounded pending customs clearance, ensure that you obtain an official receipt and try to determine where they have been put to facilitate claiming at a later date.

Shopping hours are from 8.00 am to 5.00 pm, although some stores stay open longer.

Medical services are adequate but some Zimbabweans prefer to go to South Africa or Britain for more advanced treatment and there have been some recent shortages of medical drugs. Check whether you are going to a malarial zone. Deltaprim tablets are recommended. There is a medical aid health system.

There are both nursery schools and private schools, fees for which vary considerably with waiting lists for all good schools both government and private. You would be well advised to see what strings your employer can pull.

There is an excellent system of main and feeder roads, with traffic control in cities and suburbs. Rail connections link the country with South Africa, Mozambique, Botswana and Zambia, and there are international flights connecting with the UK and South Africa, as well as domestic services from Harare to Bulawayo, Kariba, Hwange and Masvingo. A private car is, however, essential. Many models can be bought locally and there is a wide choice of French, German and Japanese cars. Automatic cars are also available and taxis are reliable. It is advisable to take a valid international driving permit. Strictly speaking, an international permit is valid for nine months; thereafter you require a Zimbabwe licence for which you will have to take a test. A UK licence is not valid because it has no photograph.

There are two English language daily papers: the *Chronicle* and the *Herald*. The telephone system is grossly overloaded and is one of the biggest frustrations. Private individuals often put up with party lines. An internal call can take a long time. Sometimes even a call booked with the operator can involve a wait of two hours. International calls are relatively easy provided you dial outside working hours. The postal service is generally good, if a little slow sometimes.

Sports clubs and golf courses abound. There are cinemas and theatres and an active amateur musical scene. Courses for adults are available at the university, polytechnic and college of music. Christianity is the main religion with a wide variety of denominations. Harare boasts Anglican and Roman Catholic cathedrals.

The American Continent

Canada

Background

Canada is one of the largest countries in the world in area, although its population is only some 29.2 million, with most people living in a 320 km wide strip along the southern border, one-third of whom live in the three main cities: Toronto, Montreal and Vancouver. The northern areas of the country 40 per cent of Canada s land mass is in the Arctic are bleak, bitterly cold for most of the year and almost completely unpopulated except for isolated settlements. Only some 17 per cent of the land surface is arable, but a third of this is very high quality indeed. Canada also has large areas of forest, mainly in British Columbia, Quebec and Ontario.

Canada, like its dominating neighbour, the USA, in the past pursued an open door policy towards immigration. The result was a large-scale influx from all over Europe, but predominantly from the British Isles; around 40 per cent of the population are of British origin. English communities are in the majority and the main provinces in central and western regions are English-speaking. Immigrants came from over 100 countries besides Britain and France, making up 30 per cent of the population. There are large German, Dutch and Ukrainian minorities. There are also ethnic minorities of Indians and, in the far north, Eskimos (or, properly, Inuit). But the biggest single population group, after those of British origin, is French, accounting for 29 per cent of the population. Nearly 6 million French live in Quebec and they form a sizeable minority in several other provinces. Canada is bilingual in the federal parliament, civil service and courts and from time to time nationalist agitation for a separate Quebec resurfaces. The majority of French speakers, however, accept that their close proximity to the USA means that the use of English is essential for business.

There are two main tiers of government federal and provincial. The provincial governments, by and large, are responsible for regional affairs, but where these overlap with federal interests (eg environmental matters, health and welfare) programmes are planned jointly.

There is a two-house parliament and the head of state is the Queen, represented by a governor-general. In October 1993, Canadians elected a Liberal government under the leadership of Mr Jean Chre tien. Canada is still in something of a constitutional limbo following the rejection by the electorate of the proposals to grant Quebec near-independence.

Exchange rate: Canadian $2.34 = £1.

The economy

Canada is basically a very rich country, but its economy in recent years has been rather patchy because of its varied nature. This variety can be illustrated by looking at the country s five main regions.

1. *The Atlantic provinces*. Largely involved in fishing and agriculture and to some extent in mining and manufacture. Oil and gas have also been found.
2. *Central Canada*. Contains some of the major cities and most of Canada s industrial and mineral capacity.
3. *The prairie provinces*. The principal sources of wealth are wheat, oil, potash and natural gas. There are also large uranium deposits.
4. *The Pacific province*. Main product is timber. Also important for fishing.
5. *The northern territories*. Contain much of Canada s vast and largely unexploited mineral wealth. Also large deposits of oil and gas.

Canada produces 20 per cent of the world s wheat; 42 per cent of the land is forested. Canada is one of the largest producers of valuable minerals and is also a major exporter of automotive, timber and paper products. Most trade is with the USA, particularly following the North American Free Trade Agreement in late 1993. Nevertheless, Canada has suffered recession recently, with some areas being very hard hit.

Personal finance
An average executive job, requiring graduate or professional-level qualifications and some five years or so of experience, would command an annual salary of between $75,000 and $100,000. A senior managerial job would be worth $125,000 to $175,000, plus 10 per cent to 30 per cent bonus. However, and unlike many other countries, cars are not normally provided as an executive fringe benefit, unless they are actually an integral part of the job. A skilled worker could expect to earn something in the region of $40,000. A university professor would be paid from $60,000. By and large, executive salaries are higher than at home, becoming more equal going down the scale.

Taxation
Normally, while you are living in Canada, all sources of revenue, whether from inside or outside the country, are liable to federal and provincial tax whether or not you are a Canadian citizen. As a separate rate of income tax is levied by each province, the total tax paid will vary somewhat, but, to take a fairly typical example, for a married employee with two children, earning $60,000, total deductions for tax and social security would come to just under $19,000.

Your identity as a taxable person (and also as a beneficiary of social benefits) is established through your Social Insurance number and you should apply for this as soon as possible after you arrive in Canada. Federal rates range from 17 to 29 per cent. A surtax on due tax of up to 8 per cent is levied. Provincial rates vary from 45 to 69 per cent of federal tax due.

Working conditions
The general working atmosphere and corporate style in Canada closely resemble those of the US, but Canadian society is more

stable, with lower crime figures. If you go to Canada intending to stay more than three months, you have to register this fact on arrival. You cannot change your status from visitor while in-country. Worker visas or applications for permanent residence must be made beforehand.

Modest increases in immigration levels are to be allowed over the next few years as a result of Canada s ageing population and falling birth rate. Many potential British immigrants fall into the family class category, with either close relatives already in Canada, or a Canadian spouse. Otherwise, they come into the independent category, and have to fulfil specific criteria: there should be a demand for their skills and they should be able to support themselves. A job offer from a Canadian employer makes a great deal of difference, as does higher education. Professional groups that are in demand include mathematicians, sales and advertising personnel, chemists and physicists. It is also possible to emigrate if you have capital available or intend to run a business in Canada under the business immigration programme. Other schemes include Temporary Employment Authorisation, Student Working Holidays, and Live-in Caregiver Programme.

In the public services preference is given to Canadian citizens and here, as well as in many private sector jobs, a knowledge of French is essential. It should not be assumed that the status of French in Canada is merely a nationalistic gesture. It is the mother language of many Canadian citizens. However, people who do not speak it may still enter public service, as provisions will be made for them to learn the language subsequently.

People who want to exercise professional skills will have to apply to the appropriate professional bodies and institutes to make sure that their qualifications are recognised. In some cases where training to achieve the qualifications in question is sub-stantially different in Canada, further examinations may have to be taken to achieve recognition. In all instances, though, docu-mentary proof of degrees, etc should be taken with you, as well as such personal documents as birth and marriage certificates. Information immigration web site on http:www.canada.org.uk\ visa-info\\. Useful publications include the Canadian Almanac and Directory (available in libraries) and the booklet *Teaching in Canada*, issued by the Canadian Teacher s Federation. The

High Commission can provide a list of many British companies operating in Canada.

Living conditions
It should be remembered that Canadian winters are much colder than anything one is accustomed to in temperate zones, although similar to Scandinavia. This is true even in the population centres in the southern part of the country. If you are to arrive in Canada any time between October and March make sure you have plenty of warm clothes. Outer winterwear is widely available, inexpensive and made to fit the climate and activities; take the minimum with you and buy the rest there. Warm clothing will not be needed indoors, as most apartments and offices are centrally heated. On the other hand, the summer (June to September) can be very warm, with temperatures averaging around 90 F in midsummer in southerly places like Toronto.

You will also have to take account of the fact that heating bills are a considerable part of the winter budget and that adequate central heating will have to be an essential feature of any house you buy. However, while you are finding your way about it is better to rent accommodation, although the availability and cost varies widely. Most apartments are unfurnished and a four-bedroomed house in Toronto would cost from $19,200 to $34,200 a year. This would include heating, hot water, electricity, a refrigerator and a stove, though it is obviously vital to check what exactly you are getting for your money when you sign a lease. Prices in major cities are in line with this figure, but it is obviously lower as you go out into suburban and country districts.

An average house costs in dollars what is paid in the UK in pounds. The houses tend to be better equipped with high insulation, hence a comparative house would be much cheaper in Canada. Many newer houses include ready-installed cookers and refrigerators as part of the price. Electricity in Canada is supplied at 120V, 60 cycles and conversion from other voltages is not really possible. Do not bring UK electrical appliances such as TV sets with you. A colour TV costs around $600.

Food prices vary from province to province and are also aggressively marketed through cost cutting. The prices listed below are roughly average; however, goods can be bought for less or more:

	$
Beer (50 cl)	1.98
Bread (1 kg)	2.53
Butter (250 gm)	1.93
Cheese, Cheddar type (500 gm)	5.96
Chicken (1 kg)	4.62
Coffee	
ground (500 gm)	6.84
instant (250 gm)	11.54
Cooking oil (1 litre)	3.65
Eggs (12)	1.74
Milk (1 litre)	1.55
Mineral water (1 litre)	1.31
Potatoes (1 kg)	1.30
Rice (1 kg)	2.44
Steak (1 kg)	14.12
Sugar (1 kg)	1.29
Tea bags (250 gm)	3.84
Whisky (75 cl)	27.56
Wine (75 cl)	11.86
Cigarettes (20)	4.04
Petrol (1 litre)	0.66

One of the principal differences between the USA and Canada is the latter s adherence to the welfare state concept. Social benefits in Canada are widespread. There is a compulsory national pension scheme with contributions related to income up to a modest, index-linked maximum. There are fairly generous allowances for each child (counting as taxable income), and there are various forms of unemployment and disability benefit. Most important, though, is the fact that Canada operates a national health insurance programme, which is administered by the provinces, for both hospital and ordinary medical (though not dental) care. In all provinces except Quebec and British Columbia, which impose a brief residence qualification (though in the case of Quebec only for hospital insurance), these are available to immigrants immediately on arrival and you should be sure to obtain details of registration and premium payments as soon as possible. Many employers pay the employee s contribution as part of the remuneration package and this is a point worth checking in any job offer.

Education in Canada is compulsory from 6 or 7 to 16 (15 in some provinces) and is free to the end of secondary schooling. Educational methods are progressive and similar to those in primary and comprehensive schools in the UK. There are also a small number of private schools. For registration you will need birth certificate, visa, vaccination certificate and previous school records. In Quebec and French-speaking Canada the medium of instruction in many schools is French, and the teaching of French is an important part of the curriculum.

Post-secondary education is not free, but repayable loans are available from the province, and there are various other forms of monetary assistance including scholarships for able students. University fees vary but are mainly low.

Social life in the cities near the US border is very like that in America and, even in the remoter regions of the north and west, many of the same features prevail: for example, the widespread use of credit facilities, shopping at drive-in, self-service supermarkets on the outskirts of towns, the high standard of material efficiency and comfort and the ubiquity of the motor car.

Conditions vary enormously between the different provinces and between urban and country areas.

Canadians do a great deal of entertaining in their homes. Many have lakeside or country cottages (perhaps built by themselves) and to have one is the ambition of most families. The scope for outdoor activity is unlimited, whether organised sport (ice hockey, Canadian football and baseball) or individual pursuits such as sailing, swimming, fishing, hunting, canoeing and mountaineering. Soccer is increasingly popular.

Liquor laws vary from province to province. In some they are pretty strict, in others, bordering on the bizarre. There are few pubs in the British sense but plenty of bars in the cities. The Canadians are easy going and informal and most British people who have settled there would probably take a great deal of persuasion to accept the fall in living standards which coming home would involve. In 1994, Canada topped the charts as the world s most developed country in the UN s Human Development Index, ahead of Switzerland and Japan.

Mexico

Background
Mexico is the largest Spanish-speaking country in the world and the third largest country in Latin America. In area it is about eight times the size of the UK. The terrain is extremely varied, ranging from near-desert to tropical rainforest. The centre of the country, where most of the population centres are, consists of high plateau between the two great mountain ranges of the Sierra Madre. There are active volcanoes and a risk of earthquake. The population is 91 million, with a growth rate of 2 per cent per year; ie, the population increases by about 1.7 million per year. The metropolitan area of Mexico City has around 18 million people, making it the most populous city in the world. Other main centres are Guadalajara, some 400 miles north-west of Mexico City and a centre for light industry, and the heavy industrial centre near the US border, Monterrey. A significant socio-political fact of life in Mexico, as in other Latin American countries, is rapid migration from the country to the cities and a birth rate which, though falling, is still too high in a country where poverty, unemployment and underemployment are endemic. However, the government has, over the past few years, been striving to modernise the economy. In the 1995 elections, the long-dominant PRI party retained control, and their candidate, Ernesto Zedillo, won the Presidential election. This administration has undertaken a programme of liberalisation in state systems.

Exchange rate: Pesos (NP) 17.22 = £1.

The economy
In late 1994, political and economic uncertainties caused an economic crisis. During 1995, Mexico suffered a severe recession and inflation and unemployment remain high, although

the economy is now recovering. Mexico is a major oil producer, but its policy is to maintain oil production at the same level and to diversify its external trade. Other prime industries are agriculture, mining, steel and motor vehicles. The major trading partners are the USA and the EU.

Membership of NAFTA, the North American Free Trade Agreement, liberalising trade between Mexico, the USA and Canada, should benefit the economy in the long term. Mexico is also seeking a similar deal with the EU.

Working conditions
Expatriate salaries in Mexico correspond to US levels. A work permit is needed which has to be applied for by the local employer; it is not easy to get because strong preference is given to Mexicans. The employer has to pay a deposit of US$2000, returnable on the employee s departure. Documentation plays a large part in the settling-in process and it is a good idea to get all major documents (eg birth and marriage certificates) certified by the Mexican Consul at this end before you arrive. It is vital that your salary should be expressed in a strong foreign currency. Tax rates start at 3 per cent and rise to 35 per cent. Tax brackets are adjusted quarterly for inflation. Foreigners employed under a technical assistance agreement are not liable to income tax. Business hours are 9am 2pm and 4pm 7pm. Siestas may be longer outside the cities.

Living conditions
The climate in Mexico is mainly hot and dry, though Mexico City is cooler because of its high altitude, although the level of air pollution is high. Altitude does produce problems of breathlessness, insomnia, etc, and those suffering from anaemia or who are overweight may encounter particular difficulties. The rainy season is from June to October.

Food prices are much lower than in the UK. Here are some examples of regular purchases:

	NP
Beer (50 cl)	2.65
Bread (1 kg)	5.03
Butter (250 gm)	4.54

Cheese, Cheddar type (500 gm)	20.69
Chicken (1 kg)	10.56
Coffee	
ground (500 gm)	16.09
instant (250 gm)	18.16
Cooking oil (1 litre)	6.91
Eggs (12)	4.76
Milk (1 litre)	2.16
Mineral water (1 litre)	3.73
Potatoes (1 kg)	7.63
Rice (1 kg)	3.91
Steak (1 kg)	36.80
Sugar (1 kg)	2.71
Tea bags (250 gm)	32.47
Whisky (75 cl)	71.47
Wine (75 cl)	40.43
Cigarettes (20)	5.64
Petrol (1 litre)	1.61

Mexico has a reputation for giving foreigners stomach upsets Montezuma s Revenge and Mexican Foxtrot . But, in the writer s experience, the hazards of diarrhoea are no worse than in any other hot country and, though ultimately unavoidable at some point, can easily be kept in check by common sense about what you eat and drink. For more serious ailments, Mexico has a good state medical service, although the degree to which it is free of charge depends on your local employer s contributions to the social security system. Since such contributions are not mandatory it is important to know where you stand in respect of medical treatment.

An unfurnished detached house (three bedrooms) would cost between NP59,600 and 64,800 per annum.

There are fluctuations in the electricity supply (100 127V, 60 cycles) so as well as checking that your equipment is adapted to these voltages you should also bring a 1KW transformer. For any portable valuables you would be well advised to take out a worldwide, all-risk insurance policy, since burglary in Mexico is not uncommon.

Among the good things to buy locally is pottery, which is attractive and cheap and makes an excellent present to bring home for people who appreciate such things. But in order to shop in markets and, indeed, to live in Mexico at all you will need to learn Spanish, preferably before you get there, even though all the professional and business people can express themselves in English. Servants, if they have worked for an English-speaking family, can often be a source of informal language lessons, especially for children. Wages are around NP250 per week for a general servant.

For people who do take children to Mexico there are a couple of good English schools in Mexico City which go right up to A-level, but fees are high; it is advisable to check the latest position.

As far as leisure is concerned, there is a great deal to see and do in Mexico, ranging from splendid unspoiled beaches to magnificent archaeological remains, though Mexico City itself is wildly overcrowded and slum-ridden. Roads are good and petrol is cheap by European standards. British cars are not readily available and cars are expensive prices are among the highest in Latin America; a new Nissan Tsuru would cost about NP49,000. British or international driving licences are valid when driving cars registered abroad, but a Mexican licence is essential to drive cars registered in Mexico. Standards of driving are not good and third-party insurance, though not compulsory, is advisable. A major improvement programme for the road network and the railways has recently been launched. Public transport in Mexico City is quick and cheap but is also one of the busiest systems in the world.

The United States of America

Background

Whether you look at it in terms of size and population, or of wealth and power, everything about the United States is big. It is a continent, rather than a country, and contains wide differences in geography, climate, people and customs.

There are about 255 million inhabitants living in a total area of 3.6 million square miles. The country as a whole is sparsely populated, with a density of only 64 inhabitants per square mile, but in some areas on the eastern seaboard (eg New Jersey) it is over 900 to the square mile.

The USA is bordered by the Atlantic, the Pacific and the Gulf of Mexico and has common frontiers with Canada and Mexico. There are wide differences in climate. During July and August the country is very hot: Washington is also humid and New York can be unbearable. The winters everywhere are cold, except in the deep south and the west and south-west.

The Americans are essentially urban dwellers and about 70 per cent of the population live in towns and cities. Many of the major cities are densely populated. Washington DC, the US capital, has only 598,000 inhabitants but it is the centre of government and of political and diplomatic activity. New York with about 7.3 million citizens (1.5 million in Manhattan alone) is the leading port and financial centre. Chicago has 3 million and Los Angeles has 3.5 million. There are many other large cities and all have conurbations of great area, adding to the numbers. The most congested part is a wide belt in the north-east stretching from Boston to Washington. Other concentrations of population are round the Great Lakes and on the west coast, associated with Chicago and Los Angeles respectively.

Between the east and west are the vast, underpopulated wheat belt and plains of the mid-west, the Rocky Mountains, Colorado and the arid land of Utah and New Mexico. There are also Alaska, Hawaii, and several territories in the Caribbean and Pacific.

The population comprises a rich variety of ethnic groups. There are about 30 million black Americans   racial discrimination is barred and equal opportunity stipulated under the law. Successive waves of immigration brought Irish, Italians, Germans, Poles, Chinese and Jews and more recently the inflow has been from Asia, the Caribbean and South America. While keeping alive their traditions, customs and sometimes their own languages, the immigrants have been absorbed down the years into the vast melting pot of American society. While English is the official language, in reality Spanish is increasingly common   there are over 22 million citizens of Hispanic origin. It has been estimated that it will not be too long before the white population will be in the minority.

The USA is a federal republic with 50 federated states. Each state has its own governor, senate and house of representatives and exercises considerable autonomy over its internal affairs. The federal government is responsible for foreign policy, defence and monetary affairs. The President is elected for a four-year term, and he may not run for more than two terms. Congress consists of the Senate and House of Representatives.

Exchange rate: US$1.61 = £1.

The economy
The USA is the richest and most successful economy in the industrialised world. There are certainly longer-term economic problems embedded in the USAs big deficits. However, the sheer size of the American market and the natural wealth of the country make it almost independent of the world economy. At the same time, there are shifts within the US economy which affect expatriates principally the growing importance of the sunbelt states in the south with their sunrise high technology industries and the relative decline of the old industrial north. Although business in the US spans every imaginable type, the largest sectors are services, finance and manufacturing. Notable industries include high-technology, automotive, oil, mineral extraction, defence, steel, chemicals and agriculture. The economy is still recovering from recession, but is stable. However, the huge Federal Budget deficit continues to be a thorn in the flesh.

Personal finance
American salaries are around 40 per cent higher than in the UK but there is nothing like the range of benefits and degree of employment protection that you get in Europe. The Medicare state health scheme is limited to the elderly and medical treatment is very expensive. Meanwhile, if insurance is not included in the remuneration package this could make quite a hole in an imposing salary. It may not be, because American executive salaries are less perk-laden than those in some other countries: for example, very few American executives get cars unless their job necessitates it.

Job advertisements in the USA, certainly at executive level, tend to demand a lot from the applicant but to be rather coy about what he or she is going to receive. Salaries, for instance, are rarely stated. It is as well to get advice from someone who has worked in the USA before accepting any offer, unless it is from a multinational, where conditions are usually fairly standard.

According to one survey, a typical middle management salary would be around $75,000, with more senior posts in the $120,000 $175,000 range plus bonus; bear in mind that the cost of living in the US is now around 20 per cent lower than in the UK. However, pay rates vary according to position, type of industry and area of the country New York, for example, is very expensive, as is Chicago. In practice, an expatriate is most likely to find a job in the USA with a multinational unless he or she has special skills in engineering, computing, R&D or electronics, a reputation in an academic discipline or is a qualified doctor (salaries offered to GPs range from £80,000 to £120,000).

There is some evidence that US firms are now seeking British managers with international experience, to establish and run European manufacturing bases. There are also opportunities with US companies that have investments in the UK, although it is also worth noting that the US is the major destination for UK investment funds.

Taxation

The American tax system is built round the idea of self-assessment, which requires a smaller bureaucracy than ours but also places more of a burden on the person making the tax return. Many people consider it impossible to complete the US self-assessment forms without professional advice. Assistance is widely available from the Internal Revenue Service through a toll-free telephone network.

Even wage and salary earners come under the self-assessment umbrella, because, although their tax is deducted initially under a form of PAYE, eventual adjustments in the form of rebates or further payment demands are based on the self-assessment return which is monitored by spot checks and computer matching with previous returns. Penalties for cheating are ferocious, but allowable deductions are rather more generous than in the

UK; and federal tax rates are lower than UK taxes. There are five levels of federal income tax: 15, 28, 31, 36 and 39.6 per cent. There are also state income taxes, so what the individual actually pays varies from state to state. Some cities also have income tax, notably New York City.

There is no VAT in the USA but there are sales taxes which vary from town to town rates are generally between 2 and 10 per cent. Since they are not shown as part of the price of the goods, as VAT usually is, this can mean a nasty shock when you get your bill for an expensive item.

Working conditions
Visitors to the USA, on business or holiday, no longer need a visa for a stay of less than 90 days.

How you set about applying for a visa that enables you to work in the USA, however, is a matter that requires a good deal of caution. Visas for permanent immigration are extremely hard to get unless you have close family ties there. Furthermore, if you make an application of this kind and are turned down, it then becomes extremely difficult to get a visa of any kind even as a visitor because the presumption is that once you get to the USA you will find some illegal way of remaining there.

If you are going to work for the British subsidiary of an American firm, or vice versa, the task is relatively easy. Your firm would apply for an L visa which would grant you residence for up to three years. Similarly, if you are proposing to invest substantial sums, at least $1 million, to start up a business venture in the USA creating employment for at least ten people (unrelated), you could apply for an immigrant investor visa.

People who merely want to go to the USA to take up a job offer must get their employer to file an application for a temporary worker s H visa. If you are going to the USA to look for a job, you have to ask the employer to do this as soon as he makes you an offer. These applications are processed within a matter of a few weeks to months.

You are allowed to take into the country your personal effects, for example, household goods which have been used for at least a year, professional books and tools of trade, cars, etc and antiques more than 100 years old.

Although the 35-hour week prevails, working conditions are a great deal more strenuous and exacting than in some firms here. American employers expect results and are fairly ruthless about removing people who do not deliver them. Senior executives come and go and it is not unusual for a shake-up at the top to work its way right down the ladder. In some firms considerable conformity with the image of the company in relation to dress, life style, etc is expected, even in the private lives of their employees. Holiday entitlement is low.

Living conditions
The overall cost of living is now lower than in the UK. Here are some sample prices (prices vary from state to state):

	$
Beer (50 cl)	1.96
Bread (1 kg)	2.68
Butter (250 gm)	1.22
Cheese, Cheddar type (500 gm)	4.93
Chicken (1 kg)	2.66
Coffee	
ground (500 gm)	6.43
instant (250 gm)	9.71
Cooking oil (1 litre)	2.68
Eggs (12)	1.24
Milk (1 litre)	0.86
Mineral water (1 litre)	1.02
Potatoes (1 kg)	1.37
Rice (1 kg)	2.29
Steak (1 kg)	11.60
Sugar (1 kg)	1.25
Tea bags (250 gm)	3.94
Whisky (75 cl)	18.08
Wine (75 cl)	9.82
Cigarettes (20)	2.33
Petrol (1 litre)	0.39

If you can wait for sales time, you will find that quality goods not buy-ins, but brand names are marked down by as much as

50 per cent and more. In fact even at ordinary shopping times, US department stores have bargain offers, particularly in clothes.

Restaurant meals can be astronomically expensive, particularly in pretentious French restaurants (there are some good ones, but many more are over-priced and of poor quality). On the other hand, the average restaurant meal is quite good and moderately priced. Standards of service in public places generally are friendlier and better than in the UK. Hotels have increased in price recently, particularly in New York, where decent hotels now cost from $200 upwards per night for a single room, though in smaller towns, less frequented by tourists, rates are only about half that.

Expatriates are likely to receive an accommodation allowance, and some employers provide free accommodation. For those who have to find their own, the monthly rent for three- to four-bedroomed unfurnished accommodation varies enormously from $800 $5,500.

Many people who work in New York prefer to live outside Manhattan. Find out about schools, shops, clubs and amenities in whatever suburb you choose. Elsewhere in the country, rents vary considerably   in Houston, Texas, for example, they are less than half New York levels.

When renting accommodation, it is usual to be asked for a month s rent in advance and another on deposit. Check the lease for such points as air conditioning, services, garbage disposal, etc   many blocks have garbage chutes   and security arrangements. The latter may come as a shock to those accustomed to the relative safety of European cities. Flats in New York City, for instance, usually have stout front doors made of heavy wood or metal, and multiple locks. Theft and more violent crimes are not uncommon and doors should be locked when you go out and at night. This even applies to the more expensive apartments that employ a porter or security guard. As for streets, they are not as unsafe as is sometimes suggested, but reasonable care has to be exercised in avoiding walking at night in badly lit or deserted ones.

Don t expect to get any domestic living-in help. You can probably get a daily for about $12 an hour, and you can hire a babysitter from $5 to $6 an hour from several agencies. A housekeeper, living in, would come to about $1000 per month for a 40-hour week. The Yellow Pages of the telephone directory in New York are infallible guides to the kind of domestic and other services you may need.

The electricity supply is generally 110 120V, AC 60 cycles. Flat three-pin plugs are normal.

You will find everything you could conceivably need in the shops, stores and supermarkets of the main centres and on the outskirts of towns. For an annual membership fee, you can try one of the discount warehouse stores, saving 20 per cent on supermarket prices for bulk buys.

Shopping hours are normally from 10 am to 9 pm, with later shopping one or two evenings a week. All shops are open on Saturday and most on Sunday. Drugstores sell not only medicines but a wide range of household goods, ice creams, toys, cosmetics, etc and some have coffee and snack bars. They stay open late.

Medical treatment is of a very high standard, but is extremely expensive. If possible, people are advised to get full medical insurance for themselves and their families before departure, even for a short stay. However, many European insurance companies no longer offer cover for expatriates and their families in the USA; instead, they advise that insurance should be arranged with a US company such as the Blue Cross.

Nursery school groups can be found in most centres. All children between 7 and 16 must attend school. The school year lasts from September to June. The system comprises public schools   there are about 90,000 in the whole country with over 50 million pupils   and there are 12 grades, 1 6 elementary, and 7 12 in secondary or high school. After the twelfth grade the pupils will probably go to college. Schools are operated by boards of education and are free.

There are fee-paying private schools and a number of boarding schools, modelled on the UK pattern, where tuition and boarding fees are usually fairly high. There are International Schools in New York (the United Nations) and Washington. The UN School takes children from kindergarten to high school age and sometimes can take in children whose parents are not UN officials. Instruction is in English and French.

The Americans have taken to the air as naturally as our great-grandfathers took to rail. Flying is the most efficient and speedy (and relatively cheap) way of getting round this vast country. All the main cities are connected by internal flights and there are frequent shuttle services between some cities (eg New York to Washington, New York to Boston and San Francisco to Los Angeles). Helicopter services are often available, as well as private plane hire.

There has recently been some revival of the railways. Long-distance coaches (usually air conditioned) are the cheapest way of travelling, if you can stand the boredom. Americans are also used to travelling long distances by car.

There are underground trains or subways in New York, Boston and Philadelphia. The famous cable cars in San Francisco are now back in service. New York city bus services are regular and frequent you need the exact fare. Cars can be rented from hire firms at airports, hotels and agencies. Few New Yorkers drive their cars in the city because of the traffic jams and parking problems, conditions which are found in all major cities.

Driving is on the right. An international or UK licence is valid for one year, but it is advisable to get an American licence from the state department of motor vehicles after a test. Most highways and super-highways have several lanes, and lane discipline is very strict as is the enforcement of speed limits. In 1995 the government repealed the national speed limits. Some states now have no restrictions.

Many expatriates buy a new or used car locally and re-sell it when they leave. The American Automobile Association (AAA) is an extremely helpful organisation for motorists. A new Toyota Corolla costs around $14,100.

Thanks to films, TV programmes and the intensive coverage of presidential elections, most British people have a pretty fair picture of the USA and the American way of life, even if they have never been there. Much of it may be an exaggerated if not distorted picture, but it does convey the sense of hustle and bustle in the big cities and gives some idea of the tensions of daily life.

The Americans are informal. They will probably call you by your first name on sight and outside Washington there is little protocol. Business is often conducted over meals, and working breakfasts are fashionable. It is worth remembering that, in fashionable society, health is all-important and smoking and even moderate drinking tend to be looked-down on. There is no strict etiquette to be followed and most appointments are made over the phone. Clothing is very much as in the UK, but remember that the American summers are hotter and the winters colder, so dress appropriately. Remember too that most houses and offices are centrally heated and air-conditioned.

American hospitality and generosity are proverbial and you may find yourself exhausted by the social round. The licensing laws vary in different states. In general, bars are open nearly all hours. In their houses, Americans tend to eat early in the evenings (5 7 pm).

There is always plenty to do in the cities, which have entertainments, theatres, opera, ballet, cinemas, museums and art galleries. TV is ubiquitous (there are over 1000 TV stations across the nation) and there is a wide choice of channels. There is naturally less in the way of cultural activity in the smaller towns, which are far removed from the cosmopolitan atmosphere of New York and San Francisco.

Opportunities for open air and indoor sports abound, and many are offered by clubs and societies. Many Americans spend weekends at the coast or lakeside, swimming, boating, fishing, etc. There is skiing in the winter in New England and in the Rockies and plenty of scope for mountaineering, camping and touring. In New York and in other large cities quite a lot of people rent summer houses in the country or at the beach.

Asia

South East Asia: Some Notes on Etiquette

It used to be said that Britain and America were two countries divided by the same language: meaning that things which appeared similar were often very different under the surface. This is even more true of South East Asia, where the cities, at any rate, have an increasingly Western appearance that nevertheless masks profound cultural differences between Asians and Europeans. The tendency is for expatriates to feel that these can be overcome by observing the ordinary niceties of social behaviour, Western-style, but these do not always translate themselves readily. In the West, for instance, it has become customary for business dealings to be conducted relatively informally indeed informality has become almost a style in itself. In the East, a good deal of ceremony is still observed and the more important the negotiations, the more ceremony will be attached to them. This is related to what people in the East would call face .

The notion of face is prevalent throughout Asia and it is a difficult term to translate. It may be, as in the instance above, the dignity of an occasion or it may be, more often, simple human dignity. The reluctance to violate your own sense of face may cause a subordinate who disagrees with you to disobey your instructions, having apparently agreed to follow them. The way to deal with such a situation is not to take issue with him or her in public but to sort it out in circumstances where no loss of face is involved for either party. This has to be done with a great deal of tact the Western notion of frankness is largely unknown to people in the Far East, who are apt to regard it merely as rudeness.

Another rich area of potential misunderstanding lies in the use of body language. As in the Middle East, it is generally considered impolite to take or offer things with the left hand, though at meals dishes can be passed with the left hand, provided it is supported by the right. Oriental people are also very wary of effusive displays of affection. Even old friends should be greeted with a certain amount of gravity and reserve. Those same qualities should also mark your relations with subordinates pointing at people with your finger or beckoning them by use of the finger is regarded as the height of bad manners. Indeed, many finger gestures are regarded as obscene, as is making points by pounding the open palm with the fist.

The Asian culture, wherever you go, is in fact one that is very nervous about familiarity and treats as familiarity many modes of behaviour that we would regard as fairly normal.* This also extends to the use of Christian (or proper) names. The Chinese style, incidentally, is for the surname to come first, the middle name second and the equivalent of the Christian name last. Thus a Chinese man by the name Goh Kee Seah would be Mr Goh, not Mr Seah.

Another way in which Asian culture differs from ours is in the importance attached to luck. Again it is important to respect this because to dismiss it as superstition would be a grievous offence against the concept of face. It can, of course, work to your favour; for instance it is considered bad luck if the first person into a shop each day leaves without making a purchase. In those shops where bargaining is part of normal transactions, this can lead to the often expressed sentiment of special price, just for you indeed having some meaning. Normally you will find that after prolonged bargaining you have ended up paying about the same as in a department store.

---

* An excellent account of this whole issue is given in a book called *Culture Shock* by Jo Ann Craig, published by Times Books International of Singapore.

A further point about shopping: Asians are, in general, slighter than Europeans, so you would be well advised to stock up on clothes before you leave.

Brunei Darussalam

Background
Brunei Darussalam is a small, prosperous sultanate on the north coast of Borneo which became an independent state in January 1984. It is about the size of Norfolk and is bounded on three sides by the Malaysian states of Sarawak and Sabah. The fourth side is bounded by the China Sea and it is on this narrow coastal strip that the main towns are located. The rest of the country is tropical rain forest. Brunei s 67 per cent Malay, 33 per cent Chinese and other indigenous population numbers 270,000, over 65 per cent of whom live in Brunei-Muara district, which includes the capital, Bandar Seri Begawan. There is a large expatriate community with a sizeable British element. The official religion is Islam and the influence of the religious element is increasing. Alcohol is banned. Brunei has very close ties with Britain, including defence. Malay is the official language, but English is spoken almost everywhere. Citizenship rules are restrictive. Islamic influence has led to Chinese emigration. There have recently been signs of political dissent to the Sultan s direct rule.

The economy
Brunei has one of the highest standards of living in South East Asia. Almost all its wealth comes from oil and gas, but the government has encouraged the use of oil money to foster the development of secondary industries and services such as fishing, agriculture, education and communications. Since 1988, government budget deficits have been recorded, but income from external reserves of over US\$27 billion helps considerably. The main trading partner is Japan, followed by the UK and Malaysia.
Exchange rate: B\$2.45 = £1.

Personal finance and taxation
The public sector employs about 50 per cent of the work force. Salaries are good and government jobs usually carry such fringe benefits as subsidised or free housing, an education allowance for children, paid home leave, free medical attention, a car or an interest-free loan to buy one and an end-of-service bonus. There is no personal tax in Brunei. There is also no restriction on remittances.

Working conditions
Entry and exit visas are not necessary for UK nationals. Employment and residence passes have to be obtained on behalf of expatriates by their employer but they are not usually difficult to obtain for UK nationals.

Living conditions
The vegetation, climate and general atmosphere of the country are typical of tropical regions of South East Asia, with high humidity and a temperature that rarely falls below 70 F and rarely rises above 90 F. New houses are being developed and accommodation is constantly improving. If you can get one, a government bungalow is excellent. Rent is charged at 10 per cent of your basic salary. Normally the houses are fully furnished and air conditioned. Non-Bruneians are normally prohibited from owning land. You will pay around B$213 a night for a single room in a four-star hotel, but your choice of hotel will be somewhat limited.

Even with air conditioning, however, the humidity gets at things like hi-fis, cameras and leather goods, so it is probably not worthwhile bringing treasured possessions with you or spending a lot of money on buying high-quality items locally, though they are available at reasonable prices. Equally, you will certainly need lightweight clothes and you should allow for plenty of changes. Again, these are available locally, but do not rely on getting them off-the-peg as oriental sizes are much smaller than European ones. Local tailors are cheap and skilful: they will run up a dress for B$15 30, exclusive of materials. Items that are not available locally, though, are shoes and sandals of size 10 or 11 for men and 7 or 8 for women, so you should take several pairs with you. Women should observe the Islamic dress code.

Good, full-time servants are hard to find but most expatriates manage to find an *amah* (domestic help) to assist with the household chores and probably to babysit. Filipino servants are available, but the problem here is that the employer is bound by contract to pay for a flight home every two years. A part-time maid would expect about B$300 a month, more for cooking duties.

Many expatriates find servants a help on shopping expeditions, particularly in the local markets where fresh fish is excellent, if no longer a cheap buy, and fruit and vegetables are both delicious and reasonably priced. The latter should be washed, though, and care is also advised with drinking water in November and December. Below are some sample prices:

	B$
Bread (1 kg)	3.50
Butter (250 gm)	2.36
Cheese, Cheddar type (500 gm)	9.82
Chicken (1 kg)	5.28
Coffee	
ground (500 gm)	13.45
instant (250 gm)	14.00
Cooking oil (1 litre)	7.07
Eggs (12)	2.58
Milk (1 litre)	3.83
Mineral water (1 litre)	1.12
Potatoes (1 kg)	3.83
Rice (1 kg)	1.50
Steak (1 kg)	21.00
Sugar (1 kg)	2.43
Tea bags (250 gm)	7.81
Cigarettes (20)	1.59
Petrol (1 litre)	0.53

Obviously you will need a car and a good choice is available locally. Japanese cars are cheaper than British and much cheaper than European models. A Toyota Corolla costs around B$27,750. Taxis, including water-taxis, and self-drive vehicles are freely available. Petrol is cheap.

Most expatriate children of secondary school age go to boarding schools in the UK, although facilities for secondary education do exist in Brunei. There are several good nursery schools as well as three good primary schools, of which the International School is the most popular.

Charges are made for state medical services but most companies employing expatriate workers provide medical insurance. Standards are reputed to be high, but there are also private medical facilities for those who prefer them. Nursing care is poor. Generally, health standards are extremely good. Innoculation requirements are minimal cholera and yellow fever are advised.

Recreational facilities are quite good, especially for water sports, with private clubs for sailing, golf and tennis. Two of the larger ones are for Shell employees, but non-Shell people are sometimes allowed to join. There are English and American films as well. Both Brunei and Malaysian colour TV can be received. TV sets and VCRs are best bought in Singapore or Brunei, as British sets will not work without adaptation. Many of the programmes are in Malay but the range of Australian, British and US programmes is improving. Videos have been regarded as a great boon to expatriates because Brunei has very little to offer in the way of night life, with no public bars or nightclubs. Although alcohol is banned, 12 cans of beer or two bottles of wine or spirits may be brought in on first arrival and subsequent visits. Electricity supply is 230V AC, 50 cycles, with both round and square three-pin plugs. The *Borneo Bulletin* is the main English-language newspaper. The government-published *Brunei Darussalam* and *The Straits Times* are also available.

The People s Republic of China

Background
China is one of the world s largest countries geographically, stretching over 4800 km from east to west and 4000 km from north to south. That obviously gives it a very varied climate subtropical in the south and hitting very cold conditions (40 C)

in the north. The coastline extends from North Korea down to Vietnam in the south, but there are also 20,000 km of boundaries: the CIS, India, Nepal, Burma, Mongolia, Pakistan, Bhutan, Vietnam, North Korea and Laos are all China s neighbours.

In addition to its sheer topographical size, China is also the world s most populous nation; its population is over 1200 million. Although only 11 per cent of the land is cultivated, China is self-sufficient in many food items and is a major agricultural exporter. Although 75 per cent of the population live in rural areas, China is highly urbanised and indeed the cities are very large Shanghai, for instance, has 12.5 million people and Beijing 11 million.

China s history in the past 40 years has been truly extraordinary. Unified after the war by Mao Zedong, it has effectively gone through several revolutions since then. Essentially, these were government-controlled, or at least government-inspired, events: the Great Leap Forward, the Cultural Revolution and the present experiment with a mixed economy, which gradually followed the ousting of the Gang of Four in 1976. The leader who emerged from all these events and undoubtedly the guiding force behind the drive towards economic development along largely Western-derived lines was Deng Xiaoping. Most Western observers were astonished by 1989 s demonstrations and subsequent massacre in Tiananmen Square. This was followed by a purge of dissidents, as conservatives increasingly gained the upper hand. There are currently tensions with the UK over Hong Kong, and the US over Taiwan, as China moves inexorably towards superpower status.

The Party Secretary and President is currently Jiang Zemin, after Deng Xiaoping s death. The Prime Minister is Zhu Rongji.

Exchange rate: Yuan 13.30 = £1.

The economy

Recent economic reforms, implemented in January 1994, included floating the currency, establishing an independent central bank, liberalising tariffs and bringing in tax reforms to narrow the gap between rich and poor and improve access to foreign capital and markets, bringing the country more into line with other economies. Foreign investment has mushroomed and enabled the construction of an industrial and communications infrastructure. In some areas the economy has become a free market in all but name, with several stock markets and Shanghai s emergence as a financial centre.

The economy has been growing at around 13 per cent, with higher exports and soaring foreign investments. The southern provinces, particularly, are booming; inflation has been as high as 23 per cent in some urban areas. However, the average rate is much lower.

The government has recently applied austerity measures in an attempt to cool down the economy, with limited success. Occasional unleashing of old-style hardliners on the political front seems to have been more effective.

There have been problems with profiteering and corruption by army officers and senior government cadres, some transferring assets into Hong Kong.

Personal finance and taxation

All foreigners whose employers are domiciled in China are liable for tax. Only business trips of under 90 days duration are exempted if the employee is on an overseas payroll. Average expatriation tax would be 10 to 13 per cent.

Working conditions

Office accommodation is scarce and very expensive. Most foreign companies at present have their offices in hotels. It has been estimated by the *China Business Review* that it costs a company around £400,000 a year to keep a small, one-man office in China. Business hours are from 8 am until midday and 2 pm until 6 pm. All foreign visitors require a visa and, for some destinations, a special permit.

Living conditions

Most expatriate business people have to live in hotels, though some expatriate housing is available in Shanghai and Beijing (Peking). Accommodation in general is in very short supply, but at least it is now possible to stay in reasonably priced, Western-built hotels. Another indication of the general improvement in conditions is the price of Western-style food; the average meal for two in the coffee shop of a Western hotel costs about £10 and a meal with wine in a French-style restaurant can be had for around £37.

Chinese restaurants, of course, are inexpensive and the food is generally excellent. Western goods can now be bought in numerous supermarkets in Beijing; there are also a few supermarkets in Shanghai. You should bring electrical goods with you and, of course, cars. These are virtually unobtainable in China though you can now get spares for some Japanese makes. Both cars and spares are subject to high rates of duty. Taxis are often the preferred mode of transport.

If you have a car it is becoming increasingly possible to get around. You need a permit to travel but these are generally granted without difficulty. The main problem is finding accommodation when you get to your destination. It is obviously a great advantage to be able to speak a little Chinese in such circumstances   and for business purposes as well   and some determined expatriates report that the standard Mandarin is not as difficult as it looks. While virtually impossible for the foreigner as far as reading and writing are concerned, it is apparently feasible to learn how to speak it well enough to get by in basic terms.

Although there are expatriate communities in the main centres, there is very little in the way of entertainment to be found in China. There is an International School in Beijing and American Schools in Guangzhou and Shanghai.

Cholera and yellow fever innoculations are advisable. An AIDS test may be required. Good medical care is available, although the equipment may not be the most modern, and proprietary medication may not be in full supply.

Hong Kong

Background

Hong Kong is not, as some people think, a unitary place, but a group of small territories and islands with a total estimated population officially given as over 6 million. However, the significant elements are: Hong Kong Island itself which is about 13 km across and 8 km wide at its maximum; Kowloon peninsula which lies on the mainland, a few minutes ferry ride from Hong Kong Island; and behind this, the New Territories, which form an area almost half the size of Greater London. They include some arable land, but most of it is too hilly to be capable of much in the way of either urban or agricultural development.

Hong Kong was a Crown colony (though the word colony is no longer officially used), administered by a Governor, an Executive Council and a Legislative Council, until July 1997 when Britain s lease ran out. Under an agreement signed in September 1984, the colony has now reverted to Chinese sovereignty, but under special conditions which should give it considerable autonomy, including the freedom to operate a free-enterprise capitalist enclave within the Communist system for a further 50 years. An important aspect of this is for Hong Kong to remain an international financial centre, outside the Chinese tax system and with a freely convertible currency. A general feeling of unease regarding Hong Kong s future has perhaps been enhanced by British attempts to democratise Hong Kong s political system, which were not well-regarded by Beijing. The businessmen of Hong Kong seem happier about the prospects for the future of Hong Kong under Chinese rule than the ordinary citizen, although many were glad to see the British go.

Exchange rate: HK$13.02 = £1.

The economy

Apart from its importance as a financial and banking centre (no fewer than 172 banks and 300 insurance companies are incorporated there and it now ranks as the world s third most important financial centre after London and New York), Hong Kong's economy is bound up principally with tourism and other service sectors. The traditional light manufacturing base is rapidly disappearing to mainland China. The biggest foreign exchange earner is tourism, with 10 million visitors in the last year, more than half coming from other Asian countries. One reason for this is the huge range of consumer goods on sale at prices now expensive to us, but still cheap to the Japanese or Taiwanese visitor. Tourist attractions are much as one might find in, say, Singapore, although perhaps more visually inspiring.

Personal finance
There are no exchange controls in Hong Kong and money is fully remittable into and out of the colony. Broadly speaking, an expatriate employee in the private sector should expect to be earning 40 to 50 per cent more than his gross UK pay. On top of this an expatriate employee should expect to get free or heavily subsidised accommodation and medical and dental attention, an education and holiday visits allowance for his children, and possibly further fringe benefits such as a car, servants and a good gratuity at the end of his contract. Public sector salaries are paid in Hong Kong dollars.

Income and other taxes
Tax is charged on all income arising in or derived from Hong Kong, and goes up by steps of 2 per cent to a theoretical top rate of 20 per cent on incomes after deductions of allowances for self, spouse and children. However, without any deduction of allowances, the maximum tax payable in practice is 15 per cent, although accommodation, when provided or subsidised by an employer, is regarded as taxable income up to a maximum of 10 per cent of total earnings. Another factor to take into account is that Hong Kong has no double taxation agreement with the UK, so income derived from there while one is resident in Britain would be liable to tax in both countries. Conversely, however, income derived from abroad while one is resident in Hong Kong is not taxable. Clearly, the need for good tax planning advice for expatriates is imperative. Further information on taxes may be found in a pamphlet, *Synopsis of Taxation in Hong Kong*, which is

available from the Inland Revenue Department, Revenue Tower, 5 Gloucester Road, Wanchai, Hong Kong.

Interest payable on foreign currency deposits placed with financial institutions carrying on business in Hong Kong is exempt from tax, as is interest on deposits in Hong Kong currency placed with such financial institutions.

Working conditions

Hong Kong s largely Chinese population (98 per cent) is impressively intelligent, skilled and hard-working, so opportunities for expatriates are limited. It is the policy of the Hong Kong government to recruit locally whenever possible. Details of teaching, academic and technical jobs are advertised in the appropriate sections of the UK press; there has recently been some demand for expatriates following the initial emigration of residents pre-1997.

Living conditions

The feature of Hong Kong life that strikes a newcomer most forcibly is the population density, impressive even by Asian standards. The population density for Hong Kong Island is 5380 persons per sq km, including barren areas (three-quarters of the whole). So Hong Kong is no place for people who feel the need for wide open spaces or who are bothered by crowds. Yet it is by no means squalid. In fact its health record is good: public places are clean and Chinese shopkeepers seem to be adept at making the most cramped premises look organised and tidy. Obviously, though, space is at a premium and this is reflected in rents which range from HK$540,000 to HK$1,680,000 a year for a three-bedroomed unfurnished flat. Most companies, however, provide free or subsidised accommodation. The latter is also the practice of the government, which gives its employees an accommodation allowance towards rent. The climate of Hong Kong warm and humid for most of the year but with a brief cool winter makes air conditioning and some heating facilities a necessity.

Hong Kong is no longer a cheap place to live, particularly if you rely on imported and frozen goods in European-style supermarkets. Shopping for food in local markets can be rewarding since prices are subject to some seasonal fluctuation, although perhaps the main advantages over supermarkets lie in variety and interest rather than price. Restaurants are excellent and quite cheap if you like Chinese food. European-style hotel meals, on the other hand, are rather expensive.

The following are sample prices:

	HK$
Beer (50 cl)	10.05
Bread (1 kg)	13.97
Butter (250 gm)	9.81
Cheese (500 gm)	32.15
Chicken (1 kg)	26.34
Coffee	
ground (500 gm)	66.59
instant (250 gm)	62.19
Cooking oil (1 litre)	21.53
Eggs (12)	10.93
Milk (1 litre)	20.92
Mineral water (1 litre)	8.25
Potatoes (1 kg)	15.99
Rice (1 kg)	10.93
Steak (1 kg)	127.20
Sugar (1 kg)	7.49
Tea bags (250 gm)	54.80
Whisky	166.99
Wine (75 cl)	105.02
Cigarettes (20)	24.70
Petrol (1 litre)	9.01

Hong Kong has two TV stations and two main radio stations providing services in both Chinese and English. There are two English TV channels and three English radio channels, two of which combine from midnight to 6.00 am, to provide a 24-hour service; there is a BBC World Service relay on another channel at night. Satellite television offers a 24-hour global news service and a cable TV channel carries locally produced programmes. A third radio station provides a service for British Forces personnel and their families. No licence fees are charged for TV or radio receivers.

Public transport and taxis are inexpensive but apt to be over-crowded, and most expatriates have cars, which in many cases are not provided as a perk that goes with the job. There are very few straight roads in Hong Kong and distances, in any case, are short, so a big car is a status symbol which also attracts a higher rate of registration tax and annual licence fees. UK driving licences are valid for a stay of up to a year, but can be exchanged for a local licence without a test. Bringing a new car into Hong Kong is hardly cheaper than buying one locally; a first registration tax is charged. However, good second-hand cars are reported to be readily available. A new Toyota Corolla costs around HK$185,364. Tax and other running costs are quite high. With electrical goods, however, the problem is that British equipment has to be adapted to Hong Kong s system (200 220V AC at 50 cycles). Household electrical goods cost about the same as in Britain in spite of the colony s duty-free port status. Experienced residents maintain, however, that it is possible to get shopping bargains in Hong Kong.

Education in Hong Kong can be a problem and expatriates are advised to make arrangements for schooling as soon as they get there, or before. Prior to arrival it is worth notifying the Education Department (9 16th Floors, Wu Chung House, 197 221 Queen s Road East, Wanchai, Hong Kong), or the English Schools Foundation (43b Stubbs Road, Hong Kong) to ask about places. This is because most of the schools cater for the predominantly Chinese population, so the medium of instruction is either Chinese or, if in English, with the emphasis on English as a foreign language. There are several independent schools offering a UK curriculum, at both primary and secondary level.

Domestic helpers (*amahs*) can be obtained in Hong Kong. Most are from the Philippines or other Asian countries as there is a trend away from domestic work by local labour.

A general, experienced, Chinese domestic helper whose responsibilities included cleaning, washing and possibly cooking and looking after one or two children, would not normally accept less than HK$3900 a month, full time and living in. In addition, she would be entitled to holidays and would expect a bonus of one month s salary at Lunar New Year. Foreign maids work on two-year contracts. Under an employment contract attested by the Labour Department, a foreign maid receives a monthly salary of not less than $3350 and paid passages. Domestic helpers working part time are also available, usually at a rate of about HK$36 $42 an hour, the minimum period of work being two hours.

Geography dictates that recreation facilities in Hong Kong are rather limited, but there are good local clubs and extensive night life facilities.

Japan

Background

This mountainous island country is the most crowded on earth, and 124.5 million people are crammed into an area one and a half times the size of Britain; because of the terrain, the majority of this population inhabit only one-quarter of the land mass. The capital, Tokyo, has a population of 7,962,000, and is on the east coast of Honshu, the largest of the four main islands (the others are Hokkaido, Shikoku and Kyushu); the area comprising Osaka, Kobe, Kyoto, Nagoya and Tokyo is almost entirely built up. To the west across the Sea of Japan is Korea, and to the east the Pacific Ocean.

Japan lies at the north-eastern end of the monsoon area. It has a temperate climate with four distinct seasons and, except in the north, winters are mild. The Pacific coast is subject to summer typhoons which bring torrential rains and violent winds. Average humidity is between 57 and 82 per cent. The country is subject to earthquakes. The most recent large-scale one hit Kobe in early 1995, causing widespread devastation and many fatalities; however new buildings are constructed to minimise damage.

Japan s history has been greatly influenced by China (whence the script derived) and has been marked by alternating periods of absorption and repulsion of foreigners, their religions, customs and inventions; the present time is a period of absorption. Buddhism and Shintoism are the dominant religions, emphasising respect for family and traditional values; their physical manifestations are seen in the shrines and temples up and down the country.

The language is written in characters (a combination of phonetic syllables and ideographs). Expatriates are employed mainly by multinational companies, but for employment with a Japanese organisation, social intercourse and cultural integration, a knowledge of Japanese is essential.

The Emperor Akihito is head of state. The Diet (parliament) has two houses, of which the dominant is the House of Representatives. The progress of politics is rather Machiavellian. In early 1996, Ryutaro Hashimoto was appointed Prime Minister in a Liberal Democrat (conservative) led coalition. This coalition is now over, and there is single party rule of 249 to 250, two short of a majority.

The government has recently been hit by scandal over the financial failure of loans companies, which looks set to cost the Japanese taxpayer up to 3 trillion yen, as the government pays off bad debts, which in many cases seem to be held by criminal elements. The problem is large enough to threaten Japan s entire financial system.

Exchange rate: Yen 212.84 = £1.

The economy

Despite Japan s almost total dependence on imported energy, the country remains one of the world s economic superpowers. Until recently Japan s readiness to adapt to new technology has been one of the secrets of its success, and the latest sign of this is that it is now the world s largest user of industrial robots. In spite of that, the unemployment rate is a low 2.5 per cent. Inflation is around zero. After a period of economic growth in the 1980s, Japan is now experiencing the worst economic crisis in its recent history. It is too early to tell how Japan will cope with this unprecedented downturn.

Japan is a highly industrialised country, only 14 per cent of which is cultivable. Fish rather than meat is the main source of protein in the diet. Rice is the staple food. Heavy investment in subsidiary manufacturing abroad has led to the peculiarity of Japan importing Japanese goods. Traditionally, Japan is very protective of its home market.

Personal finance and taxation

An expatriate executive will need double his UK salary to live at his normal standard, entertain as his job will require, and provide UK schooling for his children. Tokyo has consistently been one of the world s most expensive cities and a senior expatriate executive should strive for US$180,000 $230,000, plus 15 20 per cent overseas loading. Japanese indigenous salaries, once relatively low, are also now in the upper quartile and well above UK levels. It is advisable to arrange for some salary to be paid elsewhere to ease the tax burden and facilitate the transfer of funds to the UK.

The Japanese tax system is very complicated, but expatriates do have a concession inasmuch as they are taxed only on income arising in or remitted to Japan. The top rate (for national income tax) is 50 per cent; a typical expatriate would pay something between 30 and 50 per cent. The minimum is 10 per cent. In addition, local rates are 5 10 per cent.

Working conditions

The majority of expatriates working in Japan are employed by foreign companies, particularly as representatives; otherwise, the main source of employment is as an English language teacher. EFL teachers are likely to be recruited by Japanese language schools. Bona fide students in Japan can appeal for permission to work a limited number of hours per week (teaching EFL); pay is from £16 to £25 an hour. Some language schools underpay their full-time staff. Even a primary school teacher should be earning at least £16,000 a year, bearing in mind the cost of living.

A person wishing to enter Japan for the purposes of employment, training or study, must apply for a visa. Requirements are: a valid passport; one visa application form completed and signed; one passport-sized photograph; a certificate of eligibility (original and one photocopy). The certificate of eligibility is issued by the Ministry of Justice in Japan. It is provided by a future employer or sponsor in Japan. In certain cases additional support documents may be required.

Employment patterns in Japanese firms differ from those in the West recruitment is on traditional paternalistic lines from families with loyalty to the company and a knowledge of Japanese would be a prerequisite.

Holders of UK passports require no visas for tourist visits under 90 days, which period may be extended to a maximum of 180 days at the discretion of the authorities. A working visa is required by those who have already obtained a post. To obtain a working visa you must first have a definite job appointment in Japan. Your employer should then apply to the Ministry of Justice for a Certificate of Eligibility. Once this is received you must submit, in person, a visa application to the Japanese Consulate, together with the Certificate. Provided the documents are all in order a visa can normally be issued fairly quickly. Information is available from the Visa Section, Consulate General of Japan, 101 104 Piccadilly, London W1V 9FN. Temporary work is not permitted but, if when visiting as a tourist you receive a written offer of a permanent post, a working visa may be obtained by leaving the country and applying from outside (Korea, for example).

Booklets outlining Japanese business practices and attitudes are available for business people from JETRO London, Leconfield House, Curzon Street, London W1Y 8LQ, and may be useful for other visitors.

Living conditions

Tokyo is currently the most expensive developed city in the world. With the exception of cars, public transport (but not taxis), cigarettes and Japanese food, the vast majority of goods in Japan cost much more than in the UK. A two- or three-bedroomed unfurnished Tokyo flat will cost 6,060,000 11,760,000 yen a year to rent. Japanese-style flats are more reasonably priced. Accommodation is cheaper in the suburbs and the average Japanese expects to spend two hours a day travelling to and from work. A single four-star hotel room in Tokyo averages at 22,000 yen a night.

Measurements are metric; the electricity supply is 100V, 50 cycles AC in eastern Japan including Tokyo, and 60 cycles in western Japan, including Nagoya, Kyoto and Osaka. Hotels generally provide sockets for both 110 and 220 volts.

Expatriate wives may find life difficult because of the position of women in society, where they are expected to be self-effacing. A wife s role might be confined to formal entertaining at home, of which there is a great deal, to promote her husband s interests. Much business is done as a result of socialising, and membership of a club (usually golf, but not exclusively devoted to it) is essential; the fees are exceedingly high (around 78,000 yen a year) and usually form part of the remuneration package. Many expatriates belong to the Tokyo America Club, where annual fees are much lower but the entrance fee is around 2,200,000 yen. A Japanese wife may not ease the path of the expatriate executive, unless she is from a certain class. A successful businessman needs to be at least 45 (no one younger cuts much ice in commercial circles) and to maintain the right life style.

The expatriate who will be staying longer than a year may bring in household effects, including a car and/or boat, duty free within limits considered reasonable by the customs. The car (or boat) sales receipt must be presented to show that it has been in use for more than one year before its arrival in Japan. An international driving licence is valid for one year, after which a Japanese licence must be obtained. This involves both practical and written tests, which may be taken in English. Traffic drives on the left, and tolls are payable for motorway use. The volume of traffic is immense, but Japanese drivers are patient and disciplined, and accidents are consequently few. Signposting is inadequate (supposing one can read them) and a compass might be useful. A Toyota Corolla would cost around 1.8 million yen. All the usual forms of public and private transport are available.

A full-time maid would cost around 40,000 yen per week; cleaners and babysitters are paid about 1000 yen per hour.

Medical insurance for employees and their families is provided either by a government-managed scheme or a health insurance society. There are a number of English-speaking doctors in major cities, and Western brands of drugs are available.

There are many schools for English-speaking children but they are not geared to UK education. Most expatriates leave their children to be educated in Britain.

Some typical costs are:

	Yen
Beer (50 cl)	305
Bread (1 kg)	574
Butter (250 gm)	428
Cheese (500 gm)	967
Chicken (1 kg)	1185
Coffee	
ground (500 gm)	1608
instant (250 gm)	1973
Cooking oil (1 litre)	750
Eggs (12)	270
Milk (1 litre)	232
Mineral water (1 litre)	176
Potatoes (1 kg)	434
Rice (1 kg)	807
Steak (1 kg)	7022
Sugar (1 kg)	281
Tea bags (250 gm)	372
Whisky	2763
Wine (75 cl)	4650
Cigarettes (20)	254
Petrol (1 litre)	136

Office hours are usually from 9 am to 5 pm, banks 9 am to 3 pm Mondays to Fridays and 9 am to noon on Saturdays; many companies operate a five-day week. Shops and department stores are usually open on Sundays and public holidays, but most other businesses are closed then. There are 14 public holidays a year.

Four English language newspapers are published daily: the *Japan Times*, the *Yomiuri Daily*, the *Asahi Evening News* and the *Mainichi Daily News*. For points on etiquette and survival tips, three useful publications for intending expatriates in Japan are *Living in Japan*, *A Consumer s Guide to Prices in Japan* and *Finding a Home in Tokyo* published by the American Chamber of Commerce in Japan, Bridgestone Toranomon Building, 3 25 2, Toranomon, Minato-ku, Tokyo 105 (tel: 03 3433 5381; fax: 03 3436 1446).

Malaysia

Background
Malaysia is a federation of 13 states and two federal territories which fall into two separate geographical entities: peninsular Malaysia (the Malaya of colonial days minus Singapore) and East Malaysia which consists of Sabah and Sarawak and forms a wide strip on the northern half of what used to be Borneo Island. Peninsular Malaysia is about the size of England. East Malaysia is rather larger in area. However, a great deal of the interior in both cases is extremely mountainous and much of the coastline is swampy. East Malaysia is separated from the peninsula by about 750 km of the China Sea.

The total population of Malaysia is about 20 million, of whom about 80 per cent live in the peninsula. The largest city in the latter is the capital, Kuala Lumpur, and nearly 2 million people live in and around it. In East Malaysia, Kuching (500,000) and Sibu (250,000) are the main centres. Chinese form well over 30 per cent of the racial mix and Malays about 55 per cent. The rest are Asians, small tribal groups like Dayaks and expatriates. There is a good deal of rivalry between the tough, energetic Chinese (who have tended to dominate commerce and banking) and the Malays. Bahasa Malaysia is the official language and a knowledge of it would be useful to anyone going to live there for a long period, although English is widely spoken and understood. Various forms of Chinese and Indian languages are also spoken.

The government is partially democratically elected and partially appointed, and is headed by a titular monarch who is also elected, but only by the hereditary rulers of nine states. Under the federal system, each state has considerable autonomy. Since independence, a multiracial coalition has governed and was again returned in 1995 elections. Prime Minister Mahathir Mohammed is now in his fourth term of office. Nevertheless, ethnic and religious tensions have grown of late. Islam is the official religion of Malaysia.

The decision of the Malaysian cabinet, in February 1994, to scrap public sector deals with Britain followed three years of growing links with British businesses in both the public and private sectors.

Exchange rate: Ringgit Malaysia RM7.34 = £1.

The economy

Malaysia is a fertile country. Its economy has traditionally been associated with rubber and timber and these are still important products, particularly because of the impact of oil price rises on the synthetic rubber industry. Malaysia is also one of the few remaining sources of tropical hardwoods, grown mainly in East Malaysia. Oil palm is the most rapidly expanding new crop and Malaysia is now the world s leading exporter of oil palm products. Food crops are also grown extensively and the country is 90 per cent self-sufficient in rice. Recoverable gas reserves, however, have been found on a very large scale indeed and these have spurred industrialisation at a growing pace. Again, this country, like Japan and Russia, is going through major economic turmoil.

The other resource with which Malaysia is traditionally associated is tin, and though facing competition from synthetic substitutes, Malaysia is the West s leading supplier of this metal. The exploitation of bauxite, natural gas and copper ore reserves is growing in importance and the Federation also has oil in modest quantities.

The most rapidly expanding sector of the economy, until the recent collapse, has been manufacturing, which provided 70 per cent of exports, including electronics, office equipment, cars and consumer goods. Economic growth under the government s development programme was averaging 8 per cent. Inflation was around 4 per cent. Industrial activity has spread throughout West Malaysia with new commercial complexes in Johore and Pinang Island. Labuan Island is being established as an off-shore financial centre. Development is hampered by acute shortages of skilled labour. Unemployment is officially 4 per cent, but with the collapse of the SE Asian economy this figure is increasing rapidly

Personal finance

Broadly speaking, an expatriate should expect to be earning about 50 per cent more than his gross UK salary, taking the value of fringe benefits into account. Free or subsidised accommodation and medical care, a car, financial assistance with education and paid home leave every second year are usually provided. Expatriates on contract employment may freely remit money out of the country, though formal permission must be obtained from the Controller of Foreign Exchange for sums over RM10,000.

Taxation
Tax is levied on a PAYE basis on any income accruing in or derived from Malaysia; benefits in kind, excluding free medical treatment and the payment of passages home, are counted as part of chargeable income. Deducted from chargeable income are a broad range of allowances for a wife, dependent children, contributions to pension schemes and part of the cost of educating dependent children outside the Federation. The rate of tax begins at 2 per cent and reaches a maximum of 32 per cent. The government is encouraging companies to establish their South East Asian headquarters in Malaysia, and expatriates employed in their regional office for a short period (182 days or less) are exempt from Malaysian income tax.

Working conditions
No one may enter Malaysia to take up employment without a work permit and this can only be obtained by the employer. Dependants need a dependent pass and must also obtain permission from the immigration authorities if they wish to take up any kind of paid employment. Separate passes are issued for peninsular Malaysia, Sabah and Sarawak and they are not interchangeable. Sponsorship and a guarantee may be necessary.

The working week is usually Monday to Friday, 8.30 am to 4.30 pm, Saturday until 2.30 pm, but in some states the Moslem week, Saturday to Wednesday, or Thursday morning, is kept.

Living conditions
The climate is tropical, hot and humid, varying little (except in the highlands) from a mean of 80 F. Seasons are more related to rainfall than to temperature. Rain, averaging about 2300 mm a year, falls in short, drenching thunderstorms: about 60 per cent of it from November to March. Conditions, it will be seen, are apt to be rather trying, but air conditioning is provided nowa-

days in most homes and offices. Lightweight clothing is a necessity, but is readily available and relatively cheap. A single four-star hotel room in Kuala Lumpur is priced at around RM340 a night.

Accommodation has become somewhat easier to find and prices have been steady. Monthly rents for a large house are in the range of RM4700 RM13,500 in the Kuala Lumpur area but a good deal lower outside the principal towns. However, in most cases housing is provided as part of the contract. Where furniture and appliances are supplied as well, it is worth finding out in advance just what they consist of, so that the cost of shipping or purchasing locally can be allowed for in assessing the value of the remuneration package. Usually, cutlery, glass, linen and kitchen utensils are not provided, but household effects can be brought in free of duty if the householder has had them for more than three months. They can, however, be purchased locally and, though they will be more expensive than in the UK, it may be advisable to do this because of shipping delays. UK electrical equipment is suitable for Malaysian conditions (230V at 50 cycles AC), but perhaps not with the climate. The cost of electrical equipment is comparable with UK prices.

Food prices are higher but there are price controls on certain basic commodities. As in the case of many other developing countries, those who are not too dependent on European-style foods (cornflakes for breakfast, and the like) will find it cheaper than those who are. Some characteristic prices are:

	RM
Beer (50 cl)	6.07
Bread (1 kg)	4.05
Butter (250 gm)	3.05
Cheese, Cheddar type (500 gm)	12.14
Chicken (1 kg)	5.63
Coffee	
ground (500 gm)	19.87
instant (250 gm)	18.88
Cooking oil (1 litre)	6.83
Eggs (12)	2.61
Milk (1 litre)	2.98

Mineral water (1 litre)	2.47
Potatoes (1 kg)	3.48
Rice (1 kg)	2.30
Steak (1 kg)	34.42
Sugar (1 kg)	1.72
Tea bags (250 gm)	10.83
Whisky (75 cl)	95.36
Wine (75 cl)	55.55
Cigarettes (20)	3.57
Petrol (1 litre)	1.17

Most expatriates get domestic help for household chores. A full-time servant in Kuala Lumpur earns about RM520 per month, plus one month s bonus annually, and wages tend to be lower elsewhere.

A private car is considered a virtual necessity and the general opinion is that it is better to buy one of the makes that is locally assembled than to import a car: spares are easier to get hold of, mechanics are more familiar with the cars and they are better suited to local conditions. Moreover, there is an import duty of 100 350 per cent on cars. In the light of this, employers should be prepared to supply a company car, and as an expatriate employee you can reasonably expect that a car will go with the job. If it does not, you will find that a Proton Wira, for example, will cost about RM45,000. Petrol is cheaper than in the UK. It is advisable to take out a comprehensive insurance policy because local driving standards are poor. You will need to have a Malaysian driving licence eventually but an international driving licence is valid for one year.

Organised leisure in Sabah and Sarawak is limited to the main centres, but there is a wide choice of clubs of all kinds in the peninsula. Facilities for local leave are excellent, both in the hills and at the seaside, where some of the world s few remaining great unspoiled beaches are to be found. Scheduled coach services and long-distance taxis are cheap and efficient. A small car can be hired for around RM110 a day.

Malaysia s climate is obviously apt to present health problems for those who cannot take long spells of uninterruptedly hot, humid weather. However, the principal disease hazard, malaria, has been largely eliminated, though it still exists in some rural areas. (Yellow fever injections are required before you enter the country, and your doctor will advise you on other precautions.) Most expatriates receive free medical treatment in some form or other, either as government employees or as part of the remuneration package. Otherwise, this is a potentially major expense to be budgeted for or insured against. First-class hospital accommodation alone apart from actual treatment costs up to RM850 a day. Malaysia is very strict about drugs and trafficking in hard drugs carries the death penalty. If you are bringing medicines with you, make sure they are prescribed and labelled.

The schools situation in Malaysia is awkward for expatriates. It is difficult to get into state schools because Malaysian children have priority, and in any case the curriculum is designed for the indigenous population. There are a number of fee-paying schools catering for expatriate children, although only one, the Uplands School in Penang, offers boarding *and* a UK curriculum.

Singapore

Background

The Republic of Singapore consists of a main island and a group of islets; it lies off the southern tip of the Malay peninsula, but is close enough to be connected to it by a causeway across the Straits of Johore. In total area it is about the size of the Isle of Wight, and increasing through reclamation. It has a population of about 2.9 million, 78 per cent of whom are Chinese, 14 per cent Malay, and the rest Indian or European. The official languages are Malay, Chinese, Tamil and English, but English is the language of administration and business. In spite of its proximity to Malaysia, Singapore is a quite separate state. Its government, though democratically elected, could be described as a benevolent dictatorship and has been in power since 1959. Ideologically it practises a form of pragmatic socialism and is favourably disposed towards business while having many of the characteristics of a welfare state. Criticism of the government is unwise and political opposition is very much circumscribed. In 1993, the first direct Presidential elections were held, won by Ong Teng Cheong, of the ruling PAP party. No opposition candidates were allowed. In fact, though, the government is generally popular and has been extremely efficient in managing the economy while enacting far-reaching measures to improve health, housing, social benefits and education. Singapore is regarded as being one of the most politically stable areas of South East Asia. The official language is Malay, but English is the language of business and government.

Exchange rate: Singapore $2.80 = £1.

The economy

Traditionally Singapore, with its geographical position at the crossroads of many international trade routes, its fine natural harbour and its excellent port facilities, has served as the principal entrep t for South East Asia. It is also an important base for companies operating oil exploration and refining services. To a large extent this continues to be its role, but the government, conscious of the fact that this makes the economy somewhat too dependent on outside forces, has strongly encouraged the development of manufacturing industry. In particular, the government has fastened on to the opportunities created by the second industrial revolution of the new technology. It has deliberately fostered a high wages policy to force manufacturers to move from labour-intensive to capital-intensive activities, particularly in view of the fact that Singapore suffers from labour shortages. However, this policy has had the effect of pricing many Singapore goods out of export markets and their replacement by products from the country s Asian competitors; the rate of growth is now lagging behind that of South Korea and Taiwan. In 1993, the economy grew by 9.9 per cent of GDP. Government secrecy makes it difficult to access more recent figures.

Manufacturing industry in general has grown rapidly in recent years, sometimes at phenomenal rates. Textiles, printing, electrical goods, electronics, plastics, building materials and foodstuffs are all active sectors. The main slow-down has been in heavy industry. Sinagpore also continues to be an important financial and banking centre and, as elsewhere in Asia, tourism is a rapidly growing industry. Main trading partners are the USA, Malaysia, the EU, Hong Kong and Japan.

Personal finance

Managers of medium-sized companies might expect to earn £40,000 £50,000 a year plus fringe benefits such as free or subsidised housing, home leave, free medical treatment, school fees and a car. There are no restrictions on the amount of money that can be taken out of the country.

Taxation

Individuals resident in Singapore for tax purposes are liable to Singapore personal income tax charged on a sliding scale on income derived in or remitted to Singapore. Accommodation provided by the employer and certain benefits in kind are taxable, but not capital gains. Tax is levied at progressive rates from 2.5 to 30 per cent. There is tax relief for up to three children, but none thereafter part of Singapore s policy of keeping down family numbers.

Employment for a period or periods which together do not exceed 60 days in a calendar year is exempt from tax.

Working conditions

The British expatriate community is quite large between 7000 and 8000. Jobs are advertised in the appropriate sectors of the overseas press and are usually on a contract basis with a salary plus fringe benefits as indicated in the personal finance section. The major Singapore professional bodies are affiliated to, or otherwise closely connected with, their UK counterparts. People going to work in Singapore must have an employment pass which has to be obtained by the prospective employer. Dependants must also obtain a pass which has to be applied for by the employer. There are various immigration schemes for those with proven technical, professional or entrepreneurial skills.

Living conditions

Singapore is less than 137 km from the equator and is hot and humid for most of the year. Air conditioning is standard equipment in an executive-level house or flat, but lightweight clothing is also essential. A good cotton, off-the-peg dress costs about S$150 if locally made   much more if imported. A man s locally made tailored suit can be ordered at about S$600. Singapore abounds in small shops and stalls selling consumer durables of all kinds. However, unless you are accompanied by a Singapore citizen or are very good at bargaining you will probably find it no more expensive to shop at a department store like Tang s in Orchard Street, Singapore s main thoroughfare.

Accommodation in Singapore is becoming cheaper and easier to find and is well below the Hong Kong price levels. A single room in a four-star hotel averages S$200 a night and, although previously it was possible to reduce hotel prices by haggling (because of over-supply), this is no longer the case. This is also becoming true of rents. A three-bedroomed, unfurnished apartment would cost between S$3200 and S$9500 per month to rent. However, rents are cheaper outside the more popular residential districts. It is also possible to buy property, but there are restrictions on non-citizens doing so, except in the case of flats in high-rise buildings and condominium units. Accommodation is generally let unfurnished, but household appliances are slightly cheaper than in the UK   you can buy a large colour TV for S$1140. The electricity supply is 230 250V, 50 cycles AC. Three square pin plugs are common. Except in department stores, bargaining for expensive items is worthwhile.

Singapore is self-sufficient in many foods and it is possible to eat fairly cheaply if you buy local products. Prices vary considerably from month to month, but here are some characteristic prices:

	S$
Beer (50 cl)	4.33
Bread (1 kg)	2.15
Butter (250 gm)	2.17
Cheese (500 gm)	7.43
Chicken (1 kg)	11.15
Coffee	
ground (500 gm)	5.87
Cooking oil (1 litre)	3.99

Eggs (12)	1.67
Milk (1 litre)	2.76
Mineral water (1 litre)	1.35
Potatoes (1 kg)	4.13
Rice (1 kg)	1.95
Steak (1 kg)	13.09
Sugar (1 kg)	1.35
Tea bags (250 gm)	10.76
Whisky (75 cl)	56.77
Wine (75 cl)	26.43
Cigarettes (20)	4.67
Petrol (1 litre)	1.24

Tropical fruit is delicious and quite cheap; so are Chinese restaurants, although eating out European style is expensive. On the other hand, you can buy a delicious Chinese meal from a clean, government-inspected street stall for under S$6.

Domestic servants are now much harder to find because of Singapore s low unemployment rate. A live-in *amah*, fulfilling the functions of a maid (cooking, cleaning and babysitting), will earn around S$420 a month. On top of this, the employer has to contribute to the Central Provident Fund and, if the servant is foreign, S$300 per month tax. It is advisable to arrange workmen s compensation insurance for domestic staff such as *amahs*, drivers and gardeners. For Filipino maids, personal accident insurance is compulsory and you may also have to provide medical insurance, annual air fares home and a bond for the Immigration Department of S$5000.

The importing of cars is discouraged, and there is a duty of 45 per cent on imported cars on top of a basic additional registration fee of 150 per cent of the value of any new car, imported or otherwise. Thus it is not advisable to bring a car into Singapore from abroad, even though buying one locally is very expensive. Second-hand cars are advertised for sale in *The Straits Times*. The government is trying to limit car ownership on the island, both by fiscal policies and by placing restrictions on the use of cars in the central business district. A new Toyota Corolla is priced about S$121,570 plus certificate of entitlement (which can amount to S$45,000 50,000). On the other hand, both taxis and public transport are correspondingly inexpensive, and indeed are among the world s cheapest.

Leisure activities and participation in sport in public places are reasonably priced but membership and entrance fees at private clubs are in some cases very expensive. Top of the league is the Singapore Island Country Club, with four magnificent golf courses and an Olympic-size swimming pool. Although membership fees are high, many foreign-based employers will pay these on behalf of their senior expatriates.

As far as private entertainment is concerned, expatriates should be aware that there is censorship on moral as well as political grounds in Singapore. For instance, videotapes brought into the country have to be submitted to the board of censors. There has been some relaxation on the censorship policies. R-rated (restricted) movies are released in Singapore for adult viewing (21 years and over).

Singapore has a good health record and the government wages a somewhat draconian cleanliness campaign, which includes hefty fines for dropping even a bus ticket in the street. There are no free medical facilities but treatment in government clinics is very cheap, though most expatriates prefer to use private doctors, who charge between S$25 and S$50 (specialists S$45 $80), depending on their qualifications and what sort of treatment is involved. Surgeons and obstetricians fees start at around S$2100 and a private room in a hospital costs about S$180 a day. Medical fees, or insurance premiums to cover them, are often, in the case of expatriates, met by employers.

As in many other jobs overseas, education can be a problem, and arrangements to send children to local schools should be made as soon as possible. Government schools are very cheap, with only nominal fees for the children of Singapore residents. There are three good English private primary schools. The Singapore American School takes all ages up to 18, and there is also the United World College of South East Asia which has facilities for A-level teaching. There is an excellent university in Singapore, at which the standards of entry and the level of the courses are equivalent to UK universities. Fees vary depending on the nature of the course being taken.

Australasia

Australia

Background
Australia is the world s largest island and smallest continent. It has an area approximately equal to the continental USA and a population of about 18.5 million people. It is a highly urbanised society: 70 per cent of the population live in the ten largest cities, and nearly 7 million live in Sydney and Melbourne. Inland (up to 500 miles from the coast) there are many pleasant rural cities and towns; the remainder of the continent tends to be very sparsely populated and arid. The climate ranges from tropical in the north to temperate in the south with desert conditions in much of the interior. The capital is Canberra and the seven constituent states are New South Wales, Northern Territory, Queensland, South Australia, Tasmania, Victoria and Western Australia.

Australian government operates at two levels   State and Federal. Although considerable overlapping of responsibilities occurs, State legislature concerns education, health, justice, roads and railways, housing and agriculture while the Federal government covers matters of national importance: defence, foreign affairs, taxation, social services, etc. This system sometimes results in a conflict of political interest between Central and State Governments which may have different elected majorities. (Incidentally, the Liberal Party in Australia corresponds more to the Conservative Party in the UK while the Labour Party is somewhat to the right of its British counterpart. The Australian Democrats are broadly similar to the UK Liberal Democrats.) In spite of these rivalries, Australia is politically very stable. Parliament consists of the Queen, the Senate and the House of Representatives. In 1996, the long-ruling Labour Party under Paul Keating was heavily defeated in general elections. The current government is a Liberal National Party coalition (all conservative) under Prime Minister John Howard.

Exchange rate: A$2.67 = £1.

The economy

Australia has recovered strongly from the recession of the early 1990s. Indeed, the economy is showing the fastest growth in the western world, with gross domestic product increasing at an annual rate of 4 per cent. Inflation is hovering at around 3.5 per cent and unemployment has fallen to 8.5 per cent. However, balance of trade and foreign debt figures remain poor. The largest export industries are agricultural products and mineral extraction. Primary imports are in transportation and office equipment. Main trading partners are Japan, Korea, the US and New Zealand. Despite all this, one of the biggest revenue earners is tourism.

Despite a forecast of 4.5 per cent growth, the government is maintaining a cautious line on immigration policy. Preference is given to people with direct and close family connections, skilled and business migrants, and others accepted under refugee or special humanitarian programmes. A points system is used in some of the categories to determine a person s eligibility based on economic factors such as age, health, education, occupation and the level of skill required to undertake that occupation in Australia. All non-nationals must obtain a visa beforehand.

Additional information can be obtained from the Australian High Commission in London or the Australian Consulate in Manchester.

Taxation

Income tax is levied on a PAYE system against individuals whose source of income is derived from salary or wages. The scheme is known as standard rate taxation. Tax rates have a top marginal rate of 47 per cent.

Unearned income (dividends, interest, etc) of minors is subject to special rules. Taxable income is derived by subtracting allowable expenses, eg subscriptions to professional journals, trade union subscriptions, from total income. There is also a system of rebates which are deducted from tax payable and include dependent spouse and concessional rebate. Concessional rebate includes expenditures on life assurance and pension contributions, medical and related costs, children s education expenses, and rates and taxes on principal residence. Most are subject to an upper limit.

In addition, a family allowance is paid monthly to all resident families which include either children under 16 or full-time students aged 16 25. There is no VAT, though non-essential goods are subject to indirect taxation.

A universal health insurance scheme, Medicare, provides residents with protection against hospital, medical and optical costs. Contributions to the scheme are 1.7 per cent of taxable income (with low-income cut-off points).

Working conditions

At executive and professional levels international standards and conditions of work apply. Holidays are normally four weeks a year and some firms pay a holiday bonus. There is also often a form of sabbatical leave after ten years service with a company. Flexible working hours are quite common in Australia, particularly in the public sector. The chief difference in working conditions between Australia and other countries is that the concept of status related to specific jobs and even more, social and workplace behaviour associated with it has to be discarded. Any tendency to give yourself airs is fatal!

Australian employers will not usually recruit from a distance, but it is possible to get a good picture of the sort of employment opportunities available from Australian newspapers and particularly from the Australian migration authorities. In general the demand is for specific skills and professional or managerial qualifications (in, for example, computer work). Most British professional qualifications are recognised in Australia, but it is necessary to show documentary evidence of having obtained them.

It is fairly easy to get working holiday visas, valid for up to 12 months, if you are under 25. Apply to the Australian Commission or the nearest consulate.

It is worth noting that the new government is likely to embark on a programme of cost-cutting which may affect taxation, benefits and pay.

Living conditions

Most people s image of Australia is taken from the TV soaps: life on a housing estate with a good climate and a high standard of living. Though this is not entirely inaccurate, Australia is a very civilised place in which to live. It has excellent wines, varied and sophisticated restaurants and good cultural amenities. The major newspapers are as good as any UK daily but British and American books cost more than in the country of origin. They are not subject to import duty, however, so if you are a keen reader, it is a good idea to have an account with a British book shop. Sports are extremely popular.

Manufactured goods are expensive, for example: a 22-in colour TV for A$950, a refrigerator for A$1000 and a washing machine for A$930. This may suggest that it is worth while taking domestic appliances with you, but be careful. Electrical goods should be checked with the maker to see if they would work in Australia, because the voltage systems differ (220 250V, 50 cycles AC). Gas appliances are particularly tricky because of differences in pressure and gas composition. British TVs and video recorders do not function in Australia because of different signals and need to be professionally converted to compatibility with the Australian system.

A car, essential in Australia, is best bought there. A Ford Laser costs about A$23,300. Japanese cars are widely considered to be best buys . If you import a car you will have to make sure that it meets the safety regulations of the state to which you are going. You can drive on a British licence for the first three months. After that you will have to take a local test, but this will only be an oral one if you already hold a British or international licence. Interstate transport is usually by aeroplane, although there is also a large railway network.

Food, allowing for seasonal variations, is varied and fairly reasonable and generally much cheaper than in the UK. Many staples such as meat cost less than half UK prices.

A good up-to-date source of information on prices (as well as other facts about Australia) is a magazine available at Australia House Migration Office called *Australian Outlook.*

Fruit and vegetables vary with the season and according to the climate of the state, but can be very cheap at the appropriate times of year. Prices vary from state to state. In ascending order of cost the ranking is, roughly, Melbourne, Adelaide, Brisbane, Perth, Sydney, Canberra, Hobart, Darwin. A single room in a four-star Melbourne hotel is around A$165 a night.

Education begins at the age of 5 or 6 and is compulsory up to age 15 or 16 (depending on the state). The school session starts early in February, not September as in the UK. It must be remembered that, in the southern hemisphere, the seasons are reversed, hence the Australian Christmas is midsummer. Tuition is free in government schools, but parents generally have to provide uniforms, books and other materials, though such items can be claimed against income tax, up to a maximum of A$250 per child. As many as 25 per cent of pupils, however, attend private schools, particularly in the latter years of secondary education. Fees are reasonable (and subject to tax rebates) because these schools are aided by government grants. Allow A$4000 6000 a year for private secondary school tuition fees.

There are small tuition fees for university-level education, which is very well provided for in all states. Most Australians take a pass degree rather than honours. Standards are similar to those in the UK.

The sources for finance and house purchase are principally savings banks and building societies. Repayment periods run at between 15 and 25 years and mortgage repayment rates average around 25 per cent of income. (There are also special state schemes for families on low incomes.) As a rule the lender will provide around 75 per cent of the lender s valuation of the property (not market value) and no distinction is made in this respect between old and new houses.

The availability of houses and flats, both for rent and for sale, varies widely from state to state. The annual rental of an unfurnished, four-bedroomed house can be as high as A\$65,500 in a prime area, though A\$32,300 is a good average. Rents are substantially less in the smaller cities. About 40 per cent of Australians own their homes. To buy a quality house in a good area in most cities will cost from A\$100,000 upwards (except in Sydney where house prices tend to be 20 per cent higher than elsewhere in the country). A good up-to-date guide on house purchase and price levels in Australia is available from the Commonwealth Bank of Australia s Financial and Migrant Information Service, 1 Kingsway, London WC2B 6DU (tel: 0171 379 0955).

British migrants should note that in recent years the UK influence in Australia has diminished considerably, as witness the proposal that Australia should become a republic. While people of British descent are still in the majority, a very substantial part of the population come from other parts of Europe and there is a growing Asian minority, most of whom have arrived in the country over the last 10 15 years. Australia is now recognised officially as a multicultural society and this has led, among other things, to a wider use of a variety of languages.

New Zealand

Background
New Zealand is not, as many people seem to believe, next door to Australia, but some 1200 miles away. It is a country about the size of Italy, mostly very beautiful, mountainous and with marvellous facilities for every kind of outdoor life. It has a population of around 3.5 million, of whom nearly 75 per cent live in the North Island, specifically around the main cities of Auckland, Wellington and Hamilton. There are quite marked differences of climate between Auckland, situated in a very mild part of the North Island, and smaller cities like Dunedin or Invercargill in the South Island, where winters can be decidedly cold. Generally, the weather is maritime temperate.

The population is largely of British descent New Zealand has not attracted European settlers from other countries to the same degree as Australia and about 13 per cent of the total are Maori; however, intermarriage means that many New Zealanders have both Maori and European ancestors. There has recently been a rise in awareness of bi-culturalism and a growing politicisation of the Polynesian population in general. New Zealand also has an increasing Asian minority of mainly Chinese and South East Asian background. A long-established Indian population is also present; the large Pacific Island population continues to increase.

New Zealand is a member of the Commonwealth and the Queen is head of state, represented by a Governor-General. Parliament consists of the Single House of Representatives, which, until recently, has been elected on the British system. From 1996 on, it will be partially elected by proportional representation. Following several years of radical rule by Labour, the National party gained power in 1993 and, under Prime Minister Jim Bolger, has since undertaken a programme of reform to open up and modernise the economy.

Exchange rate: NZ$3.22 = £1.

The economy

Economic reforms have changed the economy from being highly regulated and protected to one of market economics. Deregulation, privatisation and the removal of subsidies have brought great changes. The now-independent Reserve Bank has a contract to keep inflation below 2 per cent; the welfare state has been largely dismantled. In 1994, economic growth was 5 per cent and the national debt was being steadily reduced. Unemployment is still high.

Agricultural products continue to form the core of the economy, primarily in dairy products, cattle and sheep. Fish, timber and wood pulp are increasingly important. Natural gas is the most successful resource export. Almost all power is provided by hydroelectricity. Manufacturing is being actively encouraged, but tourism is the fastest growing sector, scheduled to provide earnings of NZ$9 billion by 2000. Main trading partners are Australia, Japan, USA and the UK.

Taxation

Tax is deducted on a PAYE basis. The basic rates of income tax are 25 per cent and 33 per cent. In addition, there is a goods and services tax (GST) of 12.5 per cent which is similar to VAT.

Working conditions

Widespread means-testing has been introduced throughout the welfare state, so that only the very poor now receive free or subsidised healthcare and other benefits. Under a reciprocal arrangement with the UK, health care (including hospitalisation) is available to residents who go to live in New Zealand and have made the necessary National Insurance contributions here. Visits to the doctor, prescriptions and hospital outpatient visits are all charged in relation to the patient s ability to pay.

Applications for work permits must be supported by an offer of employment from a New Zealand employer and must be submitted at least four weeks prior to intended departure from the UK. Accommodation guarantees may be required. Further information may be obtained from the New Zealand Immigration Service, New Zealand House, Haymarket, London SW1Y 4TQ (tel: 0171 973 0366). There are no restrictions about taking money into or out of the country. Visitors from the UK, and many other nationals, do not require a visa but those intending to stay for longer must apply for a residence permit. Consideration is generally only given to applicants with skills on the Priority List.

In general, rates of pay are slightly lower than in the UK, while deductions are at about the same level. The cost of living, however, is less, so that the net result is very similar to working in the UK. Most employees receive at least three weeks holiday. The 40 hour week is universal.

Living conditions

The standard of living is high. Food is somewhat cheaper than in the UK and prices are currently falling. Bulk-buying from bins at local supermarkets is popular and economical. Most household and manufactured goods cost somewhat more than in the UK. Most supermarkets are open seven days a week, often until 8 pm on weekdays. Rates at first-class hotels are NZ$130 250 a night for a single room.

The opportunity for outdoor life in New Zealand is broader in range and cheaper to pursue than in Europe; at the same time, the larger cities provide opportunities for cultural pursuits. Hiking and trekking are particularly popular. The entire population of New Zealand is equivalent to that of a major British city but spread over an area equivalent to the British Isles, hence much of the country is sparsely populated.

There are virtually no restrictions on bringing personal effects into the country. Domestic electricity is supplied at 230V, 50HZ AC. Most electrical equipment will work in New Zealand, but some items may require a transformer to reduce voltage. British TVs *have* to be adapted as frequencies and line systems differ. However, in some instances it is possible to buy a suitable export model. A VHF modulator is required for video viewing on a normal New Zealand TV set.

People entering New Zealand to take up permanent residence for the first time may bring in a motor vehicle free of duty and GST if certain conditions are met (a leaflet is available from New Zealand House). UK driving licences are accepted for the first year of your stay, after which you have to take a test (which has written and oral parts) to obtain a New Zealand licence. Although New Zealanders drive on the left and road rules are essentially the same as in the UK, it would be advisable to check out the New Zealand road code there are differences, especially in the give-way rules. Travel by internal airline is very popular, and often the best option to more remote parts.

Primary school education begins at 5, but there is also an excellent network of pre-school education for 3-year-olds upwards. Education is compulsory from 6 to 15 and tuition is subsidised. Parents are expected to pay some fees and for uniforms, the wearing of which is customary in secondary schools. There are also private schools, mostly conducted by religious bodies. University entrance qualifications correspond to the UK and tuition is subsidised for those who reach top-level entrance qualifications. There are university scholarships for the brightest students. There are seven universities.

The typical New Zealand house is a bungalow, serviceable, with a nice garden; there is a greater range of housing in the larger cities. Rented accommodation is becoming easier to obtain and house prices remain expensive. The principal lenders are banks and Housing NZ, a former government agency now corporatised, and, though their loans carry a low rate of interest and a long repayment period, they restrict lending to first-time buyers in low income groups, which excludes many expatriates. (The national average house price is around NZ$120,000, but prices in Wellington and Auckland are considerably higher than in rural areas and rising.) New Zealand newspapers, available in New Zealand House, carry extensive real estate listings. Rentals range from NZ$400 to NZ$600 per week.

Papua New Guinea

Background

Papua New Guinea lies 160 kilometres north of Australia and has a land area of 461,700 square kilometres. The country comprises the eastern part of the main New Guinea Island and about 600 smaller islands, of which the largest are New Britain, Bougainville and New Ireland. It is geographically very diverse, with a massive mountain range running east west on the main island and large areas of tropical rain forest around its fringes. Some areas, particularly in the south, receive 200 inches of rain a year among the world s highest.

The population is estimated at 4 million, of whom about 10 per cent are non-nationals, principally Australians, Chinese, Indians, Africans and South-East Asians. The capital is Port Moresby (population 190,000) and the other major towns are the main port and commercial centre of Lae on the north-eastern coast, Madang, Rabaul and Goroka.

The official language is English, but in addition to Melanesian Pidgin and Hiri Motu, both of which are widely spoken, there are over 700 other languages about half the world s total.

Papua New Guinea has been an independent state since 1975, when power was finally transferred from Australia. There are 19 provinces, each with a provisional government that is more or less autonomous in local matters. The central government is democratically elected, has one chamber and acknowledges Queen Elizabeth II as head of state, represented by a Governor General.

Exchange rate: Kina 2.37 = £1.

The economy

Until fairly recently, the economy was based almost entirely on agriculture with no cash economy. Most of the population is occupied in this sector. Commercial crops include copra, cocoa, coffee, rubber, tea and sugar. Exports of tropical wood is a mainstay PNG is one of the few remaining countries in the region exporting unprocessed timber, but restrictions to preserve the forests have recently been imposed. The most important natural resources are copper, gold and silver. The Panguna Copper Mine in Bougainville used to provide nearly half of PNG s national income until closed by rebel action. Large-scale mining has been encouraged elsewhere. Large oil and gas reserves have also been discovered. Other industries are small-scale or absent altogether.

Personal finance and taxation

Wage-earners with only one source of income have tax deducted automatically from their pay, after deductions for dependants. Tax rates go up to 35 per cent.

There should not normally be problems with the remittability of currency from Papua New Guinea.

Working conditions

It is necessary to hold a work permit in order to gain permission to reside in the country. This is obtainable before arrival, either through the Department of Labour and Industry or through the employer. In addition, all foreign nationals must have a valid passport and visa before entering Papua New Guinea.

Many expatriate posts in the country are in government employ, and are well advertised in the UK, typically in *The Guardian*. Salaries are quite high, but the qualifications and experience demanded are equally so.

Living conditions

The climate is typically tropical and cool cotton clothes are normal year-round wear. The Highlands are cooler. Port Moresby has a dry season from May to November, the opposite of Lae s. Malaria is a problem in many areas, although Moresby is now relatively safe. Health problems have now been replaced by domestic and personal security concerns. Violent crime is a particularly serious issue and houses should be well protected. Assaults on women are also a serious problem in the major cities. Curfews are not unknown.

The Bougainville Revolutionary Army (BRA) has been active on Bougainville Island since 1988, fighting a secessionist war that has caused some 3000 deaths. This guerilla war may continue for some time to come, the Papua New Guinea Government being unlikely to relinquish control of Bougainville, which contains the largest known deposits of low-grade copper and large quantities of gold. It is advisable to investigate the level of hostilities before visiting the island.

Travel within the country is usually impossible by road (except from Lae to the principal Highland towns). Consequently, air is the normal medium for transport and Air Niugini flies to all the major centres and to many small towns; other carriers include Talair, Douglas Airways, Bougair and several other charter firms. Hire and radio cars are available in the main towns but bus services are still inefficient. There are some scenic highways, of various quality.

Although reasonably well supplied with hotels and boasting a few good restaurants, Port Moresby has little to offer by way of night life. What there is centres around the hotels, and is generally Australian in flavour. A single room in a four-star hotel would cost around K164 a night.

It is easy to get domestic servants, but it is wise to check references and make an initial provisional arrangement, as there are many urban drifters. Pay is usually around K37 a week and it should be agreed at the start how many relatives and others will be sharing it with the servant actually hired.

Imported food is expensive, but local produce is plentiful, varied and quite cheap.

Some typical prices are:

	K
Beer (50 cl)	1.71
Bread (1 kg)	1.36
Butter (250 gm)	0.90
Cheese, Cheddar type (500 gm)	4.93
Chicken (1 kg)	4.28
Coffee	
ground (500 gm)	5.99
instant (250 gm)	11.71
Cooking oil (1 litres)	3.72
Eggs (12)	2.62
Milk (1 litre)	2.25
Mineral water (1 litre)	2.03
Potatoes (1 kg)	1.36
Rice (1 kg)	0.80
Steak (1 kg)	9.24
Sugar (1 kg)	1.42
Tea bags (250 gm)	5.35
Whisky (75 cl)	36.96
Wine (75 cl)	12.92
Cigarettes (20)	1.71
Petrol (1 litre)	0.59

Accommodation is hard to find, and annual rents can be high. Port Moresby has a good water supply and in all the main centres there is safe drinking water and electricity. The telephone service is excellent but all mail must be addressed to PO boxes. There is no mains gas supply.

The education system is good, and there is a university with 3000 students at Port Moresby and a University of Technology at Lae. The language of instruction is English. There are a number of International Schools which follow a broadly New South Wales, Australia curriculum, but many expatriates send their children abroad for their education.

Further Information

Principal Sources

We are indebted to a great many sources for the information in this book, but the following not arranged in order of merit were the ones we found particularly useful.

Business Profiles. Individual booklets issued by the Hong Kong and Shanghai Banking Corporation, Public Affairs, PO Box 199, 99 Bishopsgate, London EC2P 2LA (tel: 0171 638 2366), covering many countries in some detail. They are aimed at both companies and private individuals and contain some useful information on living conditions.

Prices and Earnings Around the Globe. An excellent comparative survey of a wide variety of costs and earnings in 53 countries. Issued every three years by the Union Bank of Switzerland, 100 Liverpool Street, London EC2M 2RH (tel: 0171 901 3333, fax: 0171 901 2345).

Hints for Exporters Visiting . . . . Issued by the Department of Trade and Industry. Intended mainly for business visitors, but contain useful data on things like holidays, hotel addresses, business etiquette, climate at various times of the year, etc. Also *Country Profiles.* Contact DTI Export Publications, PO Box 55, Stratford-upon-Avon CV37 9GE (tel: 01789 296212). The Business in Europe Hotline (0117 944 4888) is also a useful contact point.

The monthly *Resident Abroad* covers both life style and money. It is published by Financial Times Magazines, Greystoke

Place, Fetter Lane, London EC4 1ND (tel: 0171 405 6969, fax: 0171 242 0263).

Barclays Country Reports, covering more than 20 OECD countries, are available from the Librarian, Economics Department, Barclays Bank plc, PO Box 12, 1 Wimborne Road, Poole, Dorset BH15 2BB. These are free to Barclays account holders. The Overseas Placing Unit of the Employment Service (Skills House, 3 7 Holy Green, Off the Moor, Sheffield S1 4AQ) produces a number of booklets on working abroad and entry conditions for specific countries.

Many pamphlets and books have been published about Europe. EU material can be obtained from the London office of the European Commission (see p. 366), or The Stationery Office. Foreign embassies based in London will also have material of value for expatriates intending to live and work in the country which they represent. Their addresses are given in the *London Diplomatic List*, available from The Stationery Office (tel: 0171 873 9090) priced £4.95 and updated every six months.

Receiving BBC World Service

Wherever you are in the world, you should be able to receive English-language radio broadcasts from the BBC World Service with BBC World Service Television now widely available too. To hear the radio programmes, you need a suitable short-wave radio, although the programmes are also available on medium wave and FM in some countries. As well as its news coverage and analysis, the World Service transmits business reports, sport, drama and stories, all kinds of music, features, comedy and quiz programmes and broad coverage of the arts and literature, science and religion. Programmes are aimed at a world audience British people abroad are a relatively small minority of listeners but news about Britain appears regularly during the day. You can ask for a free programme and frequency guide for your part of the world (please see addresses given on the following pages).

Useful Addresses

Anderson Sinclair & Co
The Leatherhead Institute
High Street
Leatherhead
Surrey KT22 8AH
Tel: 01372 379345
(Financial advisers specialising in expatriate investment and tax problems.)

BBC World Service
Bush House
Strand
London WC2B 4PH
Tel: 0171 240 3456
Fax: 0171 240 4899

BBC Worldwide Television
Woodlands
80 Wood Lane
London W12 0TT
Tel: 0181 576 2975
Fax: 0181 576 3040

BUPA International
Provident House
Essex Street
London WC2R 3AX
Tel: 0171 353 5212
Fax: 0171 836 1385

Centre for International Briefing
Farnham Castle
Farnham
Surrey GU9 0AG
Tel: 01252 721194
Fax: 01252 719277

Corona Worldwide
c/o Commonwealth Institute
Kensington High Street
London W8 6NQ
Tel: 0171 610 4407
Fax: 0171 602 7374

Council of British Independent Schools in the European Communities (COBISEC) Secretariat
c/o St Julian s British School
2777 Carcavelos Codex
Portugal
Tel: 351 1 4570140
Fax: 351 1 4566817

Department for International Development
Abercrombie House
Eaglesham Road
East Kilbride
Glasgow G75 8EA
Tel: 01355 844000
Fax: 01355 844099

Department of Social Security
Contributions Agency
International Services
Longbenton
Newcastle upon Tyne NE98 1YX
Tel: 0191 225 4811

Department of Social Security
Benefits Agency
Pensions and Overseas Benefits Directorate
Tyneview Park
Newcastle upon Tyne NE98 1BA
Tel: 0191 218 7878

Department of Social Security
Child Benefit Centre
PO Box 1
Newcastle upon Tyne NE88 1AA

Education and Guardian Advisory Services Ltd (EGAS)
11 Seaton Avenue
Mutley
Plymouth PL4 6QJ
Tel/fax: 01752 261229

Further Information

European Commission
Information Services Unit
8 Storey s Gate
London SW1P 3AT
Tel: 0171 973 1905

Europea-IMG Ltd
Provender Mill
Mill Bay Lane
Horsham
West Sussex RH12 1TQ
Tel: 01403 263860

European Council of International
Schools (ECIS)
21 Lavant Street
Petersfield
Hampshire GU32 3EL
Tel: 01730 268244
Fax: 01730 267914

Exeter Friendly Society
Beech Hill House
Walnut Gardens
Exeter EX4 4DG
Tel: 01392 477200
Fax: 01392 477235

Gabbitas Educational
Consultants Ltd
126 130 Regent Street
London W1R 6EE
Tel: 0171 734 0161
Fax: 0171 437 1764

GJW Education and Guardianship
Service
Southcote
Coreway
Sidmouth
Devon EX10 9SD
Tel: 01395 515614
Fax: 01395 514108

Going Places
Expatriate Briefing
84 Coombe Road
New Malden
Surrey KT3 4QS
Tel: 0181 949 8811

Goodhealth Worldwide Ltd
Mill Bay Lane
Horsham
West Sussex RH12 1TQ
Tel: 01403 263860
Fax: 01403 268429

The Stationery Office Books
PO Box 276
London SW8 5DT
Tel: 0171 873 9090

Independent Schools Information
Service (ISIS)
56 Buckingham Gate
London SW1E 6AG
Tel: 0171 630 8793
Fax: 0171 630 5013

International SOS Assistance
7 Old Lodge Place
St Margarets
Twickenham
Middlesex TW1 1RQ
Tel: 0181 744 0033
Fax: 0181 744 0620

National Extension College
18 Brooklands Avenue
Cambridge CB2 2HN
Tel: 01223 316644

National Savings
Lytham St Annes
Lancs FY0 1YN

Overseas Jobs Express
Premier House
Shoreham Airport
Sussex BN43 5FF
Tel: 01273 440220

Allied Pickfords
Heritage House
345 Southbury Road
Enfield EN1 1UP
Tel: 0181 219 8000

PPP Healthcare Group
Tavistock House South
Tavistock Square
London WC1H 9LJ
Tel: 0171 380 0967

RAC Travel Services
PO Box 499
Croydon
Surrey CR2 6ZH
Tel: 0800 550055

University of London
Careers Service
50 Gordon Square
London WC1H 0PQ
Tel: 0171 387 8221

Voluntary Service Overseas
317 Putney Bridge Road
London SW15 2PN
Tel: 0181 780 1331
Fax: 0181 780 1081

WES World-wide Education Service
Canada House
272 Field End Road
Eastcote
Middlesex HA4 9NA
Tel: 0181 866 4400
Fax: 0181 429 4838

Index of Advertisers

Index